Alexander Hamilton

DOCUMENTS DECODED

The ABC-CLIO series *Documents Decoded* guides readers on a hunt for new secrets through an expertly curated selection of primary sources. Each book pairs key documents with in-depth analysis, all in an original and visually engaging side-by-side format. But *Documents Decoded* authors do more than just explain each source's context and significance—they give readers a front-row seat to their own investigation and interpretation of each essential document, line by line.

TITLES IN ABC-CLIO'S DOCUMENTS DECODED SERIES

The Death Penalty: Documents Decoded
Joseph A. Melusky and Keith A. Pesto

The Abolitionist Movement: Documents Decoded
Christopher Cameron

The Great Depression and New Deal: Documents Decoded
Mario R. DiNunzio

The Democratic Party: Documents Decoded
Douglas B. Harris and Lonce H. Bailey

The Republican Party: Documents Decoded
Douglas B. Harris and Lonce H. Bailey

1960s Counterculture: Documents Decoded
Jim Willis

Founding Documents of America: Documents Decoded
John R. Vile

Presidential Power: Documents Decoded
Brian M. Harward

The Early Republic: Documents Decoded
John R. Vile

The Jacksonian and Antebellum Eras: Documents Decoded
John R. Vile

Freedom of Speech: Documents Decoded
David L. Hudson Jr.

The Civil War and Reconstruction Eras: Documents Decoded
John R. Vile

Church and State: Documents Decoded
David K. Ryden and Jeffrey J. Polet

xander Hamilton

DOCUMENTS DECODED

Christina G. Villegas

 ABC-CLIO™

An Imprint of ABC-CLIO, LLC
Santa Barbara, California • Denver, Colorado

Library of Congress Cataloging-in-Publication Data

Names: Hamilton, Alexander, 1757–1804, author. | Villegas, Christina G., editor, author.
Title: Alexander Hamilton : documents decoded / Christina G. Villegas.
Description: Santa Barbara, California : ABC-CLIO, 2018. |
Series: Documents decoded | Includes bibliographical references and index.
Identifiers: LCCN 2017056231 (print) | LCCN 2017056952 (ebook) |
ISBN 9781440857645 (ebook) | ISBN 9781440857638 (alk. paper)
Subjects: LCSH: Hamilton, Alexander, 1757–1804—Sources. |
Statesmen—United States—Biography—Sources. |
United States—Politics and government—1775–1783—Sources. |
United States—Politics and government—1783–1809—Sources.
Classification: LCC E302 (ebook) | LCC E302 .H22 2018 (print) | DDC 973.4092 [B]—dc23
LC record available at https://lccn.loc.gov/2017056231

ISBN: 978-1-4408-5763-8 (print)
978-1-4408-5764-5 (ebook)

22   21   20   19   18   1   2   3   4   5

This book is also available as an eBook.

ABC-CLIO
An Imprint of ABC-CLIO, LLC

ABC-CLIO, LLC
130 Cremona Drive, P.O. Box 1911
Santa Barbara, California 93116-1911
www.abc-clio.com

This book is printed on acid-free paper ∞

Manufactured in the United States of America

Contents

SECTION V
LEGAL PRACTICE

SECTION VI
CREATING AND DEFENDING THE CONSTITUTION

SECTION VII
SECRETARY OF THE TREASURY

SECTION VIII
THE RISE AND FALL OF THE FEDERALISTS

SECTION IX
THE NATION'S FIRST SEX SCANDAL

SECTION X
DEATH

Introduction

Few historical figures have more divergent biographical accounts of their life and influence than Alexander Hamilton. In spite of his status as a controversial figure in early American political life, there is no argument about Hamilton playing a pivotal role in the founding and establishment of the American constitutional system. In recent years, historians and political scientists have taken greater note of Hamilton's legacy, thereby raising his stature among the leading American founders. Ron Chernow (2004), for example, notes in his esteemed biography of Hamilton that "except for Washington, nobody stood closer to the center of American politics from 1776 to 1800 or cropped up at more turning points" (4). Some might even argue that the American experiment would have never succeeded without Hamilton's political foresight and devotion. Through an exploration of Hamilton's own writings which are annotated or "decoded," this volume examines Hamilton's character, ideals, afflictions, and ultimately his indispensable impact on the establishment and early unfolding of the American political order.

Section I: Early Life

What little is known of Hamilton's humble birth and childhood in the West Indies makes his remarkable rise and influential role in the nation's founding even more extraordinary.

Hamilton was born on the island of Nevis in the West Indies on January 11, 1757,[1] as the illegit-imate child of divorcée Rachael Faucett Lavien and Scottish trader James Hamilton. During his childhood, spent on the island of St. Croix, Hamilton experienced one tragedy and abandonment after another. His father deserted a young Alexander and his older brother James, and his mother died of illness a couple years later. Upon her death, Hamilton's mother's modest assets were promptly seized by her estranged former husband, Johann Michael Lavien, for his own son, Hamilton's half-brother Peter Lavien. Alexander and his brother James were placed under the legal guardianship of one of their few surviving relatives, their elder first cousin Peter Lytton. This arrangement did not last long, however, as Lytton shortly later committed suicide without making any provisions for the two orphans' care. For reasons unknown, Hamilton was taken into the home of a successful merchant, Thomas Stevens, and his wife, Ann. During this time, Hamilton developed a close friendship with the couple's son Edward that lasted through his life.

In spite of his inauspicious beginnings, Hamilton, from an early age, exhibited extraordinary talent, drive, and literary ability. Hamilton's earliest-known writings reveal his embodiment of these qualities and his fierce determination to overcome his current conditions.

Section II: Pre-Revolution

When Hamilton was nearly sixteen years old, several benefactors noted his burgeoning intellectual potential and, in 1772, sponsored his travels to the American colonies and his ensuing education. After a year of preparatory schooling in

---

[1] Hamilton's exact date of birth is uncertain. Some scholars identify his birth year as 1755 and others as 1757. This work will utilize the day Hamilton himself reported as his date of birth, January 11, 1757.

Elizabethtown, New Jersey, Hamilton enrolled at King's College (now Columbia University) on an accelerated learning plan.

Hamilton thrived as a young college student. His roommate Robert Troup later recalled that he "was studious and made rapid progress in the languages and every other branch of learning to which he applied himself" (Schachner 1947, 212). In his spare time he poured over the books in the King's College library. In addition to the works directly required for his studies, Hamilton immersed himself in the natural rights writings of theorists such as Locke, Grotius, Pufendorf, Montesquieu, Burlamaqui, Hobbes, Blackstone, and Hume. During his time in New Jersey and New York, he also fell in with a number of the country's leading Whigs, including Elias Boudinot, William Livingston, and John Jay.

Shortly after Hamilton enrolled at King's College, colonial fervor against the British government came to a head. During his first year, Hamilton witnessed the Boston Tea Party, the Sons of Liberty protests throughout the colonies, the passage of Britain's disciplinary Coercive Acts, and the meeting of the first Continental Congress in Philadelphia. As a young, ambitious college student, he was deeply interested in the political issues of the day. By mid-1774, he began speaking at political rallies, energetically supporting the patriotic cause.

In the winter of 1774–1775, Hamilton published his first major political tracts, *A Full Vindication of the Measures of Congress* and *The Farmer Refuted*. Engaging in a polemical battle with Samuel Seabury, an Anglican minister and Tory, Hamilton vigorously and effectively defended the Continental Congress and its imposition of an embargo on commercial relations with Britain. In these essays he demonstrated that, in spite of his youth, he had developed a mature knowledge of trade, political theory, law, and military strategy.

Hamilton's support for the Patriots' cause and the revolutionary activity of the Sons of Liberty, although enthusiastic, was not blind or unlimited. On at least two occasions, he risked his personal reputation by publicly resisting and denouncing the actions of mobs that sought to harm the person and property of loyalist Tories. Hamilton believed that the lawless and destructive nature of mob rule would disgrace the cause of liberty and would ultimately deprive the colonists of their justification for resisting British oppression in the first place. Thus, while he heartily endorsed the Revolution, he continually encouraged a spirit of moderation and respect for legal order.

Before completing his college degree, Hamilton, consumed with the revolutionary affairs of the budding nation, devoted himself to full-time military activity. He formed a volunteer drill company along with several of his former classmates and began to study artillery. In early 1776, he was appointed captain of a New York artillery company and, at the end of the year, he and his men reportedly crossed the Delaware with General George Washington for the surprise dawn attack on the Hessians in Trenton, New Jersey.

Section III: During the War

During the early years of the Revolution, Hamilton, having helped plant the theoretical seeds of American independence, turned his attention to full-time military service. As captain of the New York Provincial Company of Artillery, he exhibited remarkable initiative, insight, and leadership ability. With the help of his friend Hercules Mulligan, he personally recruited soldiers to staff his company and then exerted great effort to ensure that those under his command were not only well disciplined and trained but also well outfitted and compensated.

As an ambitious immigrant of illegitimate birth himself, Hamilton sought to recognize and reward dedication, ability, and achievement rather than social status. When he officially requested permission from the New York Provincial Congress to grant promotions based on merit regardless of social class or rank, his actions inspired others to follow suit. In this way, Hamilton worked to overturn the long-standing European tradition of basing military promotion on the arbitrary privileges of rank and birth, making an early and lasting democratic impact on the structure of the young nation's military.

It was not long before Hamilton's own merit drew the attention of his superiors. In January 1777, after fighting valiantly and distinguishing himself in several military campaigns, Hamilton was invited to join General George Washington's staff. He was officially appointed as aide-de-camp to the commander in chief on March 1, 1777, at which time he was also promoted in rank to lieutenant colonel. Ron Chernow (2004), noting the significance of this appointment, observes that "in fewer than five years, the twenty-two-year-old Alexander Hamilton had risen from despondent clerk in St. Croix to one of the aides to America's most eminent man" (85).

In his capacity as aide-to-camp, Hamilton was charged with writing much of Washington's official correspondence. Hamilton's responsibilities, however, soon included far more than clerical work. He quickly earned Washington's respect and became one of his principal military advisers. Washington even trusted Hamilton to serve as his proxy in many important matters and gave him a great deal of latitude to make decisions, negotiate agreements, and communicate with the Continental Congress and state governments on Washington's behalf.

Due to his extensive authority as one of the highest-ranking members of General Washington's staff, Hamilton was well positioned to observe the various military, political, and financial dimensions of the war. From critiquing the actions of the Continental Congress to suggesting the enlistment of slaves as soldiers, Hamilton was soon giving political advice to America's most prominent leaders. During this time, his sanguine vision of the future of the new country and the quality of its leaders began to diminish. Witnessing firsthand the capriciousness of the state governments and

the incompetence of the Continental Congress, Hamilton began to develop many of the political convictions that would shape his later career, including his preference for a strong union of states and energetic executive power.

After serving Washington in a largely administrative capacity for four years, Hamilton longed to return to field command. Eventually, after considerable petitioning, Hamilton was assigned to a New York battalion, which led the successful assault on Yorktown, the last major battle in the War of Independence.

By the end of the war, Hamilton had proven himself to be one of the country's most insightful, dedicated, and courageous leaders. He thus confirmed the veracity of his later statement—made in eulogy of General Nathanael Greene—that revolutions "serve to bring to light talents and virtues which might otherwise have languished in obscurity."

Although Hamilton's desire to leave Washington's staff for combat command caused a short-term rift between the two, their deep admiration for one another and mutual conviction that only a strong, united country would secure liberty and independence led them to form one of the most enduring and influential political partnerships in American history.

Section IV: Family Life

Having experienced the desertion of his father and early death of his mother, Hamilton no doubt yearned for a sense of belonging and the intimate closeness of family life that he had largely lacked as a youth. In fact, throughout his career, Hamilton's burning political ambition was rivaled only by his strong affection for his wife, children, and extended family.

Hamilton's interaction with his future in-laws, the distinguished Schuyler family, began while he was a member of Washington's staff. As Washington's aide-to-camp, Hamilton impressed many of the notable guests and high-ranking officers who visited the army headquarters. One of these, General Philip Schuyler, became not only Hamilton's father-in-law but also one of his closest political confidantes and allies.

In late 1779, General Schuyler, having been elected a delegate to the Continental Congress, traveled with his family to Philadelphia. Shortly later, his two eldest daughters, Angelica and the unwed Elizabeth, journeyed to the nearby army headquarters at Morristown, New Jersey, to visit relatives. There, they frequently came into contact with members of Washington's staff, including the young and dashing Hamilton. Although Hamilton dallied with several of the women who courted the revolutionary officers in camp, he immediately recognized in Elizabeth Schuyler the qualities he was looking for in a wife and fell deeply in love. By all accounts, including Hamilton's, Elizabeth was strong and pretty, but compassionate and modest, with unwavering convictions, a good temper, and striking black eyes. Elizabeth was equally enamored with Hamilton, and the two were married at the Schuyler manor in Albany, New York, in December 1780. As a young officer with no fortune and a questionable lineage, Hamilton thereby secured his rank in the upper society, through the wealthy and well-respected Schuyler clan.

Unfortunately, historians know little about Elizabeth (whom Hamilton frequently referred to as Betsey or Eliza) from her own accounts, as she later destroyed her own letters. She did, however, carefully preserve Hamilton's correspondence to her. The dozens of letters he sent to her during the war and his tenure in political office reveal a tender care and affection and an implicit trust in her as a confidante. As the pressures of political life increased, Hamilton often expressed a melancholy loneliness in Eliza's absence and increased dependence on her support.

In spite of his clear adoration for his "Betsey," Hamilton remained susceptible to female charms and exhibited a strong attraction to Elizabeth's older sister, the beautiful and gregarious Angelica.

Nevertheless, Hamilton's flirtatious correspondence and questionable relationship with Angelica, which some historians and many of Hamilton's political enemies have judged adulterous, did not seem to worry Elizabeth nor diminish her strong affection toward her sister—a fact which suggests that the relationship between Hamilton and Angelica was likely never more than a flirtation.

Although his career was marked by harsh political battles and a skepticism of human nature generally, Hamilton was an attentive father, who maintained a gentle and loving spirit toward his eight children. He found reprieve from the demands of public life through accompanying his children in play and delighted in encouraging their burgeoning talents and studies. Ron Chernow (2004) reports that no record exists of any of Hamilton's children ever uttering an unkind or critical word against their father either publically or privately. In a book of reminiscences, Hamilton's son James wrote of his father, "His gentle nature rendered his house a most joyous one to his children and friends. . . . His intercourse with his children was always affectionate and confiding, which excited in them a corresponding confidence and devotion."

In spite of his own father's desertion, Hamilton always spoke of him with affection and expressed unreciprocated concern for his well-being. In addition, while neither his absent brother nor father, who both continued to reside in the West Indies, showed much interest in Hamilton or his remarkable achievements, Hamilton exhibited a strong sense of family loyalty and responsibility toward them and financially assisted them from time to time.

Perhaps due to his own longing for familial rootedness, or perhaps because his political enemies often drew attention to his humble beginnings and illegitimate birth, Hamilton took great pride in his Scottish ancestry and was eager to strengthen ties with his distant paternal relatives. Thus, while Hamilton strongly advocated throughout his life that individuals be judged on the basis of merit rather than pedigree, knowledge of his father's noble lineage clearly strengthened his sense of dignity in the face of concerted attempts to discredit and belittle him for his background and birth.

Section V: Legal Practice

In late 1781, after resigning from Washington's staff and fighting heroically in the Battle of Yorktown, Hamilton left the army and began legal studies. Taking advantage of a temporary waiver for returning veterans of a three-year apprenticeship requirement for the New York Bar, Hamilton immersed himself in the study of law while simultaneously serving in his first politically appointed post as receiver of Continental taxes for New York. He pored over treatises on legal philosophy contained in his friend James Duane's extensive law library and wrote for himself a legal manual, later used as a guide for law students, to help him sort through the complexities of New York law as it evolved out of the British and colonial system. In July 1782, just six months after beginning his studies, he passed the New York Bar exam and became a licensed attorney. From this time until his death, Hamilton practiced law on and off among his other responsibilities and soon became one of the country's preeminent lawyers.

Because Hamilton planned to practice law in the busy port of New York City, he was forced to put his career on hold until the official end of British occupation. Thus, a few weeks after becoming a licensed attorney, Hamilton agreed to serve as a New York delegate to the Continental Congress. Although he served only eight months before leaving in frustration over ineptitude and cronyism, he played a pivotal role in urging Congress to accept the terms of the provisional peace treaty with Great Britain that had been signed in Paris on November 30, 1782.

The terms of the peace treaty required restoring the rights and property of former Loyalists or Tories and forbid further prosecutions against them; yet animosity in the states toward those who had remained loyal to the British remained strong, particularly in New York, which had been the citadel of British forces. Following the official end to British occupation of Manhattan in late 1783, populists associated with the Sons of Liberty scored resounding victories in New York elections. Consequently, the New York legislature, in clear violation of the peace treaty, continued to impose harsh punitive measures against remaining Tories. Three particularly oppressive measures passed during and after the Revolution included the Confiscation Act, which permitted courts to confiscate the property of those who had aided or remained loyal to Great Britain; the Citation Act, which allowed courts to suspend debts owed by Patriots to Loyalists or to permit debtors to pay their obligations in devalued paper money; and the Trespass Act, passed following negotiation of the peace treaty, which permitted Patriots to recover damages from those who had occupied their property during the war, even if such occupation was carried out under orders and in accordance with the laws of war.

As a lawyer and former revolutionary with a long-term vision for the nation's success, Hamilton was alarmed by both the treatment of Tories as a class and the blatant disregard for the authority of Congress to make and approve treaties. He believed that the obsession with vengeance, pervading the country as a whole and his state in particular, not only violated the rules of war and the terms of the peace treaty but also threatened the nation's future liberty, prosperity, and credibility. Although many prominent politicians, lawyers, and business owners privately expressed concern over the persecution of Tories, Hamilton was, for some time, alone in his willingness to publically stand against the anti-Loyalist frenzy.

In early 1784, Hamilton officially entered the public debate over the treatment of the Tories in response to a string of newspaper articles harassing former Loyalists and calling for their exile. In two pamphlets, written under the pseudonym Phocion,

Hamilton contended that retaliation against the Tories was motivated by the impulse of prejudice, revenge, and passion rather than common sense and justice. As Phocion, he made the case that the property confiscation and disenfranchisement of Tories violated the laws of nations, the Articles of Confederation, and the New York Constitution. Calling on New Yorkers to put the animus of war behind them, Hamilton emphasized that liberty, stability, and prosperity are dependent on a system of law that equally protects every citizen—not just those in the popular majority—from oppression and injury.

Determined to challenge retaliatory actions in court as well as print, Hamilton represented disenfranchised Loyalists in more than sixty cases. In one of his first and most well-known cases, *Rutgers v. Waddington*, he addressed the legality of lawsuits brought under the Trespass Act by Patriots seeking damages and back rent from Loyalists who had used their abandoned property during the British occupation. In his defense of a British merchant, Hamilton argued that the Trespass Act was a violation of the laws of war incorporated into the New York Constitution and the authority to make treaties given to Congress by the Articles of Confederation, which the states were bound to follow. He then made his first argument for judicial review, which was later fleshed out in *Federalist* 78, stating that the courts have a duty to uphold the requirements of fundamental laws, in this case the peace treaty and the New York Constitution, when they conflict with ordinary acts of legislation.

Throughout his career, Hamilton provided representation in hundreds of criminal, civil, and commercial cases. He was known for standing up against popular agitation and providing pro bono defense for those he believed had been unjustly accused in criminal cases, but he always preferred civil cases that involved disputes over legal principle or key points of constitutional law. In the last major speech of his career, Hamilton represented beleaguered journalist Harry Croswell, who had been indicted by a grand jury and found guilty by a circuit court for publishing seditious libel against President Jefferson. Arguing for an appeal before the New York Supreme Court, Hamilton contended that judgments in libel suits should account for whether or not the defamatory statements under consideration were true. Although the court upheld Croswell's conviction, Hamilton's famous speech in this case contributed to the eventual establishment in American jurisprudence of the principle of truth as a defense in libel suits.

Hamilton's keen insight of the role law plays in producing a stable, prosperous, and happy society and his willingness to stand against the tides of popular opinion in defense of key principles of justice, undoubtedly, had a profound and lasting effect on the future of the republic, but his greatest legal impact came from his involvement in shaping and defending what would become the nation's fundamental law—the U.S. Constitution.

Section VI: Creating and Defending the Constitution

Having defeated the British in the Revolutionary War, the newly formed American people faced an equal, if even greater, challenge of creating an effective republic. Independence was declared, and the Revolution was waged based on the widely held view that government ought to be rooted in the consent of the governed and designed to protect the rights of those living under it. These principles, however, were not accompanied by a clear blueprint of how the powers of such a government should be organized or allocated to achieve these twin, often conflicting goals. Thus, the task of establishing the American constitutional order was largely one of trial and error, fueled by debate, deliberation, conciliation, and compromise.

Following independence, each state adopted its own constitution and then collectively agreed to extend the authority exercised by the Continental Congress at the outset of the war to the Confederation Congress under the Articles of

Confederation. The American experience under British rule had created a general fear of strong central authority. Consequently, the Confederation Congress was vested with inadequate and poorly arranged powers and soon proved unable to meet even its limited responsibilities.

No political figure was more committed than Hamilton to promoting an energetic and perpetual union, which he believed would be necessary for the country's security, happiness, and prosperity. As early as 1780, a year before the Battle of Yorktown, he began proposing a convention of the states to strengthen the powers of Congress and to write a new constitution. Hamilton, nevertheless, understood that the creation of a stronger national government would require overcoming "mountains of prejudice." Although the Revolution had created a bond of union among the former colonists, most people still viewed their particular state as their "country." Local politicians further fed the people's trepidation of centralized authority—often out of concern for maintaining their own parochial power. Eventually, however, the inadequacies of the confederation became more apparent, and Hamilton's belief that the people should fear the collapse of a weak government as much as an overly powerful one gained credibility.

While the confederation experienced many difficulties, particularly in the realm of raising revenue, foreign relations, and military oversight, it was the failures of commerce and interstate trade that finally generated the political will for reform. In the absence of a uniform foreign and interstate trade policy, the states began levying tariffs on the imports and exports of other states in an effort to combat their own internal economic distress. Hamilton's home state of New York, one of the most egregious offenders, began imposing burdensome duties on goods headed for New Jersey and Connecticut through the port of New York.

As conflicts between the states increased and the nation teetered on the brink of civil war, Hamilton left his full-time law practice to pursue a seat in the New York legislature, so he would be well positioned to lead the fight for a stronger union. Once elected to the New York Assembly, Hamilton sought out like-minded politicians who could direct the movement for reform either in their own state or in Congress. In so doing, he found a valuable ally in Virginian congressional representative James Madison. Following a successful agreement in 1785 between Virginia and Maryland concerning trade on the Potomac River, Madison urged the Virginia legislature to sponsor a meeting of the states to recommend a federal plan for regulating commerce. The Virginia legislature complied and scheduled a convention for the following spring in Annapolis, Maryland, with the express purpose of considering "how far a uniform system [of the states] in their commercial intercourse and regulations may be necessary to their common interest and perfect harmony" (Knott and Williams 2015, 134). Because only five states sent commissioners to the Annapolis Convention, the delegates, which included Hamilton and Madison, agreed that they did not have a mandate to make decisions binding on the whole. Nevertheless, Hamilton—not wanting to squander the historic opportunity to advance the cause of union—authored an official report, signed by each of the commissioners at Annapolis, calling for a convention of states in Philadelphia the following May to consider broad revision of the Articles of Confederation.

In the months following the Annapolis Convention, the states descended even further into economic chaos, and it became clear that, unless the confederation was drastically reformed, the union would collapse and the states would be vulnerable to civil war or foreign exploitation and invasion. In early 1787, Congress finally authorized a convention to amend the Articles of Confederation.

Although Hamilton had played a decisive role in bringing about the Constitutional Convention, which convened in Philadelphia on May 25, 1787, his influence as one of New York's three delegates was minimal. The other two state delegates, Robert Yates and John Lansing, were staunch opponents of a stronger union of states. Their votes therefore nullified Hamilton's on any matter of importance. Nevertheless, when the convention faced deadlock following disagreement over the previously introduced Virginia and New Jersey Plans, Hamilton offered his own plan as an alternative. Hamilton proposed a strictly national system based loosely on a republicanized version of the British constitution, which he praised for its strength and stability. Although it had no chance of acceptance, the extremity of Hamilton's proposal in comparison to Madison's more moderate Virginia Plan redirected deliberations and encouraged conciliation and compromise. At the conclusion of the convention, Hamilton, in spite of some misgivings, believed that the chance that good would come from the new constitution far outweighed the anarchy and disorder that would likely plague the nation in its absence. He thereby pledged unwavering support for its ratification.

In order to go into effect, the proposed Constitution had to be ratified by popular ratifying conventions in at least nine of the thirteen states. Acceptance by delegates of the people, however, was by no means guaranteed, and a fierce polemical debate broke out between supporters and opponents in an effort to sway public opinion. Those who supported the proposed Constitution's division of sovereignty between an autonomous national government and the several states adopted the title Federalists, while those who preferred that ultimate sovereignty continue to reside in the states were branded Anti-Federalists. The battle for ratification was particularly intense in New York—which, as a centrally located, populous, and resource-rich state, was important not only for ratification but also for the future success of the nation. Thus, Hamilton once again entered the battlefield as a leading advocate for ratification.

Following a series of particularly virulent attacks against the proposed Constitution in the New York press, Hamilton conceived of a collaborative plan to help win ratification. He solicited fellow Federalists John Jay and James Madison to join him in authoring a series of essays defending the proposed Constitution. The series, which totaled 85 essays in all, evolved into the most comprehensive and reasoned defense of the Constitution ever produced. Following publication in New York newspapers, between October 1787 and April 1788, they were published as a book, *The Federalist*, and were circulated throughout the states. Hamilton, who wrote the bulk of the essays, focused primarily on the importance of vigor and energy in government and the need to balance order and liberty. His commentary touched on a variety of subjects, including the failures of the previous confederacy, the benefits of a strong union, military matters, commerce, taxation, the executive, the judiciary, and the Bill of Rights. In late July 1788, Hamilton—appealing to many of the arguments he had first developed in *The Federalist*—helped secure narrow approval of the proposed Constitution at the New York ratifying convention in Poughkeepsie.

Once the Constitution was scheduled to go into effect, Hamilton turned his attention to the task of putting the machine into motion. He understood that after the particularly contentious battle for ratification, the success of the new government would depend on cultivating the respect and attachment of the people. No office in this regard was more important and controversial than the newly constructed presidency. Hamilton—recognizing that George Washington's unmatched reputation for integrity and devotion to the country would legitimate the office—persistently urged Washington to once again leave retirement at Mt. Vernon and serve as the nation's first chief executive. Washington complied and on February 4, 1789, was unanimously elected the nation's first commander in chief by the Electoral College.

Section VII: Secretary of the Treasury

On September 2, 1789, shortly after assuming the presidency, Washington signed a law creating the first four executive cabinet heads: the secretary of

Treasury, the secretary of state, the secretary of war, and the attorney general. Congress, recognizing the dire straits of the nation's finances, vested the Treasury department with more extensive responsibilities and staff resources than any of the other agencies. Washington promptly nominated Hamilton, who had spent his years as Washington's aide-to-camp poring over financial treatises and contemplating the economic state of the confederation, to head this prestigious department.

Like Washington, Hamilton understood that the success of the new Constitution depended on the precedents established by the country's first administration. Thus, he immediately set out in his capacity as Treasury secretary to build respect for the new nation in the eyes of foreign nations and confidence and esteem in the hearts of its citizens. One of the most important challenges in this regard was to stabilize the country's finances that had so badly deteriorated under the previous system. Hamilton zealously took on this task, believing that a firm financial foundation would contribute not only to the nation's economic well-being but also to its security, domestic tranquility, and liberty.

Shortly after Hamilton took office, Congress directed him to devise a plan for restoring the nation's credit. In response, Hamilton presented Congress with a lengthy treatise, in which he argued that justice and necessity mandate the restoration of good fiduciary faith. He then outlined a comprehensive plan to honor current agreements, to assume the state debt acquired during the Revolution, and to realistically service the debt.

Once a congressional agreement to relocate the nation's capital to the banks of the Potomac River helped overcome Southern resistance to the federal assumption of state debt, Hamilton moved on to his next political priority, securing approval for a national bank. Hamilton easily convinced Congress that a national bank was necessary to facilitate the economic powers of the federal government, but the bank bill met stiff resistance when it landed on Washington's desk. Secretary of State

Thomas Jefferson and Attorney General Edmund Randolph fiercely contested the bank bill and urged Washington to veto it on the grounds that it exceeded the federal government's constitutional authority. In response, Hamilton provided Washington with a detailed *Report on the Constitutionality of the Bank*, in which he argued that the power to create a national bank was an implied power of the federal government derived from the necessary and proper clause of the Constitution. Hamilton's powerful counterargument sufficiently convinced Washington, and he signed the first bank of the United States into law on February 24, 1791.

With the passage of the national bank secure, Hamilton quickly settled in on a third major priority, promoting domestic manufacturing. The new American republic was completely reliant on foreign nations for its military supplies and other essential goods, which Hamilton believed put the country in a vulnerable position economically and politically. In the midst of establishing the Coast Guard and writing regulations for customs collectors, Hamilton researched the status of the country's various forms of industries. On December 5, 1791, in compliance with a request from the House of Representatives, Hamilton submitted his comprehensive *Report on the Subject of Manufacturers* to Congress. Although Hamilton emphasized his commitment to free market principles in the report, he contended that minimal protective tariffs and government subsidies would spur the development of America's manufacturing capability and thereby contribute to industrial growth.

Like his plans for the federal assumption of the revolutionary debt and the establishment of a national bank, Hamilton's call for government subsidies for manufacturing was viewed by many as part of a broader plan to line the pockets of Northern financiers, weaken the power and influence of the states, and destroy the agricultural economy of the South. Consequently, the schisms that developed in response to Hamilton's initial financial proposals set the stage for the formation of parties in the 1790s and the vicious political battles that ensued over competing visions of the republic's future and the type of political order best suited for protecting liberty.

Section VIII: The Rise and Fall of the Federalists

Initially, most of the nation's founders—among them Hamilton, Madison, and Jefferson—ardently opposed the formation of political parties, viewing them as factional and corrosive to the public good. Nevertheless, the lack of consensus among political leaders over the nation's first domestic and foreign policies inevitably resulted in the formation of opposing political camps, which eventually evolved into the nation's first political parties: the Federalists and the Democratic-Republicans.

In 1791, Thomas Jefferson and James Madison spurred this transformation by launching the *National Gazette*, which they intended to counteract the pro-Hamilton stance of the *Gazette of the United States*. Madison and Jefferson recruited former poet laureate Philip Freneau as editor in chief of the newspaper and then secured a position for him as a translator at the state department to subsidize his salary. Freneau immediately began publishing editorials classifying Hamilton as an undercover monarchist, who sought to destroy republicanism and subvert liberty. Hamilton defended himself against such charges in both public and private correspondence. In a letter to his friend and Virginian political ally, Edward Carrington, Hamilton lamented his split with his former collaborator James Madison and contended that Jefferson and Madison (acting as Jefferson's lackey) were the true enemies of the American experiment in a republican government.

As the press wars increased in intensity, Washington, who sought to remain above the partisan fray, pleaded with his secretary of Treasury and secretary of state to cease their journalist warfare but to no avail. In spite of Jefferson's incessant attacks on Hamilton and his funding system,

however, Washington retained full confidence in Hamilton's patriotism and foresight. Like Hamilton, Washington believed that the success of the American republic depended on the establishment of a firm and energetic union; and, although he thoughtfully considered the competing views of all of his secretaries, he continued to seek and follow Hamilton's advice on nearly every major issue of his presidency.

Toward the end of Washington's first term, conflict over foreign policy began to overshadow domestic disputes. In fall of 1792, French revolutionaries overthrew the French monarchy and early the next year decapitated King Louis XVI. As the newly constituted French republic sought both to defend itself against forces seeking to restore the monarchy and to expand the Revolution beyond its borders, war broke out between France and an alliance of European monarchical powers, including Great Britain. In response to popular sympathy for the French Revolution in America, French leaders sought to capitalize on the treaty of alliance negotiated between France and the United States during the American Revolution. In spite of a general consensus that the United States should not directly involve itself in the European war, the Washington administration, Congress, and the public at large still erupted into vigorous debate over the proper course of American foreign policy.

Stephen F. Knott and Tony Williams (2015) astutely observe that "the foreign policy debate over how to respond to the French Revolutionary Wars was one of ideology as well as constitutional power" (194). Although the Jeffersonian Republicans were somewhat disturbed by the French Reign of Terror—in which churches were forcibly transformed into "temples of reason" and anyone representing the old order, including nuns, priests, aristocrats, and suspected counterrevolutionaries were purged or executed—they were enamored with the spirit of the movement and believed that supporting the newly minted republic was the best way to promote the progress of liberty and to diminish the power of Great Britain. Hamilton, on the other hand, was shocked at the unbridled ferociousness with which the revolutionaries annihilated suspected counterrevolutionaries and sought to overturn the old order. He accurately foresaw that the licentiousness unleashed in France would culminate not in a free society but in despotism. He, therefore, urged Washington to avoid any alliance between the United States and France that might threaten its commercial relationship with Great Britain.

Washington, recognizing that the fragile American republic would not survive the division and turmoil caused by involvement in a foreign war, announced a policy of U.S. neutrality in the war between Britain and France. Washington's pronouncement, which became known as the Neutrality Proclamation of 1793, unleashed a political firestorm that further divided the country along partisan lines. Whereas the Hamiltonian Federalists supported the proclamation, Jefferson and Madison declared that Washington had usurped the power of Congress to declare war. In a series of controversial essays, written under the pseudonym Pacificus, Hamilton defended the Neutrality Proclamation both as good policy and as a legitimate exercise of presidential power. The president, Hamilton argued, possessed the rightful authority not only to enforce the law but also to determine the conditions necessary for maintaining peace with other nations under the obligations of treaties and the law of nations.

In 1794, following an intense congressional investigation by Democratic-Republicans into his tenure as Treasury secretary, Hamilton was prepared to resign from Washington's cabinet, when a rebellion broke out in Western Pennsylvania. In protest of federal excise taxes on whiskey, thousands of armed militants expelled federal tax collectors and threatened to burn Pittsburg to the ground. Hamilton argued, in several short essays published under the pseudonym Tully, that the whiskey rebels were undermining constitutional government, democracy, and the rule of law, by attempting to forcefully overthrow laws that had

been constitutionally enacted by a majority of the people's representatives in Congress. Hamilton urged Washington to quickly suppress the insurrection. After several failed efforts at conciliation, Washington agreed to a military showdown, raising over 12,000 infantry and cavalrymen from the militias of several states. In order to emphasize the gravity of the mission, both he and Hamilton accompanied the militia into the heart of the uprising. The massive show of federal force was sufficient to dispel the rebels without fighting or bloodshed. In the end, Washington pardoned all who had been arrested and convicted as a result of the expedition. Forrest McDonald (1979) observes that the "combination of both strength and clemency" exhibited in the federal mission "had a salutary effect throughout the land: a wave of enthusiasm for the administration swept the country, and with few exceptions seditious and even libelous talk virtually ceased" (302). In a show of support for the Washington administration, voters reelected Federalist majorities to both houses of Congress that year.

Having placed the nation's finances and public credit in good order, having kept the country free of dangerous foreign entanglements, and having helped establish reverence for federal law, Hamilton issued his official resignation from Washington's cabinet and prepared to return to his family and law practice. Despite his departure, however, Hamilton continued to serve as one of Washington's closest advisers. He played a prominent role in the campaign to ratify the Jay Treaty, which—though extremely unpopular at the time—helped to prevent war with Great Britain over its seizure of U.S. ships. Washington was immensely grateful for Hamilton's contributions to the success of his administration and his role in helping erect a solid foundation for the new and fragile nation. In a letter to Hamilton just following his official resignation, Washington acclaimed, "In every relation which you have borne to me, I have found that my confidence in your talents, exertions, and integrity has been well placed." In a last major service to his mentor and confidante, Hamilton drafted Washington's Farewell Address, emphasizing the themes that had consumed the pair's attention throughout Washington's two presidential terms—the blessings of union and the threats that endangered it.

In contrast with the amicable and close relationship Hamilton had maintained with Washington, his relationship with John Adams, the nation's second president, was far more tenuous. Hamilton thought Adams disagreeable and impulsive, and Adams disdained Hamilton's low birth, distrusted his ambition, and resented his influence with Washington.

Shortly after John Adams was elected as the nation's second president, tensions with France began to escalate. The French, viewing the U.S. Jay Treaty with Great Britain as a threat to their own commercial power, increased their practice of privateering American ships. Adams responded by sending a diplomatic mission to France, consisting of John Marshall, Charles Cotesworth Pinckney, and Elbridge Gerry. When French officials rejected overtures of peace by publically degrading these notable emissaries, war seemed inevitable. Adams correspondingly began to rebuild the military, nominating Washington as its commander in chief. Only after Washington insisted did Adams begrudgingly appoint Hamilton as the second in command with a rank of major general.

In 1799, Adams greatly astounded and angered Washington, Hamilton, and other leading Federalists, when he seemingly abandoned overnight his tough, saber-rattling stance toward France and instead dispatched a peace delegation to France without consulting anyone in his cabinet or his party. While historians have argued that Adams's decision to pursue peace at any cost proved profitable in the end, the secretive, unilateral manner in which he conducted the mission, which resulted in a lop-sided agreement in favor of France, aggravated the growing divisions in his party. When members of his cabinet and fellow Federalists expressed skepticism at his peace overtures, Adams publically questioned their patriotism and loyalty,

vindictively fired a couple prominent members of his cabinet, and cut off further interaction with his fellow partisans, retreating to his home in Quincy for more than half the year.

Following Washington's death in December 1799, Hamilton became even less restrained in his dealings with his perceived adversaries, most notably President Adams. In the election of 1800, Hamilton secretly opposed Adam's bid for reelection, hoping to convince fellow Federalists to support vice-presidential candidate Charles Cotesworth Pinckney over Adams for the presidency. Exhibiting an extreme lack of foresight, Hamilton circulated a letter enumerating Adam's "defects of character" among leading Federalists. The letter eventually made it into the hands of Republican vice-presidential candidate Aaron Burr, who ensured that it was widely published as evidence of the Federalists' lack of faith in their own candidate. Although it is unclear whether or not Hamilton's ill-timed letter directly diminished Adam's chance at reelection, it clearly contributed to Hamilton's own political decline and to the downfall of the party he had helped create.

When the election results came in, Adams and Pinckney narrowly lost to the Democratic-Republican ticket of Jefferson and Burr, who tied with seventy-three electoral votes each. The tie resulted in a crisis when Burr—although clearly intended as the Republican's vice-presidential candidate—refused to accede the presidency. Consequently, the Federalist-controlled House of Representatives was forced to resolve the dilemma in a series of run-off elections. While most Federalists decided to cast their lot with Burr, Hamilton's disdain for the largely unprincipled Burr was even greater than his long-standing hatred for Jefferson. He, thus, worked furiously to persuade Federalists to cast blank ballots instead of giving their votes to Burr. Eventually, after the House had gone through multiple rounds of balloting, Hamilton convinced Congressman James Bayard of Delaware, the only state with a single vote, to cast a blank ballot and Jefferson was elected president.

With Jefferson's remarkably pacific inauguration, Hamilton's own political career and the vitality of his party had come to an end.

Section IX: The Nation's First Sex Scandal

In addition to his imprudent attack on Adams at the height of a presidential election, another major factor contributing to Hamilton's rapid decline in political influence was his own exposition of an extramarital affair he had carried on with Maria Reynolds early in his tenure as Treasury secretary.

The affair dated back to the summer of 1791, when Hamilton's wife Eliza and their children left the sweltering heat of Philadelphia to stay with extended family in upstate New York. Hamilton, residing alone in the nation's temporary capital, was approached by twenty-three-year-old Maria Reynolds, who portrayed herself as a fellow New Yorker in dire need of aid. Appealing to Hamilton's chivalrous nature, Maria entreated his financial assistance, telling him that her abusive husband had recently abandoned her without the means to return to her friends and family. After acquiring a bank note, Hamilton visited Maria's apartment and the affair between the two commenced.

The affair lasted several months before Maria's husband James returned. On discovering the affair, James actually encouraged it to continue, while demanding that Hamilton pay him small installments in bribes. Eventually, Hamilton, suspecting that Maria and her husband were acting in concert against him, ended the affair in August 1792. The affair might have remained private were it not for the federal arrest and imprisonment of James Reynold and his business partner Jacob Clingman. In late 1792, Treasury comptroller Oliver Wolcott discovered that Reynolds and Clingman were engaged in perjury and fraud and brought suit against the pair. Hoping to escape long-term imprisonment in exchange for providing evidence of corruption in the Treasury department, Clingman sought the ear of his former employer, House Speaker Frederick Muhlenberg. Clingman and Reynolds presented Muhlenberg with proof that Hamilton had made payments to Reynolds and argued that the payments consisted of funds from the public Treasury used for illicit purposes.

Muhlenberg shared the matter with Senator James Monroe and Congressman Abraham Venable, who decided to first address Hamilton before presenting the charges of corruption to Washington. When the three confronted Hamilton with the evidence against him, he confessed the details of his affair with Maria and successfully convinced them that he had not engaged in corrupt activities as head of the Treasury. The congressional delegation left satisfied that Hamilton's dealings with the Reynolds were solely a matter of personal infidelity and agreed that the issue would be put to rest.

Hamilton's affair, thus, remained private until June 1797 when James Callender, a gossip-mongering columnist who at the time was favorable to the Democratic-Republicans, published a series of articles resurrecting the charges that Hamilton, as Treasury secretary, had engaged in illicit investments with James Reynolds. After James Monroe refused to confirm his earlier belief that Hamilton was innocent of such charges, Hamilton concluded that the only way to vindicate his public reputation was to publish a detailed account of his affair with Maria Reynolds and his corresponding dealings with her husband James.

Far from vindicating Hamilton in the eyes of the public, however, Hamilton's revelation of his long-ended extramarital affair merely provided his adversaries with the ammunition needed to destroy any future aspirations he might have had for the presidency. Jefferson was delighted by Hamilton's public admission and remained convinced that he was additionally guilty of corrupt speculation. Many of Hamilton's fellow Federalists likewise condemned him for foolishly divulging such a humiliating account.

In spite of the abandonment of many of his former Federalist allies, two important individuals remained by Hamilton's side in the wake of the scandal—his wife, Eliza, and former president George Washington. In a subtle letter, sent along with the gift of a wine cooler, Washington emphasized his unwavering regard for his former adviser and confidante. Eliza was so resentful of James Monroe—whom she held personally responsible for terminating her husband's political ambitions—that she refused to accept him into her drawing room when he called on her years later.

Section X: Death

Following the termination of his own political aspirations, Hamilton largely focused his energies on his growing family and law practice. He did, nevertheless, continue to dally in New York politics and even founded a newspaper, the *New York Evening Post*, as an outlet for political attacks against Democratic-Republicans. One of the first stories the *Post* ran was an account of the death of Hamilton's beloved eldest son Philip. Philip was fatally shot in November 1801, while defending his father's honor in a duel with Republican George Eaker. Hamilton, overcome with depression and despair by what he described as "the most afflicting" event of his life, found solace in a renewed dedication to his Christian faith. Although he expressed a growing disaffection with American politics, he simultaneously became more obsessed with preventing Aaron Burr from making a political comeback.

While Hamilton and Burr got along on a personal level and even represented clients together in several legal cases, Hamilton never wavered in his conviction that Burr's unprincipled ambition would eventually threaten the American union—the preservation of which was the greatest object of Hamilton's own ambition. In the year leading up to the 1804 gubernatorial elections in New York, Hamilton's opposition to Burr took on a new sense of urgency. During this period, Northern Federalists, fearful that Jefferson's purchase of the Louisiana Territory would strengthen the

political influence of Southern Republicans and tip the balance of power toward the South, began to flirt with the idea of seceding and forming a new country made up of the New England states and New York. In such a state of affairs, Vice President Burr, who had recently severed all ties with Jefferson, saw an avenue for reviving his largely moribund political career. New York Federalists, who at this point were too weak to field their own candidate, agreed to support Burr in the New York gubernatorial race based on subtle indications that he would willingly lead a breakaway confederacy with New York as its head. Hamilton, appalled by threats of disunion, intensely campaigned against Burr in favor of the Democratic-Republican candidate Morgan Lewis, who won the gubernatorial election by a large margin. Although Hamilton's impact on the race is unknown, Burr held Hamilton personally responsible for destroying his career and became obsessed with exacting revenge. Such an opportunity soon presented itself when, weeks after his electoral defeat, Burr read a letter from Dr. Charles D. Cooper published in the *Albany Register*, recounting how Hamilton had slandered Burr at a dinner party. Burr immediately sent an emissary to Hamilton demanding an explicit apology or satisfaction in a duel.

Hamilton, in preceding years, had repeatedly condemned the practice of dueling as abhorrent, yet, when faced with Burr's demands for an apology, he refused to accede. Instead, he requested a short delay to put his affairs in order. During this time, Hamilton penned a justification of his decision to proceed with the duel, arguing that such action was necessary to preserve his ability to be politically useful in the future. Hamilton believed that avoiding the duel would deprive him of the credibility and respect he would need to oppose the growing secessionist threat. He also wrote to his wife, however, that he did not want the guilt of taking away another's life. Therefore, he was determined not to kill Burr but to purposelessly shoot to miss.

On the morning of July 11, 1804, Hamilton and Burr met in Weehawken, New Jersey, and exchanged fire. Burr's bullet pierced Hamilton's liver and lodged in his spine, while Hamilton's hit an overhead tree branch. A mortally wounded Hamilton died the following day in the company of his friends and family. In his last recorded statement, Hamilton uttered a brief statement commemorating the object to which he had devoted his life's ambition, even to the point of death: "If they break this union, they will break my heart" (Chernow 2004, 708). In the end, Hamilton had played a decisive role in creating and sustaining the republican experiment that outlived Hamilton's personal decline in influence and power to become one of the most free and mighty political edifices in the history of the world.

SECTION I

Early Life

Letter to Edward Stevens on Ambition

November 11, 1769

INTRODUCTION

Hamilton addressed this earliest surviving letter to Edward Stevens, his dear friend and the son of his guardian, who had traveled to New York to study medicine at King's College. The letter reveals young Hamilton's dissatisfaction with his lowly social status and his fear that it might stymie his ambition to live a noteworthy and glorious life. He resolves to overcome the constraints of ill-fortune and to work ardently to improve his future station.

St Croix Novembr. 11th 1769
Dear Edward

This just serves to acknowledge receipt of yours per Cap Lowndes which was delivered me Yesterday. . . . As to what you say respecting your having soon the happiness of seeing us all,[1] I wish, for an accomplishment of your hopes provided they are Concomitant with your welfare, otherwise not, tho doubt whether I shall be Present or not for to confess my weakness, Ned, my Ambition is prevalent that I contemn the grov'ling and condition of a Clerk or the like, to which my Fortune &c. condemns me[2] and would willingly risk my life tho' not my Character to exalt my Station.[3] Im confident, Ned that my Youth excludes me from any hopes of immediate Preferment nor do I desire it, but I mean to prepare the way for futurity. Im no Philosopher you see and may be jusly said to Build Castles in the Air. My Folly makes me ashamd and beg youll Conceal it, yet Neddy we have seen such Schemes successfull when the Projector is Constant I shall Conclude saying I wish there was a War.[4]

I am Dr Edward Yours
Alex Hamilton

[1] Hamilton is responding to a letter from Stevens announcing a visit home to St. Croix.

[2] Hamilton identifies his ambition as a dominant trait but worries that his impoverished social station, and the legal system that artificially sustains it, will impede his advancement.

[3] Hamilton reveals the great lengths he is willing to go to overcome his lot but also piously recognizes that even the most ardent ambition should be limited by the higher end of preserving good character.

[4] Hamilton does not seek unmerited favor but believes that during a period of war his true talent and ability would enable him to rise out of obscurity.

CONCLUSION

Hamilton eventually received the opportunity to escape the ill-fortune of his youth when several benefactors, who had taken notice of his initiative and promising talents, encouraged and sponsored his education in the American colonies.

Source: Hamilton Papers, Library of Congress.

Letter to Nicholas Cruger on Duties as a Clerk

February 24, 1772

INTRODUCTION

Shortly before his cousin and guardian Peter Lytton committed suicide, Hamilton began working as a clerk for the mercantile house of two New York traders, Nicholas Cruger and David Beekman (who was later replaced by Cornelius Kortright). As an apprentice clerk for Beekman & Cruger, Hamilton proved remarkably dependable, self-reliant, and insightful. When Hamilton was only fourteen, Nicholas Cruger traveled to New York for health reasons and left Hamilton to manage his affairs for several months. In spite of his youth, Hamilton successfully discharged this trust with exceptional competency, authority, and good judgment. He bought, sold, and assessed the quality of cargoes; kept a precise record of imports and exports; issued orders; and made business decisions and recommendations requiring considerable discernment. Hamilton reported the details of these activities in occasional letters to Cruger.

Mr. Nicholas Cruger
St Croix February 24 177<2>
Dr. Sir Lightbourn

Herewith you have duplicate of my two last Letters of the 27 November & 10th Ulto. and I now congratulate myself upon the pleasure of addressing you again, but am sorry I shall be obligd to communicate some dissatisfactory occurrencies.

Your Sloop Thunderbolt[1] arrivd here the 29th of the preceding Month with 41 More Skeletons. A worse parcel of Mules never was seen;[2] she took in at first 48 & lost 7 on the passage. I sent all that were able to walk to pasture, in Number 33. The other 8 could hardly stand for 2 Minutes together & in spite of the greatest care 4 of them are now in Limbo. The Surviving 4 I think are out of Danger, and shall likewise be shortly sent to pasture. I refusd two great offers made me upon their first landing to Wit 70 ps. a head for the Choice of 20, and 15 ps. a Head for the abovementiond Invalids, which may

[1] Most of Hamilton's correspondence with Nicholas Cruger concerned the cargo carried by the *Thunderbolt*, a sloop (a fast-sailing vessel) partially owned by the Cruger family.

[2] Hamilton put much care into obtaining a cargo of mules in time for harvest season. Here Hamilton expresses his disgust that the load contained only forty-one emaciated mules unfit to be sold for their intended purpose or price. Undaunted in admonishing his superiors, Hamilton sent an earlier letter instructing the ship's captain, William Newton, to "reflect continually on the unfortunate voyage you have just made and endeavor to make up for the considerable loss" (Hamilton 1961, vol. 1, 24).

give you a proper idea of the condition they were in. Taking this along with it—that if they had been such as we had reason to hope they would be—I could with pleasure have had £40 round, so unfortunate has the Voyage been. However by sending them to pasture I expect to get £100 round for those now alive. 17 are already gone at that price and as they recruit fast the rest I hope will soon go at the same. I pay 2 ps. a Head Montly for pasturage. The Sloop was 27 days on her passage from the Main—not for want of swiftness, for tis now known she Sails well, but from continual Calms & the little wind she had was quite against her. Capt Newton seemd to be much concernd at his Ill luck tho I believe he had done all in his power to make the voyage Successful. But no Man can command the Winds. The Mules were pretty well chosen & had been once a good parcel. I receivd only a few lines from your Brother: no Sales nor anything else; he excusd himself being Sick. I desird him as directed to furnish the Sloop with a few Guns but she went intirely defenceless to the Main;[3] notwithstanding several Vessells had been obligd to put back to get out of the way of the Launches with which the Coast swarms. When Capt Newton urgd him to hire a few Guns for the Sloop He replied to this effect—that I only had mentiond the matter to him but that you had never said a word about it. This last time I mentiond it again & begd the Captain to hire 4 Guns himself if your Brother did not which he has promisd to do.[4] The Expence will not be above 15. or 20 ps., and one escape may not be followd by a second, neither do I see any reason to run the risque of it. I sent down on your account 10 Hhds Codfish, 8 Hhds Rum, 40 Philad. barrels & 8 Teirces Bread. The Rum Cost 2/7½ & is worth 5 bits a Gallon at Curacoa. I believe those Articles will answer pretty well. . .

Brig Nancys Accounts are inclosd. The Tea is arrivd; it Cost 20¼ Sti, but there is a discount of 4 Ct. for prompt payment. I shall send Copy of the Invoice &c. to Mess[rs.] Walton & Cruger. The Lumber you contracted for is arrivd & I am a good deal puzzled to fulfil your engagements; it is rather early you know to receivd & Cash is scarce. Mr Beekman would Ship on freight which would ease the matter but he can receive none yet. However I must manage some how or other. It would be a pity to pay dead freight.

As to introducing Wine, it depends upon Circumstances. There is none here at present and if yours could be brought while the scarcity continues, it would not be difficult to obtain permission to land

[3] Hamilton refers to the request he sent to Nicholas's brother Tileman, who oversaw the Cruger operation in Curaçao. Hamilton had advised Tileman to arm the *Thunderbolt* with guns to ensure the cargo's safe passage along the Spanish Main—South America's northern Caribbean coast. The area was patrolled by the Spanish Guarda Costa and was swarming with pirates and privateers.

[4] Hamilton explains that he instructed Captain Newton to directly hire four armed guards should Tileman Cruger fail to comply with his request to equip the ship against possible attack.

it. Other-wise it will be impracticable, unless our General[5] who is momently expected should bring any new indulgence concerning that article. But the whole is a chance.

Many changes of Officers are talkd of; in particular tis said Judge Sevel will be superceded by Jeger the informer—& the Collector by the present Comptroler, which is all that occurs to me now.[6] Therefore Ill conclude wishing you safe passage out.

I am Sir Your Obdt Serv
AH

[5] Hamilton is referring to the governor general appointed by the king of Denmark to govern the Danish West Indies, including St. Croix.

[6] Hamilton informs Cruger of expected political changes in St. Croix following the death of a superior court judge.

CONCLUSION

Although Hamilton did not envision a future as a merchant and was eager to leave behind his life as a clerk, his role at Kortright & Cruger provided him with an invaluable education in foreign and domestic trade, global banking and monetary policy, administration, and general leadership. He later recounted to his son that this experience had been "the most useful of his education" (Hendrickson 1981, 29).

Source: Hamilton Papers, Library of Congress.

Letter to the *Royal Danish American Gazette* Describing a Hurricane

September 6, 1772

INTRODUCTION

During his tenure as a mercantile clerk, Hamilton also began studying under the tutelage of the Reverend Hugh Knox, a learned Presbyterian minister who had taken notice of Hamilton's intellectual potential. As a young scholar, Hamilton frequently reflected on what he read and observed in letters and poetry. In late August 1772, the worst hurricane in St. Croix's recorded history struck the island. After hearing the Reverend Knox's own account of the horrific storm in a public sermon to survivors, Hamilton wrote a letter to his absent father poetically ruminating on the hurricane's catastrophic effects.

The Reverend Knox was impressed with Hamilton's letter and submitted it for publication to the *Royal Danish American Gazette* with the introduction: "The following letter was written the week after the late Hurricane, by a Youth of this Island, to his Father; the copy of it fell by accident into the hands of a gentleman, who, being pleased with it himself, shewed it to others to whom it gave equal satisfaction, and who all agreed that it might not prove unentertaining to the Publick. The Author's modesty in long refusing to submit it to Publick view, is the reason of its making its appearance so late as it now does."

St. Croix, Sept. 6, 1772
Honoured Sir,

I take up my pen just to give you an imperfect account of one of the most dreadful Hurricanes that memory or any records whatever can trace, which happened here on the 31st ultimo at night.

It began about dusk, at North, and raged very violently till ten o'clock. Then ensued a sudden and unexpected interval, which lasted about an hour. Meanwhile the wind was shifting round to the South West point, from whence it returned with redoubled fury and continued so 'till near three o'clock in the morning. Good God! what horror and destruction. It[']s impossible for me to describe or you to form any idea of it. It seemed as if a total dissolution of nature was taking place. The roaring of the sea and wind, fiery meteors flying about it in the air, the prodigious glare of almost perpetual lightning, the crash of the falling houses, and the ear-piercing shrieks of the distressed, were sufficient to strike astonishment into Angels. A great part of the buildings throughout the Island are levelled to the ground, almost all the rest very much shattered; several persons killed and numbers utterly ruined; whole families running about the streets, unknowing where to find a place of shelter; the sick exposed to the keeness of water and air without a bed to lie upon, or a dry covering to their bodies; and our harbours entirely bare. In a word, misery, in all its most hideous shapes, spread over the whole face of the country. A strong smell of gunpowder added somewhat to the terrors of the night; and it was observed that the rain was surprizingly salt. Indeed the water is so brackish and full of sulphur that there is hardly any drinking it.

My reflections and feelings on this frightful and melancholy occasion, are set forth in the following self-discourse.

Where now, oh! vile worm, is all thy boasted fortitude and resolution? What is become of thine arrogance and self sufficiency?[1] Why dost thou tremble and stand aghast? How humble, how helpless, how contemptible you now appear. And for why? The jarring of elements—the discord of clouds? Oh! impotent presumptuous fool! how durst thou offend that Omnipotence, whose nod alone were sufficient to quell the destruction that hovers over thee, or crush thee into atoms? See thy wretched helpless state, and learn to know thyself.[2] Learn to know thy best support. Despise thyself, and adore thy God. How sweet, how unutterably sweet were now, the voice of an approving conscience; Then couldst thou say, hence ye idle alarms, why do I shrink? What have I to fear? A pleasing calm suspense! A short repose from calamity to end in eternal bliss? Let the Earth rend. Let the planets forsake their course. Let the Sun be extinguished and the Heavens burst asunder. Yet what have I to dread? My staff can never be broken—in Omnip[o]tence I trusted.

He who gave the winds to blow, and the lightnings to rage—even him have I always loved and served. His precepts have I observed. His commandments have I obeyed—and his perfections have I adored. He will snatch me from ruin. He will exalt me to the fellowship of Angels and Seraphs, and to the fullness of never ending joys.

[1] Hamilton's anger in describing hurricane's destructive force against mankind could be directed against his father for deserting his family more than five years before.

[2] Following a vivid depiction of the hurricane and its devastation, Hamilton delivers a moral commentary on mankind's complete dependency on an omnipotent deity. Likely inspired by the Reverend Knox, Hamilton portrays the hurricane as a divine admonishment of human arrogance.

But alas! how different, how deplorable, how gloomy the prospect! Death comes rushing on in triumph veiled in a mantle of tenfold darkness. His unrelenting scythe, pointed, and ready for the stroke. On his right hand sits destruction, hurling the winds and belching forth flames: Calamity on his left threatening famine disease and distress of all kinds. And Oh! thou wretch, look still a little further; see the gulph of eternal misery open. There mayest thou shortly plunge—the just reward of thy vileness. Alas! whither canst thou fly? Where hide thyself? Thou canst not call upon thy God; thy life has been a continual warfare with him.

Hark—ruin and confusion on every side. 'Tis thy turn next; but one short moment, even now, Oh Lord help. Jesus be merciful!

Thus did I reflect, and thus at every gust of the wind, did I conclude, 'till it pleased the Almighty to allay it. Nor did my emotions proceed either from the suggestions of too much natural fear, or a conscience over-burthened with crimes of an uncommon cast. I thank God, this was not the case. The scenes of horror exhibited around us, naturally awakened such ideas in every thinking breast, and aggravated the deformity of every failing of our lives. It were a lamentable insensibility indeed, not to have had such feelings, and I think inconsistent with human nature.

Our distressed, helpless condition taught us humility and contempt of ourselves. The horrors of the night, the prospect of an immediate, cruel death—or, as one may say, of being crushed by the Almighty in his anger—filled us with terror. And every thing that had tended to weaken our interest with him, upbraided us in the strongest colours, with our baseness and folly. That which, in a calm unruffled temper, we call a natural cause, seemed then like the correction of the Deity. Our imagination represented him as an incensed master, executing vengeance on the crimes of his servants. The father and benefactor were forgot, and in that view, a consciousness of our guilt filled us with despair.

But see, the Lord relents. He hears our prayer. The Lightning ceases. The winds are appeased. The warring elements are reconciled and all things promise peace. The darkness is dispell'd and drooping nature revives at the approaching dawn. Look back Oh! my soul, look back and tremble. Rejoice at thy deliverance, and humble thyself in the presence of thy deliverer.

Yet hold, Oh vain mortal! Check thy ill timed joy. Art thou so selfish to exult because thy lot is happy in a season of universal woe? Hast thou no feelings for the miseries of thy fellow-creatures? And art thou incapable of the soft pangs of sympathetic sorrow? Look around thee and shudder at the view. See desolation and ruin where'er thou turnest thine eye! See thy fellow-creatures pale and lifeless; their bodies mangled, their souls snatched into eternity, unexpecting. Alas! perhaps unprepared! Hark the bitter groans of distress. See sickness and infirmities exposed to the inclemencies of wind and water! See tender infancy pinched with hunger and hanging on the mother[']s knee for food! See the unhappy mother[']s anxiety. Her poverty denies relief, her breast heaves with pangs of maternal pity, her heart is bursting, the tears gush down her cheeks. Oh sights of woe! Oh distress unspeakable! My heart bleeds, but I have no power to solace! O ye, who revel in affluence, see the afflictions of humanity and bestow your superfluity to ease them.[3] Say not, we have suffered also, and thence withold your compassion. What are you[r] sufferings compared to those? Ye have still more than enough left. Act wisely. Succour the miserable and lay up a treasure in Heaven.

I am afraid, Sir, you will think this description more the effort of imagination than a true picture of realities. But I can affirm with the greatest truth, that there is not a single circumstance touched upon, which I have not absolutely been an eye witness to.

Our General has issued several very salutary and humane regulations, and both in his publick and private measures, has shewn himself *the Man*.[4]

[3] Hamilton draws a stark contrast between the storm's effects on the wealthy, who were left largely unscathed, and the poor, who bore the brunt of the devastation. Hamilton is particularly disdainful toward St. Croix's affluent class, whom he likely views as the undeserving beneficiaries of an arbitrarily imposed social structure.

[4] Hamilton reveals an early predilection for assessing statesmanship and political rule.

CONCLUSION

Hamilton's lyrical account of St. Croix's devastating hurricane proved particularly advantageous to his unceasing efforts to rise above his low social station. The intellectual aptitude reflected in his youthful account likely strengthened the resolve of a group of benefactors—including the Reverend Knox, Nicholas Cruger, and Hamilton's elder cousin Ann Lytton—to finance Hamilton's travel to mainland America and his ensuing preparatory and college education in New York.

Source: *The Royal Danish American Gazette*, October 3, 1772.

SECTION II

Pre-Revolution

A Full Vindication of the Measures of Congress

December 15, 1774

In the months following the Boston Tea Party, the British Parliament issued a series of harsh retaliatory measures against Massachusetts intended to squash dissent and discourage colonial resistance elsewhere. These acts, collectively titled the Coercive Acts, included the following:

- The Boston Port Act, which shut down Boston Harbor
- The Massachusetts Government Act, which increased the powers of the royally appointed governor, replaced the elected council with one appointed by the king, and restricted the right of assembly
- The Administration of Justice Act, which allowed royal officials charged with capital crimes in the colonies to stand trial in England
- The Quartering Act, which authorized the quartering of troops in colonists' homes

These acts, referred to by Patriots as the "Intolerable Acts," only strengthened colonial resolve. In September 1774, all of the colonies except Georgia sent delegates to the First Continental Congress in Philadelphia. Congress adjourned the following month, having established a Continental Association to enforce a trade embargo against the British Isles and West Indies. The embargo restricted importation, exportation, and consumption of goods until Parliament reopened the port of Boston and repealed the Coercive Acts.

The gathering of the Continental Congress provoked a visceral reaction from New York's loyalist Tories. The Reverend Samuel Seabury, an Anglican priest who later became the first bishop of the U.S. Episcopal Church, sharply attacked the proceedings of Congress and its delegates in a widely distributed pamphlet initially published in James Rivington's newspaper the *New York Gazeteer*. In his *Free Thoughts on the Proceedings of the Continental Congress*, Seabury, writing under the pseudonym "A Westchester Farmer," referred to the association assigned to oversee the embargo as a "brood of scorpions" and argued that Congress had betrayed not only the British Crown but also the colonies by subjecting them to possible economic ruin and war.

Alexander Hamilton, armed with books and pamphlets supplied by a local Sons of Liberty leader, took on the task of defending the legitimacy of the Continental Congress and the judiciousness of the embargo.

New-York 1774
FRIENDS AND COUNTRYMEN,

It was hardly to be expected that any man could be so presumptuous, as openly to controvert the equity, wisdom, and authority of the measures, adopted by the congress: an assembly truly respectable on every account! . . . But, however improbable such a degree of presumption might have seemed, we find there are some, in whom it exists. Attempts are daily making to diminish the influence of their decisions, and prevent the salutary effects, intended by them. . . . But lest they should have a tendency to mislead, and prejudice the minds of a few; it cannot be deemed altogether useless to bestow some notice upon them.

And first, let me ask these restless spirits, whence it arises that violent antipathy they seem to entertain, not only to the natural rights of mankind; but to common sense and common modesty.[1] That they are enemies to the natural rights of mankind is manifest, because they wish to see one part of their species enslaved by another. That they have an invincible aversion to common sense is apparent in many respects: They endeavour to persuade us, that the absolute sovereignty of parliament does not imply our absolute slavery; . . . and even, that our contest with Britain is founded entirely upon the petty duty of 3 pence per pound on East India tea; whereas the whole world knows, it is built upon this interesting question, whether the inhabitants of Great-Britain have a right to dispose of the lives and properties of the inhabitants of America, or not?[2] And lastly, that these men have discarded all pretension to common modesty, is clear from hence, first, because they, in the plainest terms, call an august body of men, famed for their patriotism and abilities, fools or knaves, and of course the people whom they represented cannot be exempt from the same opprobrious appellations. . .

A little consideration will convince us, that the congress instead of having "ignorantly misunderstood, carelessly neglected, or basely betrayed the interests of the colonies," have, on the contrary, devised and recommended the *only* effectual means to secure the freedom, and establish the future prosperity of America upon a solid basis. . .

Before I proceed to confirm this assertion by the most obvious arguments, I will premise a few brief remarks. The only distinction

[1] Hamilton's three-pronged critique of his polemical opponents closely mirrors his critique of Parliament and its Coercive Acts.

[2] Hamilton emphasizes that the dispute with Great Britain is not motivated by mere economic interest (i.e., avoiding a small tax on tea). Instead, it is rooted in the more fundamental issue of whether or not the American colonists have a right to their lives and property.

between freedom and slavery consists in this: In the former state, a man is governed by the laws to which he has given his consent, either in person, or by his representative: In the latter, he is governed by the will of another.[3] In the one case his life and property are his own, in the other, they depend upon the pleasure of a master. It is easy to discern which of these two states is preferable. No man in his senses can hesitate in choosing to be free, rather than a slave.

That Americans are intitled to freedom, is incontestible upon every rational principle. All men have one common original: they participate in one common nature, and consequently have one common right. No reason can be assigned why one man should exercise any power, or pre-eminence over his fellow creatures more than another; unless they have voluntarily vested him with it.[4] Since then, Americans have not by any act of their's impowered the British Parliament to make laws for them, it follows they can have no just authority to do it.

Besides the clear voice of natural justice in this respect, the fundamental principles of the English constitution are in our favour. . . . Nor is this all, our charters, the express conditions on which our progenitors relinquished their native countries, and came to settle in this, preclude every claim of ruling and taxing us without our assent. . .[5]

What then is the subject of our controversy with the mother country? It is this, whether we shall preserve that security to our lives and properties, which the law of nature, the genius of the British constitution, and our charters afford us; or whether we shall resign them into the hands of the British House of Commons, which is no more privileged to dispose of them than the Grand Mogul?[6] . . .

The only scheme of opposition, suggested by those, who have been, and are averse from a non-importation and non-exportation agreement, is, by Remonstrance and Petition. The authors and abettors of this scheme, have never been able to *invent* a single argument to prove the likelihood of its succeeding. On the other hand, there are many standing facts, and valid considerations against it.

In the infancy of the present dispute, we had recourse to this method only. We addressed the throne in the most loyal and respectful manner, in a legislative capacity; but what was the consequence? Our address was treated with contempt and neglect. . .

[3] According to Hamilton, when humans are governed by a system in which they have no input, they are entirely dependent on the arbitrary whim of those in power and, thus, live as slaves.

[4] Here Hamilton lays out a Lockean argument for natural human equality and the just establishment of political authority. There are neither gods nor beasts among men; therefore, all human beings are, in Locke's words, "creatures of the same species and rank" (Locke 1690, sec. 4). In other words, nature has not established a clear distinction between those who are to govern and those who are governed—no one is born the natural lord over others, just as no one is born a natural slave. Thus, the only legitimate foundation of political authority is consent. On these grounds, Parliament has no right to rule over the colonists without their consent.

[5] In defending the legitimacy of the trade embargo, Hamilton appeals both to the natural rights of mankind and to the legal rights of Englishmen under the British constitution and the terms of the colonial charters (agreements in which the king granted governing powers to proprietors or settlement companies).

[6] Hamilton declares that since the colonists are not represented in the British House of Commons, Parliament has no more of a legitimate claim to tax the colonists than would the ruler of the Moghul Empire in India.

There is less reason now than ever to expect deliverance, in this way, from the hand of oppression. . . . The Premier has advanced too far to recede with safety: He is deeply interested to execute his purpose, if possible: we know he has declared, that he will never desist, till he has brought America to his feet; and we may conclude, nothing but necessity will induce him to abandon his aims.[7] In common life, to retract an error even in the beginning, is no easy task. Perseverance confirms us in it, and rivets the difficulty; but in a public station, to have been in an error, and to have persisted in it, when it is detected, ruins both reputation and fortune. . . .

This being the case, we can have no resource but in a restriction of our trade, or in a resistance *vi & armis* . . . Our congress, therefore, have imposed what restraint they thought necessary. . .

I shall now examine the principal measures of the congress, and vindicate them fully from the charge of injustice or impolicy.[8]

. . . There is no law, either of nature, or of the civil society in which we live, that obliges us to purchase, and make use of the products and manufactures of a different land, or people. It is indeed a dictate of humanity to contribute to the support and happiness of our fellow creatures and more especially those who are allied to us by the ties of blood, interest, and mutual protection; but humanity does not require us to sacrifice our own security and welfare to the convenience, or advantage of others.[9] Self-preservation is the first principle of our nature. When our lives and properties are at stake, it would be foolish and unnatural to refrain from such measures as might preserve them, because they would be detrimental to others.

. . . It remains now to be examined, whether [the measures of Congress also have] the sanction of good policy.

To render it agreeable to good policy, three things are requisite. First, that the necessity of the times require it: Secondly, that it be not the probable source of greater evils, than those it pretends to remedy: And lastly, that it have a probability of success.

That the necessity of the times demands it needs but little elucidation. We are threatened with absolute slavery; it has been proved, that resistance by means of Remonstrance and Petition, would not be efficacious, and of course, that a restriction on our trade, is the only peaceable method, in our power, to avoid the impending mischief: It follows therefore, that such a restriction is necessary.

That it is not the probable source of greater evils than those it pretends to remedy, may easily be determined. The most abject slavery, which comprehends almost every species of human misery, is what it is designed to prevent.

The consequences of the means are a temporary stagnation of commerce, and thereby a deprivation of the luxuries and some of the conveniencies of life. The necessaries, and many of the conveniencies, our own fertile and propitious soil affords us.

No person, that has enjoyed the sweets of liberty, can be insensible of its infinite value, or can reflect on its reverse, without horror and detestation. . .

Were not the disadvantages of slavery too obvious to stand in need of it, I might enumerate and describe the tedious train of calamities, inseparable from it. I might shew that it is fatal to religion and morality; that it tends to debase the mind, and corrupt its noblest springs of action. I might shew, that it relaxes the sinews of industry, clips the wings of commerce, and introduces misery and indigence in every shape. . .[10]

[10] Hamilton critiques slavery not only for being an unjust form of political rule but also for causing moral degradation and deficiency of character in the enslaved population.

The evils which may flow from the execution of our measures, if we consider them with respect to their extent and duration, are comparatively nothing. In all human probability they will scarcely be felt. Reason and experience teach us, that the consequences would be too fatal to Great Britain to admit of delay.[11] There is an immense trade between her and the colonies. The revenues arising from thence are prodigious. The consumption of her manufactures in these colonies supplies the means of subsistence to a vast number of her most useful inhabitants. The experiment we have made heretofore, shews us of how much importance our commercial connexion is to her; and gives us the highest assurance of obtaining immediate redress by suspending it.

[11] Hamilton begins to consider whether the economic sanctions against Great Britain will successfully accomplish their objectives. In the ensuing discussion, he highlights the various ways that the sanctions will harm Great Britain economically. Furthermore, he argues that in the event that Great Britain chooses to resort to force, the Americans would be well positioned to defeat Great Britain in war.

From these considerations it is evident, she must do something decisive. She must either listen to our complaints, and restore us to a peaceful enjoyment of our violated rights; or she must exert herself to enforce her despotic claims by fire and sword. To imagine she would prefer the latter, implies a charge of the grossest infatuation of madness itself. Our numbers are very considerable; the courage of Americans has been tried and proved. Contests for liberty have ever been found the most bloody, implacable and obstinate. The disciplined troops Great Britain could send against us, would be but few, Our superiority in number would over balance our inferiority in discipline. It would be a hard, if not an impracticable task to subjugate us by force. . .

But should we admit a possibility of a third course, as our pamphleteer supposes, that is, the endeavouring to bring us to a compliance by putting a stop to our whole trade: Even this would not be so terrible as he pretends. We can live without trade of any kind. Food and clothing we have within ourselves. Our climate produces cotton, wool, flax and hemp. . . . We have sheep, which, with due care in improving and increasing them, would soon yield a sufficiency of wool. The large quantity of skins, we have among us, would never let us want a warm and comfortable suit. . . . Those hands, which may be deprived of business by the cessation of commerce, may be occupied in various kinds of manufactures and other internal improvements. If by the necessity of the thing, manufactures should once be established and take root among us, they will pave the way, still more, to the future grandeur and glory of America, and by lessening its need of external commerce, will render it still securer against the encroachments of tyranny. . .[12]

Thus have I clearly proved, that the plan of opposition concerted by our congress is perfectly consonant with justice and sound policy; and will, in all human probability, secure our freedom against the assaults of our enemies.

But, after all, it may be demanded why they [The Second Continental Congress] have adopted a non-exportation; seeing many arguments tend to shew that a non-importation alone would accomplish the end desired?

I answer, that the continuance of our exports is the only thing which could lessen, or retard the efficacy of a non-importation. It is not indeed probable it should do that to any great degree; but it was

[12] Hamilton conjectures that a restriction on trade with Great Britain would promote long-term economic development within the colonies because it would foster the growth of domestic manufacturing previously suppressed by British mercantile policy. Such development would make America even more formidable in future conflicts.

adviseable to provide against every possible obstruction. Besides this, the prospect of its taking place, and of the evils attendant upon it, will be a prevailing motive with the ministry to abandon their malignant schemes. It will also serve to convince them, that we are not afraid of putting ourselves to any inconveniencies, sooner than be the victims of their lawless ambition. . .

I am now to address myself in particular to the Farmers of New York.

My good countrymen,

The reason I address myself to you, in particular, is, [not] because I am one of your number, or connected with you in interest more than with any other branch of the community. I love to speak the truth, and would scorn to prejudice you in favour of what I have to say, by taking upon me a fictitious character as other people have done. I can venture to assure you, the true writer of the piece signed A. W. Farmer, is not in reality a Farmer. He is some ministerial emissary, that has assumed the name to deceive you, and make you swallow the intoxicating potion he has prepared for you. But I have a better opinion of you than to think he will be able to succeed . . .

'Tis my maxim to let the plain naked truth speak for itself. . .[13] I am neither merchant, nor farmer. I address you, because I wish well to my country, and of course to you, who are one chief support of it; and because an attempt has been made to lead you astray in particular. You are the men too who would lose most should you be foolish enough to counteract the prudent measures our worthy congress has taken for the preservation of our liberties. Those, who advise you to do it, are not your friends, but your greatest foes. They would have you made slaves, that they may pamper themselves with the fruits of your honest labour. 'Tis the Farmer who is most oppressed in all countries where slavery prevails. . .

Are you willing then to be slaves without a single struggle? Will you give up your freedom, or, which is the same thing, will you resign all security for your life and property, rather than endure some small present inconveniencies? . . .

Pray who can tell me why a farmer in America, is not as honest and good a man, as a farmer in England? or why has not the one as good

[13] The oppressive measures imposed on the colonies by Parliament and the Continental Congress's non-importation, non-exportation, and non-consumption agreement were likely to burden farmers in particular. Thus, Hamilton concludes his vindication of the trade embargo by directly addressing such farmers. He suggests that Seabury chose the pseudonym A.W. Farmer to hoodwink local farmers into believing that he was one of them. In contrast, Hamilton says that rather than pretentiously appealing to their prejudice as Seabury has done, he will attempt to persuade them to support the Continental Association through reason and sound argument.

a right to what he has earned by his labour, as the other? I can't, for my life, see any distinction between them. And yet it seems the English farmers are to be governed and taxed by their own Assembly, or Parliament; and the American farmers are not. The former are to choose their own Representatives from among themselves, whose interest is connected with theirs, and over whom they have proper controul. The latter are to be loaded with taxes by men three thousand miles off; by men, who have no interest, or connexions among them; but whose interest it will be to burden them as much as possible. . .

You have, heretofore experienced the benefit of being taxed by your own Assemblies only. Your burdens are so light, that you scarcely feel them. You'd soon find the difference if you were once to let the Parliament have the management of these matters. . .

But being ruined by taxes is not the worst you have to fear. What security would you have for your lives? How can any of you be sure you would have the free enjoyment of your religion long? [W]ould you put your religion in the power of any set of men living? Remember civil and religious liberty always go together, if the foundation of the one be sapped, the other will fall of course. . .[14]

The Farmer cries, "tell me not of delegates, congresses committees, mobs, riots, insurrections, associations; a plague on them all. Give me the steady, uniform, unbiassed influence of the courts of justice. I have been happy under their protection, and I trust in God, I shall be so again."

I say, tell me not of the British Commons, Lords, ministry, ministerial tools, placemen, pensioners, parasites. I scorn to let my life and property depend upon the pleasure of any of them. Give me the steady, uniform, unshaken security of constitutional freedom; give me the right to be tried by a jury of my own neighbours, and to be taxed by my own representatives only.[15] What will become of the law and courts of justice without this? The shadow may remain, but the substance will be gone. I would die to preserve the law upon a solid foundation; but take away liberty, and the foundation is destroyed. . .

The sort of men I am opposing give you fair words, to persuade you to serve their own turns; but they think and speak of you in common in a very disrespectful manner.[16] I have heard some of their party talk

[14] Hamilton identifies British restriction of the colonists' civil liberty as a threat to all of their freedoms—including freedom of conscience.

[15] Hamilton demands safeguards against the abuse of unchecked power, including both substantive legal protections and electoral representation.

[16] Hamilton appeals to the farmers' pride to counteract Seabury's populist rhetorical strategy. He believes that, if properly directed, pride would lead the farmers to subject their immediate passions and pecuniary interests in service of a more elevated cause.

of you, as the most ignorant and mean-spirited set of people in the world. They say, that you have no sense of honour or generosity; that you don't care a farthing about your country, children or any body else, but yourselves; and that you are so ignorant, as not to be able to look beyond the present; so that if you can once be persuaded to believe the measures of your congress will involve you in some little present perplexities, you will be glad to do any thing to avoid them; without considering the much greater miseries that await you at a little distance off. This is the character they give of you. Bad men are apt to paint others like themselves. For my part, I will never entertain such an opinion of you, unless you should verify their words, by wilfully falling into the pit they have prepared for you. I flatter myself you will convince them of their error, by shewing the world, you are capable of judging what is right and left, and have resolution to pursue it. . .

May God give you wisdom to see what is your true interest, and inspire you with becoming zeal for the cause of virtue and mankind.

A Friend to America.

CONCLUSION

At a mere seventeen years of age, Hamilton began to establish himself as a formidable figure in American political life. The effectiveness of his first political tract was confirmed when Seabury, unaware of Hamilton's authorship, found it necessary to promptly and directly respond.

Source: *A Full Vindication of the Measures of Congress from the Calumnies of their Enemies; In Answer to a Letter, Under the Signature of A.W. Farmer. Whereby His Sophistry Is Exposed, His Cavils Confuted, His Artifices Detected, and His Wit Ridiculed; in a General Address to the Inhabitants of America, and A Particular Address to the Farmers of the Province of New York. Veritas Magna Est and Prevalebit—Truth Is Powerful and Will Prevail* (New York: Printed by James Rivington, 1774).

The Farmer Refuted

February 23, 1775

INTRODUCTION

Less than a month after Hamilton published his *Full Vindication on the Measures of Congress*, Seabury issued a scathing response, contending that the very title "colony" implies a dependence on a mother country and that the American colonies are, thus, subject to the "supreme legislative authority of Great Britain."

In his second response to Seabury, Hamilton provides a more detailed defense of representative government and justifies colonial resistance on theoretical and legal grounds by invoking the authority of natural law, Lockean social contract theory, the English constitution, and the colonial charters.

New-York 1775

Sir,

I resume my pen, in reply to the curious epistle, you have been pleased to favour me with; and can assure you, that, notwithstanding, I am naturally of a grave and phlegmatic disposition, it has been the source of abundant merriment to me. The spirit that breathes throughout is so rancorous, illiberal and imperious: The argumentative part of it so puerile and fallacious: The misrepresentations of facts so palpable and flagrant: The criticisms so illiterate, trifling and absurd . . . that I will venture to pronounce it one of the most ludicrous performances, which has been exhibited to public view, during all the present controversy. . .[1]

I shall, for the present, pass over to that part of your pamphlet, in which you endeavour to establish the supremacy of the British Parliament over America. After a proper eclaircissement of this point, I shall draw such inferences, as will sap the foundation of every thing you have offered.

The first thing that presents itself is a wish, that "I had, explicitly, declared to the public my ideas of the *natural rights* of mankind. Man, in a state of nature (you say) may be considered, as perfectly

[1] Seabury had mocked Hamilton's earlier pamphlet *Vindication on the Measures of Congress* as adolescent and ignorant. In response, Hamilton viscerally rebukes Seabury, contending that he is the one who is ill-informed and infantile. As Ron Chernow (2004) observes, "This slashing style of attack would make Hamilton the most feared polemicist in America, but it won him enemies as well as admirers" (60).

40

free from all restraints of *law* and *government*, and, then, the weak must submit to the strong."

I shall, henceforth, begin to make some allowance for that enmity, you have discovered to the *natural rights* of mankind. For, though ignorance of them in this enlightened age cannot be admitted, as a sufficient excuse for you; yet, it ought, in some measure, to extenuate your guilt. If you will follow my advice, there still may be hopes of your reformation. Apply yourself, without delay, to the study of the law of nature. I would recommend to your perusal, Grotius. Puffendorf, Locke, Montesquieu, and Burlemaqui. I might mention other excellent writers on this subject; but if you attend, diligently, to these, you will not require any others.

There is so strong a similitude between your political principles and those maintained by Mr. Hobbs, that, in judging from them, a person might very easily *mistake* you for a disciple of his. His opinion was, exactly, coincident with yours, relative to man in a state of nature. He held, as you do, that he was, then, perfectly free from all restraint of *law* and *government*. Moral obligation, according to him, is derived from the introduction of civil society; and there is no virtue, but what is purely artificial, the mere contrivance of politicians, for the maintenance of social intercourse.[2] But the reason he run into this absurd and impious doctrine, was, that he disbelieved the existence of an intelligent superintending principle, who is the governor, and will be the final judge of the universe.

As you, sometimes, swear *by him that made you*, I conclude, your sentiment does not correspond with his, in that which is the basis of the doctrine, you both agree in; and this makes it impossible to imagine whence this congruity between you arises. To grant, that there is a supreme intelligence, who rules the world, and has established laws to regulate the actions of his creatures; and, still, to assert, that man, in a state of nature, may be considered as perfectly free from all restraints of *law* and *government*, appear to a common understanding, altogether irreconcileable.

Good and wise men, in all ages, have embraced a very dissimilar theory. They have supposed, that the deity, from the relations, we stand in, to himself and to each other, has constituted an eternal and immutable law, which is, indispensibly, obligatory upon all mankind, prior to any human institution whatever.[3]

[2] Hamilton accuses his opponent of adopting the Hobbesian view that moral obligation and justice do not exist by nature and are, therefore, merely conventional. If justice and morality are artificial conventions rooted in history and law, then the colonists would have no grounds to justify their actions outside of British law.

[3] In contrast to the Hobbesian view that political obligations are rooted in law, Hamilton maintains that pre-conventional rules of justice dictate how humans ought to treat one another based on their status in nature. These eternal and unchangeable laws, which he says are dictated by God or an "intelligent superintending principle," can be discovered by reason and are superior in authority to civil law.

4 Although Hamilton's case for a system of natural laws that limit the just foundation, scope, and character of political power is distinctly Lockean, he repeatedly quotes William Blackstone in support of his position. Perhaps, Hamilton believed that Blackstone's authority as a conservative English jurist would bolster his argument among Loyalist sympathizers.

5 Hamilton explains that human beings possess natural rights by virtue of their common humanity. He later elaborates that these rights, which include personal liberty and safety, exist because no man has a natural political or moral authority "to deprive another of his life, limbs, property, or liberty." In this particular passage, Hamilton explains that human beings are endowed with rational faculties so they might exercise their rights to pursue self-preservation and to improve or beautify their existence.

6 The purpose of civil government, according to Hamilton, is to secure the "absolute" or natural rights of the ruled. Furthermore, since no one individual has the right to rule over another by nature, the only just basis for political authority is consent. Consequently, governments that fail to protect the liberty and safety of their citizens or that assert authority that has not been voluntarily granted can be legitimately resisted or replaced.

This is what is called the law of nature, "which, being coeval with mankind, and dictated by God himself, is, of course, superior in obligation to any other. It is binding over all the globe, in all countries, and at all times. No human laws are of any validity, if contrary to this; and such of them as are valid, derive all their authority, mediately, or immediately, from this original." BLACKSTONE.[4]

Upon this law, depend the natural rights of mankind, the supreme being gave existence to man, together with the means of preserving and beatifying that existence.[5] He endowed him with rational faculties, by the help of which, to discern and pursue such things, as were consistent with his duty and interest, and invested him with an inviolable right to personal liberty, and personal safety.

Hence, in a state of nature, no man had any *moral* power to deprive another of his life, limbs, property or liberty; nor the least authority to command, or exact obedience from him; except that which arose from the ties of consanguinity.

Hence also, the origin of all civil government, justly established, must be a voluntary compact, between the rulers and the ruled; and must be liable to such limitations, as are necessary for the security of the *absolute rights* of the latter; for what original title can any man or set of men have, to govern others, except their own consent?[6] To usurp dominion over a people, in their own despite, or to grasp at a more extensive power than they are willing to entrust, is to violate that law of nature, which gives every man a right to his personal liberty; and can, therefore, confer no obligation to obedience.

"The principal aim of society is to protect individuals, in the enjoyment of those absolute rights, which were vested in them by the immutable laws of nature; but which could not be preserved, in peace, without that mutual assistance, and intercourse, which is gained by the institution of friendly and social communities. Hence it follows, that the first and primary end of human laws, is to maintain and regulate these *absolute rights* of individuals." BLACKSTONE.

If we examine the pretensions of parliament, by this criterion, which is evidently, a good one, we shall, presently detect their injustice. First, they are subversive of our natural liberty, because an authority is assumed over us, which we by no means assent to. And secondly, they divest us of that moral security, for our lives and properties, which we are intitled to, and which it is the primary end of society to bestow. For such security can never exist, while we have no part in making the laws, that are to bind us; and while it may be the interest of our uncontroled legislators to oppress us as much as possible.[7]

To deny these principles will be not less absurd, than to deny the plainest axioms: I shall not, therefore, attempt any further illustration of them.

You say, "when I assert, that since Americans have not, by any act of theirs, impowered the British parliament to make laws for them, it follows they can have no just authority to do it, I advance a position subversive of that dependence, which all colonies must, from their very nature, have on the mother country." The premises from which I drew this conclusion, are indisputable. You have not detected any fallacy in them; but endeavor to overthrow them by deducing a false and imaginary consequence. My principles admit the only dependence which can subsist, consistent with any idea of civil liberty, or with the future welfare of the British empire, as will appear hereafter. . .

In what sense, the dependance of the colonies on the mother country, has been acknowledged, will appear from those circumstances of their political history, which I shall, by and by, recite. The term colony signifies nothing more, than a body of people drawn from the mother country, to inhabit some distant place, or the country itself so inhabited. As to the degrees and modifications of that subordination, which is due to the parent state, these must depend upon other things, besides the mere act of emigration, to inhabit or settle a distant country. These must be ascertained, by the spirit of the constitution of the mother country, by the compacts for the purpose of colonizing, and, more especially, by the law of nature, and that *supreme law* of every society—*its own happiness*.[8] . . .

But you deny, that "we can be liege subjects to the King of Great-Britain, while we disavow the authority of parliament." . . . [T]he King of Great Britain . . . is King of America, by virtue of a compact between us and the Kings of Great-Britain. These colonies were planted and settled by the Grants, and under the Protection of English Kings, who entered into covenants with us for themselves,

[7] Hamilton argues that, under the authority of the laws of nature, the American colonists have the legitimate right to resist the actions of Parliament. The British Parliament violated the just foundation and end of civil government by exerting authority that had never been granted and by subverting, rather than protecting, the colonists' right to their lives and properties. Furthermore, as long as members of Parliament are permitted to exercise unconstrained power over the colonies, they will continue to oppress the colonists as much as possible for their own benefit.

[8] Seabury had claimed that colonies, by their very nature, are dependent on and subordinate to the mother country. Hamilton responds by acknowledging that the American colonies have a long political history of dependence on Great Britain. He continues to point out, however, that every people group has a right to base its continued political obligations on what will best secure its welfare and happiness. Thus, for the British Empire to merit continued loyalty and obedience, it must promote civil liberty and representative government.

9 After maintaining that, based on the terms of the colonial charters, the colonies owed allegiance to the British king, but not to Parliament, Hamilton makes the classic social contract argument of allegiance for protection, which is that people have a duty to obey the laws in exchange for the protection they receive under the law. Therefore, in so far as the king provides protection for the lives and properties of the American colonists from external threat and invasion, they are obligated to obey him. In the event, however, that the king fails to secure or directly invades the rights of the colonists, they are no longer obligated to obey him.

their heirs and successors; and it is from these covenants, that the duty of protection on their part, and the duty of allegiance on ours arise. . .

The law of nature and the British constitution both confine allegiance to the person of the King; and found it upon the principle of protection. . . . Hence it is evident, that while we enjoy the protection of the King, it is incumbent upon us to obey and serve him, without the interposition of parliamentary supremacy.[9] . . .

The fundamental source of all your errors, sophisms and false reasonings is a total ignorance of the natural rights of mankind. Were you once to become acquainted with these, you could never entertain a thought, that all men are not, by nature, entitled to a parity of privileges. You would be convinced, that natural liberty is a gift of the beneficent Creator to the whole human race, and that civil liberty is founded in that; and cannot be wrested from any people, without the most manifest violation of justice. *Civil liberty, is only natural liberty, modified and secured by the sanctions of civil society.* It is not a thing, in its own nature, precarious and dependent on human will and caprice; but is conformable to the constitution of man, as well as necessary to the *well-being* of society.

Upon this principle, colonists as well as other men, have a right to civil liberty. . . . The practice of Rome, towards her colonies, cannot afford the shadow of an argument against this. That mistress of the world was often unjust. And the treatment of her dependent provinces is one of the greatest blemishes in her history. Through the want of that civil liberty, for which we are now so warmly contending, they groaned under every species of wanton oppression. If we are wise, we shall take warning from thence; and consider a like state of dependence, as more to be dreaded, than pestilence and famine.[10]

The right of colonists, therefore, to exercise a legislative power, is an inherent right. It is founded upon the right of all men to freedom and happiness. For civil liberty cannot possibly have any existence, where the society, for whom laws are made, have no share in making them; and where the interest of their legislators is not inseparably interwoven with theirs. Before you asserted, that the right of legislation was derived "from the indulgence or grant of the parent state," you should have proved two things, that all men have not a natural right to freedom, and that civil liberty is not advantageous to society. . .

. . . I have taken a pretty general survey of the American Charters; and proved to the satisfaction of every unbiassed person, that they are intirely, discordant with that sovereignty of parliament, for which you are an advocate. . . . It is true, that New-York has no Charter. But, if it could support it's claim to liberty in no other way, it might, with justice, plead the common principles of colonization: for, it would be unreasonable, to seclude one colony, from the enjoyment of the most important privileges of the rest. There is no need, however, of this plea: The sacred rights of mankind are not to be rummaged for, among old parchments, or musty records. They are written, as with a sun beam, in the whole *volume* of human nature, by the hand of the divinity itself; and can never be erased or obscured by mortal power.[11]

The nations of Turkey, Russia, France, Spain, and all other despostic kingdoms, in the world, have an inherent right, when ever they please, to shake off the yoke of servitude, (though sanctified by the immemorial usage of their ancestors;) and to model their government, upon the principles of civil liberty.

. . . When the first principles of civil society are violated, and the rights of a whole people are invaded, the common forms of municipal law are not to be regarded. Men may then betake themselves to the law of nature; and, if they but conform their actions, to that standard, all cavils against them, betray either ignorance or dishonesty. There are some events in society, to which human laws cannot extend; but when applied to them lose all their force and efficacy. In short, when human laws contradict or discountenance the means, which are necessary to preserve the essential rights of any society, they defeat the proper end of all laws, and so become null and void. . .[12]

Whatever opinion may be entertained of my sentiments and intentions, I attest that being, whose all-seeing eye penetrates the inmost recesses of the heart, that I am not influenced (in the part I take) by any unworthy motive—that, if I am in an error, it is my judgment, not my heart, that errs. That I earnestly lament the unnatural quarrel, between the parent state and the colonies; and most ardently wish for a speedy reconciliation, a perpetual and *mutually* beneficial union, that I am a warm advocate for limited monarchy, and an unfeigned well-wisher to the present Royal Family.[13]

[11] Hamilton appeals to historical documents and the colonial charters to defend the colonists' right to liberty and representation under British law. Ultimately, however, he concludes that the absence of legal charters (such as in the case of New York, which had no colonial charter) is irrelevant. The rights to liberty and representation are not legal privileges granted by government but are rights established by divine ordinance. Therefore, as he proceeds to explain, any people from any country have an equal right to throw off the "yoke of servitude" no matter how long they have lived under oppressive rule.

[12] The legitimacy of human laws should always be based on an assessment of whether or not they are in accordance with the higher natural law and the rights of human beings.

[13] Hamilton concludes by expressing his support for "limited monarchy" and his hope for amicable reconciliation based on the restoration of the colonists' rights.

But on the other hand, I am inviolably attached to the essential rights of mankind, and the true interests of society. I consider civil liberty, in a genuine unadulterated sense, as the greatest of terrestrial blessings. I am convinced, that the whole human race is intitled to it; and, that it can be wrested from no part of them, without the blackest and most aggravated guilt.

I verily believe also, that the best way to secure a permanent and happy union, between Great-Britain and the colonies, is to permit the latter to be as free, as they desire. To abridge their liberties, or to exercise any power over them, which they are unwilling to submit to, would be a perpetual source of discontent and animosity. A continual jealousy would exist on both sides. This would lead to tyranny, on the one hand, and to sedition and rebellion, on the other. Impositions, not really grievous in themselves, would be thought so; and the murmurs arising from thence, would be considered as the effect of a turbulent ungovernable spirit. These jarring principles would, at length, throw all things into disorder; and be productive of an irreparable breach, and a total disunion.

That harmony and mutual confidence may speedily be restored, between all the parts of the British empire, is the favourite wish of one, who feels the warmest sentiments of good will to mankind, who bears no enimity to you, and who is, A sincere Friend to America.

CONCLUSION

Hamilton's *Full Vindication* and *Farmer Refuted* made such an impression on the public mind that many assumed they were written by well-established Whigs such as John Adams, John Jay, or William Livingston. Once it became known that the youthful Hamilton was in fact the author, he was praised as an oracle of the Revolution and became known throughout the colonies as "The Vindicator" (Hendrickson 1981).

Source: *The Farmer Refuted: Or a More Impartial and Comprehensive View of the Dispute between Great-Britain and the Colonies, Intended as a Further Vindication of the Congress: In Answer to a Letter from A.W. Farmer, Intitled A View of the Controversy between Great-Britain and Her Colonies: Including a Mode of Determining the Present Disputes Finally and Effectually, &c . . .* (New York: Printed by James Rivington, 1775).

Letter to John Jay on Lawlessness of a Mob

November 26, 1775

INTRODUCTION

In late 1775, a militia led by Sons of Liberty leader Isaac Sears—wishing to take revenge on outspoken Loyalists—kidnapped and terrorized Samuel Seabury and his family in Connecticut. The angry band then proceeded to New York where they attacked printer James Rivington and raided his print shop, destroying his press and stealing his property.

Although Hamilton thought Seabury and Rivington detestable and their views dangerous, he was outraged by the lawless actions of the Patriot mob, which he felt compelled to denounce. He wrote to his friend John Jay, who was currently serving as a delegate in the Second Continental Congress. Hamilton hoped Jay might use his political clout to ensure a public condemnation of Sears and his men.

New York Novem 26. 1775
Dear Sir

I take the liberty to trouble you with some remarks on a matter which to me appears of not a little importance; doubting not that you will use your influence in Congress to procure a remedy for the evil I shall mention, if you think the considerations I shall urge are of that weight they seem in my judgment to possess.

You will probably ere this reaches you have heard of the late incursion made into this city by a number of horsemen from New England under the command of Capt Sears, who took away Mr. Rivington's types, and a Couteau or two. Though I am fully sensible how dangerous and pernicious Rivington's press has been, and how detestable the character of the man is in every respect, yet I cannot help disapproving and condemning this step.

In times of such commotion as the present, while the passions of men are worked up to an uncommon pitch there is great danger of fatal extremes. The same state of the passions which fits the multitude, who have not a sufficient stock of reason and knowlege to guide

47

Hamilton worries that the passions unleashed in just resistance to British oppression might cause the multitude to disregard the importance of authority and established order in general—in which case tyranny would merely be replaced by anarchy.

In periods of political turmoil, it is essential that prudent leaders direct people's passions toward the proper ends of justice and the common good.

Allowing militias from neighboring states to trample on the rights and property of certain citizens of New York, whoever they might be, would build impunity for criminal behavior that eventually would threaten the rights of all citizens—Patriots and Loyalists alike.

them, for opposition to tyranny and oppression, very naturally leads them to a contempt and disregard of all authority.[1] The due medium is hardly to be found among the more intelligent, it is almost impossible among the unthinking populace. When the minds of these are loosened from their attachment to ancient establishments and courses, they seem to grow giddy and are apt more or less to run into anarchy. These principles, too true in themselves, and confirmed to me both by reading and my own experience, deserve extremely the attention of those, who have the direction of public affairs. In such tempestuous times, it requires the greatest skill in the political pilots to keep men steady and within proper bounds,[2] on which account I am always more or less alarmed at everything which is done of mere will and pleasure, without any proper authority. Irregularities I know are to be expected, but they are nevertheless dangerous and ought to be checked, by every prudent and moderate mean. From these general maxims, I disapprove of the irruption in question, as serving to cherish a spirit of disorder at a season when men are too prone to it of themselves . . .

Besides this, men coming from a neighbouring province to chastise the notorious friends of the ministry here, will hold up an idea to our ennemies not very advantageous to our affairs.[3] They will imagine that the New Yorkers are totally, or a majority of them, disaffected to the American cause, which makes the interposal of their neighbours necessary: or that such violences will breed differences and effect that which they have been so eagerly wishing, a division and qurrelling among ourselves. Every thing of such an aspect must encourage their hopes.

Upon the whole the measure is condemned, by all the cautious and prudent among the whigs, and will evidently be productive of secret jealousy and ill blood if a stop is not put to things of the kind for the future.

All the good purposes that could be expected from such a step will be answered; and many ill consequences will be prevented if your body gently interposes a check for the future . . .

A favourable idea will be impressed of your justice & impartiality in discouraging the encroachments of any one province on another; and the apprehensions of prudent men respecting the ill-effects of an ungoverned spirit in the people of New England will be quieted. Believe me sir it is a matter of consequence and deserves serious attention . . .

I am sir with very great Esteem—Your most hum servant
A. Hamilton

CONCLUSION

Jay communicated the concerns spelled out in Hamilton's letter to Nathaniel Woodhull, president of the Provincial Congress of New York. The Provincial Congress in response issued a sharp rebuke of Isaac Sears's actions.

Source: Alexander Hamilton Papers, Manuscript and Archives Division, The New York Public Library.

SECTION III

During the War

Letter to the New York Congress on Merit-Based Promotions

August 12, 1776

INTRODUCTION

In early 1776, the New York Provincial Congress appointed Hamilton command of the New York Provincial Company of Artillery. Hamilton took great care in this role to ensure that his men were not only well trained and disciplined but also well fed and compensated. When he learned that the men in his provincial company received lower pay and rations than their counterparts in the Continental Artillery, Hamilton constructed two thoughtful letters of complaint to the New York Provincial Congress. He convinced the members that they were legally obliged to rectify the discrepancy, since provincial troops were subject to the same regulations as the soldiers in the Continental Army.

In a third letter to the New York Provincial Congress, written just over a month after independence was declared, Hamilton sought to improve his soldiers' future prospects by challenging the long-standing military custom of basing promotion on birth and rank. By requesting to promote an enlisted man to the position of commissioned officer based on merit alone, Hamilton helped ensure that the exemplary service and achievements of soldiers would be recognized and rewarded.

Gentlemen

It is necessary I should inform you that there is at present a vacancy in my company, arising from the promotion of Lieutenant Johnson to a captaincy in one of the row-gallies.[1] . . . As artillery officers are scarce in proportion to the call for them, and as myself and my remaining officers sustain an extraordinary weight of duty on account of the present vacancy, I shall esteem it a favour if you will be pleased, as soon as possible, to make up my deficiency by a new appointment. It would be productive of much inconvenience, should not the inferior officers succeed in course, and from this consideration. . . . I would beg the liberty warmly to recommend to your attention Thomas Thompson, now first sergeant in my company, a

[1] Hamilton identifies an open lieutenant position in his company because one of his men was promoted as captain of an armed watercraft on Lake Champlain.

53

[2] Hamilton encourages the Provincial Congress to promote worthy men from the lower ranks and requests that the vacant position in his company be filled by Sergeant Thomas Thompson. He then explains that Thompson's qualifications make him a deserving candidate.

[3] Hamilton contends that promoting Thompson from the lower ranks, based on his achievements and qualifications, will inspire others from the lower ranks to serve more valiantly, based on the hope of their own future advancement.

man highly deserving of notice and preferment.[2] He has discharged his duty in his present station with uncommon fidelity, assiduity and expertness. He is a very good disciplinarian, possesses the advantage of having seen a good deal of service in Germany; has a tolerable share of common sense, and is well calculated not to disgrace the rank of an officer and gentleman. In a word, I verily believe he will make an excellent lieutenant, and his advancement will be a great encouragement and benefit to my company in particular, and will be an animating example to all men of merit, to whose knowledge it comes.[3]

Myself and my officers will be much obliged to the Honourable Convention to favour us with our commissions with all convenient speed, as they may be highly requisite under some circumstances, that may possibly hereafter arise.

I am, with the utmost respect, gentlemen, Your most obedient and most humble servant,

A Hamilton,
Captain of N. Y. Artillery.
Augt. 12th, 1776.

The Honourable the Convention of the State of New-York.

CONCLUSION

Hamilton's request to promote a sergeant to a lieutenant was so unprecedented that the New York Provincial Congress sent Colonel Peter Livingston to meet with Hamilton and carefully consider his proposal. Following this meeting, the Provincial Congress not only approved Thomas Thompson's appointment as a lieutenant but also issued a directive—publicized throughout the province of New York and the army in general—adopting merit as the official standard for promotion. Thus, Hamilton inspired a practice that overturned age-old European tradition and greatly influenced the future development of the American armed forces.

Source: *Journals of the Provincial Congress of the State of New York*, vol. II. Albany: Thurlow Weed, 1842, 278.

Letter to the New York Congress on Leaving the Artillery

March 6, 1777

INTRODUCTION

On March 1, 1777, Hamilton was officially appointed as an aide-de-camp to General George Washington and was offered a double promotion to the rank of lieutenant colonel. A few days later, writing from the army headquarters in Morristown, Hamilton informed the New York Provincial Congress of his change in commission and gave an account of the artillery company formerly under his command.

The change in my own circumstances and in those of your company of Artillery lately under my command make it necessary I should inform you of the present state of things, respecting it; in order that you may determine as to the future disposal of it; and I should be happy as speedily as convenient to know your pleasure on the subject.

His Excellency has been pleased to appoint me one of his Aid du Camps. Capt Lieutenant James Moore, a promising officer, and who did credit to the state he belonged to, died the 25th of December, after a short but excruciating fit of illness. Lieut. Gilliland, from domestic inconveniences, and *other motives*, resigned his Commission to General Washington about three weeks before. There remain now only two officers Lieutenant Bean & Lieutenant Thompson. Mr. Johnson began the enlistment of the Company, contrary to his orders from the convention, for the term of a year, instead of during the war; a circumstance I was unacquainted with till lately, but which, with deaths and desertions; reduces it at present to the small number of 25 men.[1]

If you think proper to retain the company on its present establishment it will be necessary to fill up the vacancies and make provision to have the number of men completed. In this case I would beg leave to recommend to your attention Lieutenant Thompson, as far as a Capt Lieutenancy; but Mr. Bean though a brave man, has a failing that disqualifies him for any farther preferment.[2] As to the new

[1] After announcing his appointment to Washington's staff, Hamilton provides an account of his company. He explains that—following the military campaigns of the previous year and the death, desertions, and enlistment expirations that ensued—his company of ninety-three had dwindled to as few two officers and twenty-five enlisted men.

[2] Of the two remaining officers in his company, Hamilton recommends that the Provincial Congress promote Lieutenant Thompson as captain. Although he does not give specifics, Hamilton asserts that Lieutenant Bean has a character flaw, making him unfit for promotion. Another version of this letter claims that "Mr. Bean is so incurably addicted to a certain failing."

[3] Hamilton acknowledges that, in its paltry state, his former company would be more of a financial burden than a benefit to New York and that the state would likely transfer its authority over to the Continental Army. (It did so on March 17.)

[4] In his last few months as artillery captain, Hamilton was plagued by severe illness. Although nearly bedridden, he still mustered the strength to lead his men with Washington across the Delaware and fight the Hessians in Trenton, New Jersey. Hamilton's fortitude in this regard no doubt influenced Washington's decision to personally invite Hamilton to join his staff as a top aide.

arrangement for the Artillery, if I am not misinformed, the number of officers is increased to six & the pay of both officers and men is raised to a fourth part more than the other troops. As the rest of the Company can hardly answer any special good purposes to the state I imagine you will resolve to resign it. There will be no difficulty in having it transferred to the Continental establishment.[3]

I should have advised you earlier of these [changes] but, am just recovered from a long and severe fit of [illness].[4]

I have the honor to be with the most sincere respect Gentlemen

Yr. most Obedient Ser

CONCLUSION

Hamilton's appointment to Washington's staff—where promotion was allocated based on talent and virtue rather than birth—marked an important turning point in Hamilton's career. Had he remained a captain of the Provincial Artillery Company, it is doubtful he would have ever experienced such a rapid rise in status and influence.

Source: Hamilton Papers, Library of Congress.

Letter to George Clinton on the Failures of Congress

February 13, 1778

INTRODUCTION

Hamilton's proximity to General Washington enabled him to observe firsthand the military and political affairs of the nation. Although Hamilton remained an idealist who full-heartedly supported the revolutionary cause, he soon became frustrated and disillusioned by his fellow countrymen and their leaders. In late 1777, after uncovering a cabal originating in the Continental Congress that sought to replace Washington with General Horatio Gates, Hamilton began to seriously doubt the wisdom and virtue of the members of Congress.

Hamilton's disenchantment with the Continental Congress only increased when, after recovering from a near-fatal illness following an arduous diplomatic mission, he returned to the army's winter headquarters in Valley Forge. On arriving, Hamilton found his fellow soldiers in extremely dire straits, starving, nearly frozen, and on the verge of mutiny—having gone weeks without sufficient food, clothing, and shelter. In a letter to New York governor George Clinton, Hamilton attributed the sufferings of the troops to mismanagement, incompetence, and corruption in Congress and the various committees that had been charged with overseeing the war.

Head Quarters Feb'y 13, 1778.
Dear Sir,

. . . There is a matter, which often obtrudes itself upon my mind, and which requires the attention of every person of sense and influence, among us. I mean a degeneracy of representation in the great council of America.[1] It is a melancholy truth Sir, and the effects of which we dayly see and feel, that there is not so much wisdom in a certain body, as there ought to be, and as the success of our affairs absolutely demands. Many members of it are no doubt men in every respect, fit for the trust, but this cannot be said of it as a body. Folly, caprice a want of foresight, comprehension and dignity, characterise the general tenor of their actions. Of this I dare say, you are sensible, though you have not perhaps so many opportunities of knowing it as I have. Their conduct with respect to the

[1] Once made up of high-caliber representatives—including men who had authorized the Continental Army, appointed George Washington as its commander in chief, and signed the Declaration of Independence—the Continental Congress, according to Hamilton, was now facing a failure of leadership.

[2] Congress had exhibited a lack of foresight in its treatment of the army. In an attempt to reduce expenditures, it withheld the provisions necessary to attract quality officers and prevent dissolution and mutiny.

[3] Hamilton harshly criticizes Congress's capricious granting of non-meritorious promotions. He is particularly critical of the favoritism granted to foreigners.

[4] Having been a leading defender of independence and republicanism, Hamilton laments that the irresponsibility of the nation's principal representative body degrades not only the reputation of republican government, generally, but also his personal honor.

[5] According to Hamilton, the quality of Congress deteriorated because the most talented and distinguished members of the early Congress left to occupy positions in their respective state governments or in the army, thereby handing control of the nation's governing body to largely mediocre and disreputable characters.

army especially is feeble indecisive and improvident—insomuch, that we are reduced to a more terrible situation than you can conceive. False and contracted views of economy have prevented them, though repeatedly urged to it, from making that provision for officers which was requisite to interest them in the service;[2] which has produced such carelessness and indifference to the service, as is subversive of every officer-like quality. They have disgusted the army by repeated instances of the most whimsical favouritism in their promotions; and by an absurd prodigality of rank to foreigners and to the meanest staff of the army.[3] They have not been able to summon resolution enough to withstand the impudent importunity and vain boasting of foreign pretenders; but have manifested such a ductility and inconstancy in their proceedings, as will warrant the charge of suffering themselves to be bullied, by every petty rascal, who comes armed with ostentatious pretensions of military merit and experience. Would you believe it Sir, it is become almost proverbial in the mouths of the French officers and other foreigners, that they have nothing more to do, to obtain whatever they please, than to assume a high tone and assert their own merit with confidence and perserverance? These things wound my feelings as a republican more than I can express; and in some degree make me contemptible in my own eyes.[4]

By injudicious changes and arrangements in the Commissary's department, in the middle of a campaign, they have exposed the army frequently to temporary want, and to the danger of a dissolution, from absolute famine. At this very day there are complaints from the whole line, of having been three or four days without provisions; desertions have been immense, and strong features of mutiny begin to show themselves. It is indeed to be wondered at, that the soldiery have manifested so unparalleled a degree of patience, as they have. If effectual measures are not speedily adopted, I know not how we shall keep the army together or make another campaign. . .

America once had a representation, that would do honor to any age or nation.[5] The present falling off is very alarming and dangerous. What is the cause? or how is it to be remedied? are questions that the welfare of these states requires should be well attended to. The great men who composed our first council; are they dead, have they deserted the cause, or what has become of them? Very few are dead and still fewer have deserted the cause;—they are all except the few who still remain in Congress either in the field, or in the civil offices of their respective states; far the greater part are engaged in the latter. The only remedy then is to take them out of these employments and return them to the place, where their presence is infinitely more important.

Each State in order to promote its own internal government and prosperity, has selected its best members to fill the offices within itself, and conduct its own affairs. Men have been fonder of the emoluments and conveniences, of being employed at home, and local attachment, falsely operating, has made them more provident for the particular interests of the states to which they belonged, than for the common interests of the confederacy. This is a most pernicious mistake, and must be corrected.[6] However important it is to give form and efficiency to your interior constitutions and police; it is infinitely more important to have a wise general council; otherwise a failure of the measures of the union will overturn all your labours for the advancement of your particular good and ruin the common cause. You should not beggar the councils of the United States to enrich the administration of the several members. Realize to yourself the consequences of having a Congress despised at home and abroad. How can the common force be exerted, if the power of collecting it be put in weak foolish and unsteady hands? How can we hope for success in our European negociations, if the nations of Europe have no confidence in the wisdom and vigor, of the great Continental Government? This is the object on which their eyes are fixed, hence it is America will d[e]rive its importance or insignificance, in their estimation. . .

The sentiments I have advanced are not fit for the vulgar ear; and circumstanced as I am, I should with caution utter them except to those in whom I may place an entire confidence. But it is time that men of weight and understanding should take the alarm, and excite each other to a proper remedy.[7] For my part, my insignificance, allows me to do nothing more, than to hint my apprehensions to those of that description who are pleased to favour me with their confidence. In this view, I write to you. . .

I am with great regard & respect, Sir, Your most Obed. servant
Alex. Hamilton

[6] Indicating his early preference for nationalism, Hamilton argues that the most competent leaders have erroneously preferred employment in the affairs of their particular states, when their talents would be utilized far more profitably in service to the common cause and the union as a whole. He further contends that the future well-being and success of the states in their individual capacity is dependent on a strong union of states and the competency of the national council.

[7] Hamilton writes to Governor Clinton, hoping that he, and others in positions of influence, will persuade more qualified figures to seek office in Congress. Although Clinton indicated in response that he, too, was concerned with the defects in Congress, Clinton eventually became an ardent supporter of states' rights and one of Hamilton's most bitter political enemies.

CONCLUSION

Hamilton and Washington's efforts to convince leaders in Congress and the state governments to quickly provide adequate relief for the troops suffering at Valley Forge were largely in vain. During the winter of 1777–1778, approximately 2,500 men died of starvation, disease, and exposure; hundreds of others resigned their posts or deserted altogether. This early demonstration of the incompetence of the Continental Congress, and the failures of the congressional committees charged with overseeing the war effort, helped shape Hamilton's understanding of effective political power and his later vision for an energetic, unified executive.

Source: *Public Papers of George Clinton*, vol. II. New York and Albany, 1900, 860–864.

Letter to John Jay on Slaves as Soldiers

March 14, 1779

INTRODUCTION

Hamilton formed several intimate friendships with members of Washington's military family during his tenure as aide-de-camp. Colonel John Laurens was the closest and dearest of these friends. The two were united ideologically on many subjects, including their mutual antagonism toward the institution of slavery. In fact, both men viewed the fight for emancipation as part of the larger struggle for natural freedom and equality being waged in the war against Great Britain by the American colonists.

From the time he joined Washington's staff, Laurens fervently advocated freeing slaves in exchange for their service to Continental Army. By the end of 1778, acceptance of his proposals became more probable as the British began to move into and capture parts of the South. British invasion put Southern slave owners in a precarious position. Defense of their homeland required military service, but many slave owners feared a slave revolt if they left their homes and families unattended. Thus, it seemed plausible that even the most ardent slavery advocates might support the enlistment of slaves as soldiers in exchange for future emancipation.

In 1779, Laurens resigned from Washington's staff to help defend South Carolina. On his journey home, he first traveled to Philadelphia to solicit congressional approval for a plan to raise between two and four battalions of Negro troops in South Carolina. Hamilton wholeheartedly endorsed the plan. He sent Laurens with a letter addressed to John Jay, the recently elected president of the Continental Congress, urging Congress to put the Negro battalions on the Continental payroll.

Dear Sir,

Col Laurens, who will have the honor of delivering you this letter, is on his way to South Carolina, on a project, which I think, in the present situation of affairs there, is a very good one and deserves every kind of support and encouragement. This is to raise two three or four batalions of negroes; with the assistance of the government of that state, by contributions from the owners in proportion to the number they possess. If you should think proper to enter upon the subject

61

with him, he will give you a detail of his plan. He wishes to have it recommended by Congress to the state; and, as an inducement, that they would engage to take those batalions into Continental pay.

It appears to me, that an expedient of this kind, in the present state of Southern affairs, is the most rational, that can be adopted, and promises very important advantages. Indeed, I hardly see how a sufficient force can be collected in that quarter without it;[1] and the enemy's operations there are growing infinitely serious and formidable. I have not the least doubt, that the negroes will make very excellent soldiers, with proper management; and I will venture to pronounce, that they cannot be put in better hands than those of Mr. Laurens. He has all the zeal, intelligence, enterprise, and every other qualification requisite to succeed in such an undertaking. It is a maxim with some great military judges, that with sensible officers soldiers can hardly be too stupid; and on this principle it is thought that the Russians would make the best troops in the world, if they were under other officers than their own. The King of Prussia is among the number who maintain this doctrine and has a very emphatical saying on the occasion, which I do not exactly recollect. I mention this, because I frequently hear it objected to the scheme of embodying negroes that they are too stupid to make soldiers. This is so far from appearing to me a valid objection that I think their want of cultivation (for their natural faculties are probably as good as ours) joined to that habit of subordination which they acquire from a life of servitude, will make them sooner became soldiers than our White inhabitants.[2] Let officers be men of sense and sentiment, and the nearer the soldiers approach to machines perhaps the better.

I foresee that this project will have to combat much opposition from prejudice and self-interest. The contempt we have been taught to entertain for the blacks, makes us fancy many things that are founded neither in reason nor experience;[3] and an unwillingness to part with property of so valuable a kind will furnish a thousand arguments to show the impracticability or pernicious tendency of a scheme which requires such a sacrifice. But it should be considered, that if we do not make use of them in this way, the enemy probably will;[4] and that the best way to counteract the temptations they will hold out will be to offer them ourselves. An essential part of the plan is to give them their freedom with their muskets. This will secure their fidelity, animate their courage, and I believe will have a good influence upon

1 Hamilton initially advises support for Laurens's proposal by pragmatically appealing to expediency and self-interest.

2 Hamilton dismisses as fallacy the claim that blacks are genetically inferior and would therefore make poor soldiers. Instead, he argues that any intellectual shortcomings stem from a lack of cultivation caused by social and political subordination. Toward the end of his letter, he further argues that, given the promise of freedom, black slaves will be more loyal, courageous, and disciplined as soldiers than free whites.

3 Hamilton correctly predicts that both prejudice and self-interest will produce strong resistance to any plan to arm and emancipate slaves. Repudiating bigotry as ungrounded in reason or experience, he explains that contempt for and prejudice toward blacks is cultivated to justify the self-interest of those who benefit from keeping them in a subordinated state.

4 Predicting that if Southern slaveholders do not emancipate and arm their slaves the British surely will, Hamilton attempts to combat self-interest by appealing to fear.

those who remain, by opening a door to their emancipation. This circumstance, I confess, has no small weight in inducing me to wish the success of the project; for the dictates of humanity and true policy equally interest me in favour of this unfortunate class of men. . .[5]

With the truest respect & esteem I am Sir Your most Obed servant Alex Hamilton

[5] While Hamilton opens his letter by pragmatically arguing that emancipation will help supply necessary manpower, here he argues that emancipation is also required by the dictates of justice and humanity. Thus, as Chernow (2004) aptly observes, "In typical Hamiltonian manner, he placed political realism at the service of a larger ethical framework" (122).

CONCLUSION

In spite of the clearly beneficial role that Negro troops would have played in stopping British advancement in the South, Laurens's plan received virtually no support from Southern delegates. It was therefore ignored by the Continental Congress and rejected by South Carolina's legislature. Hamilton's prediction that the British would offer emancipation in exchange for their military service, if the South did not, became a reality. Thousands of slaves accepted the British offer and eventually settled as free men in the Caribbean following the war. Hamilton continued to abhor slavery throughout his life and eventually became one of the leading members of the New York Society for Promoting the Manumission of Slaves.

Source: William Jay. *The Life of John Jay*, vol. II. New York: J. & J. Harper, 1833, 31–32.

Letter to James Duane on the Defects of the Confederation

September 3, 1780

INTRODUCTION

In 1780, as deficiencies in the Continental Army became more apparent and the political and financial state of the country more tenuous, the state legislatures began to send more capable and nationally minded representatives to serve in the Continental Congress. That same year, a convention was scheduled to consider full ratification of the Articles of Confederation. With this upcoming convention in mind, James Duane, a New York delegate to the Continental Congress, wrote to Hamilton soliciting his views concerning what reforms he thought would be necessary to win the war and save the country from political and fiscal ruin.

Hamilton responded to Duane's inquiry with a comprehensive assessment of the defects of the current confederation and a vision to substantially overhaul the nation's political, administrative, and financial institutions. In so doing, Hamilton presented the first official proposal for national over state sovereignty.

Dr. Sir

[1] Hamilton acknowledges that his proposals have little chance of acceptance given the current state of public opinion. Nevertheless, he lays out his vision for the future republic in hopes that Duane, and other political leaders, might strive to implement his suggestions bit by bit.

Agreeably to your request and my promise I sit down to give you my ideas of the defects of our present system, and the changes necessary to save us from ruin. They may perhaps be the reveries of a projector rather than the sober views of a politician. You will judge of them, and make what use you please of them.[1]

The fundamental defect is a want of power in Congress. It is hardly worth while to show in what this consists, as it seems to be universally acknowleged, or to point out how it has happened, as the only question is how to remedy it. It may however be said that it has originated from three causes—an excess of the spirit of liberty which has made the particular states show a jealousy of all power not in their own hands; and this jealousy has led them to exercise a right of judging in the last resort of the measures recommended

64

by Congress, and of acting according to their own opinions of their propriety or necessity, a diffidence in Congress of their own powers, by which they have been timid and indecisive in their resolutions, constantly making concessions to the states, till they have scarcely left themselves the shadow of power; a want of sufficient means at their disposal to answer the public exigencies and of vigor to draw forth those means;[2] which have occasioned them to depend on the states individually to fulfil their engagements with the army, and the consequence of which has been to ruin their influence and credit with the army, to establish its dependence on each state separately rather than *on them*, that is rather than on the whole collectively.

It may be pleaded, that Congress had never any definitive powers granted them and of course could exercise none—could do nothing more than recommend. The manner in which Congress was appointed would warrant, and the public good required, that they should have considered themselves as vested with full power *to preserve the republic from harm*. They have done many of the highest acts of sovereignty, which were always chearfully submitted to—the declaration of independence, the declaration of war, the levying an army, creating a navy, emitting money, making alliances with foreign powers, appointing a dictator &c. &c.—all these implications of a complete sovereignty were never disputed, and ought to have been a standard for the whole conduct of Administration.[3] Undefined powers are discretionary powers, limited only by the object for which they were given—in the present case, the independence and freedom of America. . .

[T]he confederation itself is defective and requires to be altered; it is neither fit for war, nor peace.[4] The idea of an uncontrolable sovereignty in each state, over its internal police, will defeat the other powers given to Congress, and make our union feeble and precarious. . .

The confederation gives the states individually too much influence in the affairs of the army; they should have nothing to do with it. The entire formation and disposal of our military forces ought to belong to Congress. It is an essential cement of the union; and it ought to be the policy of Congress to des⟨troy⟩ all ideas of state attachments in the army and make it look up wholly to them. For this purpose all appointments promotions and provisions whatsoever ought to be made by them. It may be apprehended that this may be dangerous to liberty. But nothing appears more evident to me, than that we

[2] Hamilton lists three reasons for the ineptitude and weakness of the Continental Congress. The first one is that the fear of centralized power generated by the Revolution had created a hesitancy among American political leaders to diminish the prerogatives of their own state governments; therefore, they were reticent to endow the nation's governing body with sufficient power. Second, members of the Continental Congress lacked the political will to decisively exercise even their legitimate powers. Thus, they continually made concessions to the states and had abdicated much of their responsibility over the war to the states. Finally, Congress did not have the resources or means to carry out its intended functions and was thus dependent on the arbitrary, haphazard willingness of each state to comply with its requests. Hamilton concludes that the nation's success in peace and war will require that Congress be vested with complete legal authority and the means to execute that authority in all areas concerning the states collectively—including war, foreign affairs, trade, and finance.

[3] Because the pre-Confederation Congress lacked a formal legal declaration of specific powers, the argument could be made that it only possessed the authority to recommend measures. Hamilton argues the contrary, that since the Continental Congress was created to secure "the independence and freedom of America," it rightly possessed the authority to finance and direct the war effort. He explains that "undefined powers are discretionary powers, limited only by the object for which they were given." In other words, a body created to achieve a specific objective, implicitly possesses the discretionary authority necessary to achieve that end. Congress had initially acted according to this implied sovereignty by declaring independence, establishing a military, and engaging in diplomatic relations with foreign countries.

[4] The Articles of Confederation left too much control over important functions, such as finance and arms, in the hands of the state governments. Consequently, the

proposed confederation would not be fit to effectively wage war or to maintain order and stability among the states.

5 In response to concerns that vesting full control over the armed forces in the central government would jeopardize liberty, Hamilton aims to demonstrate that lovers of liberty have more to fear from a weak and disunited government.

6 Hamilton explains the difference between a unitary system, in which a single sovereign holds comprehensive and unlimited power over the parts, and a confederation, in which the parts maintain their own individual governments and constitutions. Under the latter system, it is more likely that people will favor the level of government representing their parochial or partial interests and that the common government will not have sufficient power to unite the parts and promote the happiness of the whole.

7 Hamilton cites the ancient Greek confederations as an example of how insufficient central power threatens liberty and public happiness. History had shown that loosely united republics were frequently the victim of internal turmoil and foreign subjugation.

8 The eventual adoption of a confederacy, vested with legal authority to arbitrate between and compel obedience from the individual states, would be necessary to avoid the calamities that plagued ancient confederacies and to preserve harmony between the states.

run much greater risk of having a weak and disunited federal government, than one which will be able to usurp upon the rights of the people.[5] Already some of the lines of the army would obey their states in opposition to Congress notwithstanding the pains we have taken to preserve the unity of the army—if any thing would hinder this it would be the personal influence of the General, a melancholy and mortifying consideration.

The forms of our state constitutions must always give them great weight in our affairs and will make it too difficult to bend them to the persuit of a common interest, too easy to oppose whatever they do not like and to form partial combinations subversive of the general one. There is a wide difference between our situation and that of an empire under one simple form of government, distributed into counties provinces or districts, which have no legisla(tures) but merely magistratical bodies to execute the laws of a common sovereign. Here the danger is that the sove[re]ign will have too much power to oppress the parts of which it is composed. In our case, that of an empire composed of confederated states each with a government completely organised within itself, having all the means to draw its subjects to a close dependence on itself—the danger is directly the reverse. It is that the common sovereign will not have power sufficient to unite the different members together, and direct the common forces to the interest and happiness of the whole.[6]

The leagues among the old Grecian republics are a proof of this.[7] They were continually at war with each other, and for want of union fell a prey to their neighbours. They frequently held general councils, but their resolutions were no further observed than as they suited the interests and inclinations of all the parties and at length, they sunk intirely into contempt. . .

Our own experience should satisfy us. We have felt the difficulty of drawing out the resources of the country and inducing the states to combine in equal exertions for the common cause. The ill success of our last attempt is striking. Some have done a great deal, others little or scarcely any thing. The disputes about boundaries &c. testify how flattering a prospect we have of future tranquillity, if we do not frame in time a confederacy capable of deciding the differences and compelling the obedience of the respective members.[8]

The confederation too gives the power of the purse too intirely to the state legislatures. It should provide perpetual funds in the disposal of Congress—by a land tax, poll tax, or the like. All imposts upon commerce ought to be laid by Congress and appropriated to their use, for without certain revenues, a government can have no power; that power, which holds the purse strings absolutely, must rule.[9] This seems to be a medium, which without making Congress altogether independent will tend to give reality to its authority.

Another defect in our system is want of method and energy in the administration. This has partly resulted from the other defect, but in a great degree from prejudice and the want of a proper executive.[10] Congress have kept the power too much into their own hands and have meddled too much with details of every sort. Congress is properly a deliberative corps and it forgets itself when it attempts to play the executive. It is impossible such a body, numerous as it is, constantly fluctuating, can ever act with sufficient decision, or with system.[11] Two thirds of the members, one half the time, cannot know what has gone before them or what connection the subject in hand has to what has been transacted on former occasions. The members, who have been more permanent, will only give information, that promotes the side they espouse, in the present case, and will as often mislead as enlighten. The variety of business must distract, and the proneness of every assembly to debate must at all times delay.

Lately Congress, convinced of these inconveniences, have gone into the measure of appointing boards. But this is in my opinion a bad plan. A single man, in each department of the administration, would be greatly preferable. It would give us a chance of more knowlege, more activity, more responsibility and of course more zeal and attention.[12] Boards partake of a part of the inconveniencies of larger assemblies. Their decisions are slower their energy less their responsibility more diffused. They will not have the same abilities and knowlege as an administration by single men. Men of the first pretensions will not so readily engage in them, because they will be less cospicuous, of less importance, have less opportunity of distinguishing themselves.[13] The members of boards will take less pains to inform themselves and arrive to eminence, because they have fewer motives to do it. All these reasons conspire to give a preference to the plan of vesting the great executive departments of the state in the hands of individuals. As these men will be of course at all times

[9] A primary reason for Congress's ineptitude was its lack of an independent power to tax. Congress would requisition the states for funds, but the states were often unwilling or unable to comply. Hamilton explains that true sovereignty cannot exist without the ability to raise revenue. Thus, Congress must be vested with an independent means of taxation.

[10] Hamilton emphasizes that, in addition to vesting the national government with competent power, it is necessary to divide the legislative and executive functions of government so they might be exercised effectively.

[11] Hamilton argues that numerous views and fluctuation of membership in Congress encourage deliberation and sound policymaking—however, these same qualities are actually deleterious to the vigor and dispatch necessary for execution.

[12] According to Hamilton, concentrating administrative authority under single heads of distinct executive departments, including war, finance, and foreign affairs, would promote competent and decisive execution. Vesting the authority of each department under a single minister would also ensure responsibility by making it easier to ascribe praise and blame for that department's successes and failures.

[13] Assigning the various aspects of executive power to distinct department heads, as opposed to multiple member committees, would also help attract ambitious, capable individuals motivated by a desire to distinguish themselves by their superior service.

[14] Although Hamilton later makes the case in *The Federalist Papers* for an independent executive, here he proposes that each executive department head would be appointed by, and therefore dependent on, Congress. He contends that this would help ensure the republican advantage of accountability combined with the monarchical advantage of secrecy and dispatch in execution.

[15] Without access to basic provisions, the morals and discipline of soldiers had largely succumbed to the appetites of brute necessity. This resulted in an army that at times exhibited mob-like tendencies and threatened the very rights of property the Revolution was meant to secure.

under the direction of Congress, we shall blend the advantages of a monarchy and republic in our constitution. . .[14]

A third defect is the fluctuating constitution of our army. This has been a pregnant source of evil; all our military misfortunes, three fourths of our civil embarrassments are to be ascribed to it. The General has so fully enumerated the mischief of it in a late letter to Congress that I could only repeat what he has said, and will therefore refer you to that letter.

The imperfect and unequal provision made for the army is a fourth defect which you will find delineated in the same letter. Without a speedy change the army must dissolve; it is now a mob, rather than an army, without cloathing, without pay, without provision, without morals, without discipline.[15] We begin to hate the country for its neglect of us; the country begins to hate us for our oppressions of them. Congress have long been jealous of us; we have now lost all confidence in them, and give the worst construction to all they do. Held together by the slenderest ties we are ripening for a dissolution.

The present mode of supplying the army—by state purchases—is not one of the least considerable defects of our system. It is too precarious a dependence, because the states will never be sufficiently impressed with our necessities. Each will make its own ease a primary object, the supply of the army a secondary one. The variety of channels through which the business is transacted will multiply the number of persons employed and the opportunities of embezzling public money. . .

These are the principal defects in the present system that now occur to me. There are many inferior ones in the organization of particular departments and many errors of administration which might be pointed out; but the task would be troublesome and tedious, and if we had once remedied those I have mentioned the others would not be attended with much difficulty.

I shall now propose the remedies, which appear to me applicable to our circumstances, and necessary to extricate our affairs from their present deplorable situation.

The first step must be to give Congress powers competent to the public exigencies. This may happen in two ways, one by resuming and exercising the discretionary powers I suppose to have been originally vested in them for the safety of the states and resting their conduct on the candor of their country men and the necessity of the conjuncture: the other by calling immediately a convention of all the states with full authority to conclude finally upon a general confederation,[16] stating to them beforehand explicity the evils arising from a want of power in Congress, and the [impossibility] of supporting the contest on its present footing. . .

The confederation in my opinion should give Congress complete sovereignty; except as to that part of internal police, which relates to the rights of property and life among individuals and to raising money by internal taxes.[17] It is necessary, that every thing, belonging to this, should be regulated by the state legislatures. Congress should have complete sovereignty in all that relates to war, peace, trade, finance, and to the management of foreign affairs, the right of declaring war of raising armies, officering, paying them, directing their motions in every respect, of equipping fleets and doing the same with them, of building fortifications arsenals magazines &c. &c., of making peace on such conditions as they think proper, of regulating trade, determining with what countries it shall be carried on, granting indulgencies laying prohibitions on all the articles of export or import, imposing duties granting bounties & premiums for raising exporting importing and applying to their own use the product of these duties, only giving credit to the states on whom they are raised in the general account of revenues and expences, instituting Admiralty courts &c., of coining money, establishing banks on such terms, and with such privileges as they think proper, appropriating funds and doing whatever else relates to the operations of finance, transacting every thing with foreign nations, making alliances offensive and defensive, treaties of commerce, &c. &c. . .

The second step I would recommend is that Congress should instantly appoint the following great officers of state—A secretary for foreign affairs—a President of war—A President of Marine—A Financier—A President of trade; instead of this last a board of Trade may be preferable as the regulations of trade are slow and gradual and require prudence and experience (more than other qualities), for which boards are very well adapted.

Congress should choose for these offices, men of the first abilities, property and character in the continent—and such as have had the best opportunities of being acquainted with the several branches. . .

[16] It is essential, Hamilton contends, that Congress be given more extensive powers than those granted under the proposed Articles of Confederation. Since Congress would not likely exercise its rightful implied powers without a formal legal declaration, Hamilton proposes calling another convention to institute a stronger confederation. This convention, he later explains, should vest Congress with unambiguous sovereignty and competent powers in the areas of war, finance, trade, and foreign affairs. The convention should additionally establish clear administrative units to be led by "men of first abilities" and adopt a financial system that would produce fiscal solvency.

[17] Hamilton provides an illustrative list of powers that he says should be completely delegated to Congress, but he concedes that the state legislatures should retain significant sovereignty to accomplish their own delegated ends.

Another step of immediate necessity is to recruit the army for the war, or at least for three years. . . . Congress should endeavour, both upon their credit in Europe, and by every possible exertion in this country, to provide cloathing for their officers, and should abolish the whole system of state supplies. The making good the depreciation of the currency and all other compensations to the army should be immediately taken up by Congress, and not left to the states. . .

The advantages of securing the attachment of the army to Congress, and binding them to the service by substantial ties are immense. We should then have discipline, an army in reality, as well as in name. Congress would then have a solid basis of authority and consequence, for to me it is an axiom that in our constitution an army is essential to the American union.[18]

The providing of supplies is the pivot of every thing else (though a well constituted army would not in a small degree conduce to this, by giving consistency and weight to government). There are four ways all which must be united—a foreign loan, heavy pecuniary taxes, a tax in kind, a bank founded on public and private credit. . .[19]

If a Convention is called the minds of all the states and the people ought to be prepared to receive its determinations by sensible and popular writings, which should conform to the views of Congress. There are epochs in human affairs, when *novelty* even is useful. If a general opinion prevails that the old way is bad, whether true or false, and this obstructs or relaxes the operation of the public service, a change is necessary if it be but for the sake of change. This is exactly the case now. 'Tis an universal sentiment that our present system is a bad one, and that things do not go right on this account. The measure of a Convention would revive the hopes of the people and give a new direction to their passions,[20] which may be improved in carrying points of substantial utility. . .

You will perceive My Dear Sir this letter is hastily written and with a confidential freedom, not as to a member of Congress, whose feelings may be sore at the prevailing clamours; but as to a friend who is in a situation to remedy public disorders, who wishes for nothing so much as truth, and who is desirous of information, even from those

[18] Maintaining a permanent military, completely financed by and under the authority of Congress, would draw the loyalty of both soldiers and officers and strengthen the bond of the union.

[19] Hamilton contends that any viable plan for a stronger, more effective union must include restructuring the nation's financial system. Here, he proposes a system of public finance and sound currency based on foreign loans, various forms of taxation, and a national bank funded by government and private investment.

[20] Hamilton cautions that a lack of faith in the governing system makes citizens reticent to fight for, invest in, or make sacrifices on behalf of their country. A change in system would "revive the hopes of the people" and help produce the public confidence and national morale needed to wage war, secure independence, and administer government effectively.

less capable of judging than himself. I have not even time to correct and copy and only enough to add that I am very truly and affectionately D Sir Your most Obed ser

A. Hamilton
Liberty Pole
Sept. 3d 1780

CONCLUSION

Following ratification of the Articles of Confederation by all thirteen states in 1781, Hamilton and other nationalist-minded leaders continued to highlight the inadequacy of the central government and to press for a national government vested with competent powers. The country had to undergo further turmoil and political unrest, however, before Hamilton's call for a convention to establish a stronger union was eventually authorized nearly a decade later in 1787 in Philadelphia.

Source: Hamilton Papers, Library of Congress.

Letter to George Washington Requesting Field Command

November 22, 1780

INTRODUCTION

Hamilton's intense ambition was never fully satisfied in his position of aide-de-camp to Washington. In spite of his prestigious and powerful role as secretary, adviser, and proxy to the commander in chief, Hamilton was convinced that his future advancement and glory would be secured only on the battlefield. Finally, after nearly four years in Washington's service, Hamilton wrote directly to Washington requesting reassignment to field command.

Dear Sir,

Sometime last fall when I spoke to your Excellency about going to the Southward, I explained to you candidly my feelings with respect to military reputation, and how much it was my object to act a conspicuous part in some enterprise that might perhaps raise my character as a soldier above mediocrity.[1] You were so good as to say you would be glad to furnish me with an occasion. When the expedition to Staten Island was on foot a favourable one seemed to offer. There was a batalion without a field officer, the command of which I thought, as it was accidental, might be given to me without inconvenience. I made an application for it through the Marquis, who informed me of your refusal on two principles—one that giving me a whole batalion might be a subject of dissatisfaction, the other that if an accident should happen to me, in the present state of your family, you would be embarrassed for the necessary assistance.[2]

The project you now have in contemplation affords another opportunity. I have a variety of reasons that press me to desire ardently to have it in my power to improve it. I take the liberty to observe, that the command may be proportionned to my rank, and that the second objection ceases to operate, as during the period of establishing our winter quarters there will be a suspension of material business;

[1] Hamilton believed that his services to Washington, no matter how valuable to the revolutionary cause, were insufficient to secure his future advancement. He would only be able to make a name for himself and demonstrate his true worth by winning distinction in battle.

[2] Washington, perhaps judging that Hamilton's unique talents were better applied in his current role, spurned his request to lead a battalion in the Marquis de Lafayette's raid on Staten Island. Washington justified the refusal on the grounds that placing Hamilton as head of a battalion might displease higher-ranking officers and that he could not afford to furlough Hamilton from his valuable services at headquarters.

besides which, my peculiar situation will in any case call me away from the army in a few days. . .[3]

I flatter myself also that my military character stands so well in the army as to reconcile the officers in general to the measure. All circumstances considered, I venture to say any exceptions which might be taken would be unreasonable.

I take this method of making the request to avoid the embarrassment of a personal explanation; I shall only add that however much I have the matter at heart, I wish your Excellency intirely to consult your own inclination; and not from a disposition to oblige me, to do any thing, that may be disagreeable to you. . .

I have the honor to be very sincerely, and respectfully Yr Excellencys Most Obed Servant

A Hamilton

[3] Believing that his military career would be stymied if he was not assigned to active service before the war's end, Hamilton continued to relentlessly plead his case for field command. Here, he identifies another possible combat assignment and rebuts Washington's previous reasons for refusal. Furthermore, Hamilton writes that Washington would inevitably have to learn to make due in his absence as he would soon be taking leave for his upcoming marriage to Elizabeth Schuyler.

CONCLUSION

Hamilton officially resigned from Washington's staff in February 1781, but he was forced to wait several months before being assigned to active command. He spent this time continuing to petition for a military appointment and writing political tracts. Finally, in July 1781, he was granted command of a New York light infantry battalion. He soon received the opportunity to earn his long-sought-after military glory in the Battle of Yorktown, the grand finale of the Revolutionary War.

Source: George Washington Papers, Library of Congress.

Letter to John Laurens on Service in Congress

August 15, 1782

INTRODUCTION

Shortly following his election as a New York delegate to the Continental Congress, Hamilton wrote to his closest friend John Laurens urging him to seek a position in Congress. Now that victory in the war and a peace treaty with Great Britain were at hand, Hamilton envisioned the two fighting side by side in the political arena to secure a prosperous future for the newly independent states.

I received with great Pleasure, My Dear Laurens, the letter which you wrote me in last.

Your wishes in one respect are gratified; this state has pretty unanimously delegated me to Congress.[1] My time of service commences in November. . . . We have great reason to flatter ourselves peace on our own terms is upon the carpet. The making it is in good hands. It is said your father is exchanged for Cornwallis and gone to Paris to meet the other commissioners and that Grenville on the part of England has made a second trip there, in the last instance, vested with Plenipotentiary powers.

I fear there may be obstacles but I hope they may be surmounted.

Peace made, My Dear friend, a new scene opens. The object then will be to make our independence a blessing. To do this we must secure our *union* on solid foundations; an herculean task and to effect which mountains of prejudice must be levelled![2]

It requires all the virtue and all the abilities of the Country. Quit your sword my friend, put on the *toga*, come to Congress.[3] We know each others sentiments, our views are the same: we have fought side by side to make America free, let us hand in hand struggle to make her happy.[4]

[1] Hamilton informs Laurens of his recent election as a delegate from New York to the Continental Congress.

[2] The War for Independence having been won, the country now faced the equally great, if not greater, challenge of consolidating the union and nation building.

[3] To carry out the task at hand successfully would require the country's most virtuous characters and greatest minds, among which Hamilton counts himself and Laurens. Appealing to the grandeur of classical statesmanship, Hamilton urges his friend to join him for battle in Congress.

[4] The newly secured freedom from British rule alone would not ensure the long-term public happiness. Such happiness, Hamilton believed, would depend on a strong union and well-designed institutions of government.

Remember me to General Greene with all the warmth of a sincere attachment.

Yrs for ever

A Hamilton
Albany Aug. 15. 1782

CONCLUSION

Having fought at Yorktown, Laurens returned to South Carolina and was killed in a military skirmish there in late August 1782. He likely never read Hamilton's letter, and Hamilton was left to battle for the establishment of a stronger, more unified country without his most devoted political ally and dearest friend.

Source: Gertrude Atherton. *A Few of Hamilton's Letters*. New York: The MacMillan Company, 1903, 127–128.

SECTION IV

Family Life

Letter to Margarita Schuyler on Courtship with Elizabeth

February 1780

INTRODUCTION

After interacting with Elizabeth Schuyler over the course of a several weeks at the army headquarters in Morristown, the smitten Hamilton was convinced she should be his bride and was thus eager to obtain the favor of her family. When Elizabeth requested that Hamilton dispatch a letter she had written to her younger sister, he used the opportunity to introduce himself and profess his love for Elizabeth and her many fine qualities.

In obedience to Miss Schuylers commands I do myself the pleasure to inclose you a letter, which she has been so obliging as to commit to my care, and I beg your permission to assure you that many motives conspire to render this commission peculiarly agreeable.[1] Besides the general one of being in the service of the ladies which alone would be sufficient, even to a man of less zeal than myself, I have others of a more particular nature. I venture to tell you in confidence, that by some odd contrivance or other, your sister has found out the secret of interesting me in every thing that concerns her;[2] and though I have not the happiness of a personal acquaintance with you, I have had the good fortune to see several very pretty pictures of your person and mind which have inspired me with a more than common partiality for both. Among others your sister carries a beautiful copy constantly about her elegantly drawn by herself, of which she has two or three times favoured me with a sight.[3] You will no doubt admit it as a full proof of my frankness and good opinion of you, that I with so little ceremony introduce myself to your acquaintance and at the first step make you my confident. But I hope I run no risk of its being thought an impeachment of my discretion. Phlegmatists may say I take too great a license at first setting out, and witlings may sneer and wonder how a man the least acquainted with the world should show so great facility in his confidences—to a lady.[4] But the idea I have formed of your character places it in my estimation above the insipid maxims of the former or the ill-natured jibes of the latter.

[1] Although this letter contains no addressee, the assumed recipient is Elizabeth's younger sister Margarita, often known as Peggy. Angelica Schuyler Church, with whom Hamilton frequently exchanged correspondence, was currently in Morristown with Hamilton and Elizabeth.

[2] Having interacted with Elizabeth for little over a month, Hamilton expresses astonishment at how quickly he was enraptured by her.

[3] Hamilton compliments Margarita and, at the same time, draws attention to Elizabeth's talent as a portrait artist.

[4] While phlegmatists—those with a more tranquil and dispassionate character—might critique him as rash and overly confident, Hamilton boasts of his bold, uninhibited pursuit of Betsy's affections.

[5] Hamilton proceeds to enumerate Elizabeth's most admirable qualities. The list Hamilton provides here—although lacking jesting statements about appearance, virginity, and sex—is nearly identical to a list of traits, which he claimed to be looking for in a wife that he had sent to his friend John Laurens the previous year.

[6] Hamilton claims that Elizabeth's fine qualities had transformed him from a playboy, reluctant to settle down, into an eager husband and family man.

I have already confessed the influence your sister has gained over me; yet notwithstanding this, I have some things of a very serious and heinous nature to lay to her charge.[5] She is most unmercifully handsome and so perverse that she has none of those pretty affectations which are the prerogatives of beauty. Her good sense is destitute of that happy mixture of vanity and ostentation which would make it conspicuous to the whole tribe of fools and foplings as well as to men of understanding so that as the matter now stands it is little known beyond the circle of these. She has good nature affability and vivacity unembellished with that charming frivolousness which is justly deemed one of the principal accomplishments of a *belle*. In short she is so strange a creature that she possesses all the beauties virtues and graces of her sex without any of those amiable defects, which from their general prevalence are esteemed by connoisseurs necessary shades in the character of a fine woman. The most determined adversaries of Hymen can find in her no pretext for their hostility, and there are several of my friends, philosophers who railed at love as a weakness, men of the world who laughed at it as a phantasie, whom she has presumptuously and daringly compelled to acknowlege its power and surrender at discretion. I can the better assert the truth of this, as I am myself of the number. She has had the address to overset all the wise resolutions I had been framing for more than four years past, and from a rational sort of being and a professed con[d]emner of Cupid has in a trice metamorphosed me into the veriest inamorato you perhaps ever saw. . .[6]

CONCLUSION

Hamilton's courtship with Elizabeth in the winter of 1780 marked a turning point in Hamilton's life, as he was wholeheartedly accepted and embraced as a permanent member of the Schuyler family.

Source: Allan McClane Hamilton. *The Intimate Life of Alexander Hamilton*. New York: Charles Scribner's Sons, 1910, 97–99.

Letter to Elizabeth Schuyler on Being a Poor Man's Wife

August 1780

INTRODUCTION

During the same summer that Hamilton began requesting field command, he also sent several swooning love letters to Elizabeth Schuyler, leading up to their impending marriage that fall. In a letter written sometime in August, Hamilton humorously and candidly forewarns Elizabeth of the life she may endure as the wife of a wartime officer and a man of little fortune.

Impatiently My Dearest have I been expecting the return of your father to bring me a letter from my charmer with the answers you have been good enough to promise me to the little questions asked in mine by him. I long to see the workings of my Betseys heart, and I promise my self I shall have ample gratification to my fondness in the sweet familiarity of her pen. . .[1]

Meade just comes in and interrupts me by sending his love to you. He tells you he has written a long letter to his widow asking her opinion of the propriety of quitting the service; and that if she does not disapprove it, he will certainly take his final leave after the campaign. You see what a fine opportunity she has to be enrolled in the catalogue of heroines, and I dare say she will set you an example of fortitude and patriotism. I know too you have so much of the Portia in you, that you will not be out done in this line by any of your sex, and that if you saw me inclined to quit the service of your country, you would dissuade me from it. I have promised you, you recollect, to conform to your wishes, and I persist in this intention. It remains with you to show whether you are a *Roman* or an *American wife*.[2]

Though I am not sanguine in expecting it, I am not without hopes this Winter will produce a peace and then you must submit to the mortification of enjoying more domestic happiness and less fame. This I know you will not like, but we cannot always have things as we wish.

[1] Hamilton chides Elizabeth for writing him too infrequently.

[2] Portia was the wife of Marcus Junius Brutus, one of the Roman senators who assassinated Julius Caesar in an attempt to restore the republic. Portia's devotion to her husband and to Rome was so strong that Brutus entrusted her with advance knowledge of the assassination plot. In questioning whether Elizabeth will be a *Roman* or an *American* wife, Hamilton might be asking Elizabeth whether she will have the fortitude to support his prominent role in the establishment of a new republic. He pledges to resign from public service if Elizabeth so requests, but he hopes that she will emulate the heroines of antiquity who esteemed their husbands' honor and courageous service to country over domestic happiness.

3 Hamilton expresses optimism that, with
the promise of French military and naval
reinforcements, the Continental Army
might soon be victorious. Nevertheless,
Britain's obstinacy could inevitably extend
the war.

The affairs of England are in so bad a plight that if no fortunate events attend her this campaign, it would seem impossible for her to proceed in the war. But she is an obstinate old dame, and seems determined to ruin her whole family, rather than to let Miss America go on flirting it with her new lovers, with whom, as giddy young girls often do, she eloped in contempt of her mothers authority. . .[3]

But now we are talking of times to come, tell me my pretty damsel have you made up your mind upon the subject of housekeeping? Do you soberly relish the pleasure of being a poor mans wife? Have you learned to think a home spun preferable to a brocade and the rumbling of a waggon wheel to the musical rattling of a coach and six? Will you be able to see with perfect composure your old acquaintances flaunting it in gay life, tripping it along in elegance and splendor, while you hold an humble station and have no other enjoyments than the sober comforts of a good wife? Can you in short be an Aquileia and chearfully plant turnips with me, if fortune should so order it?[4] If you cannot my Dear we are playing a comedy of all in the wrong, and you should correct the mistake before we begin to act the tragedy of the unhappy couple.

I propose you a set of new questions my lovely girl; but though they are asked with an air of levity, they merit a very serious consideration, for on their being resolved in the affirmative stripped of all the colorings of a fond imagination our happiness may absolutely depend. I have not concealed my circumstances from my Betsey; they are far from splendid; they may possibly even be worse than I expect, for every day brings me fresh proof of the knavery of those to whom my little affairs are entrusted. They have already filed down what was in their hands more than one half, and I am told they go on diminishing it, 'till I *fear* they will reduce it below my *former fears*.[5] An indifference to property enters into my character too much, and what affects me now as my Betsey is concerned in it, I should have laughed at or not thought of at all a year ago. But I have thoroughly examined my own heart. Beloved by you, I can be happy in any situation, and can struggle with every embarrassment of fortune with patience and firmness. I cannot however forbear entreating you to realize our union on the dark side and satisfy, without deceiving yourself, how far your affection for me can make you happy in a privation of those elegancies to which you have been accustomed. If fortune should smile upon us, it will do us no harm to have been prepared for adversity; if she frowns upon us, by being prepared, we shall encounter it without the chagrin of disappointment. Your future rank in life is a perfect lottery;[6] you may move in an exalted you may move in a very humble sphere; the last is most probable; examine well your heart. And in doing it, dont figure to yourself a cottage in romance, with the spontaneous bounties of nature courting you to enjoyment. Dont imagine yourself a shepherdess, your hair embroidered with flowers a crook in your hand tending your flock under a shady tree, by the side of a cool fountain, your faithful shepherd sitting near and entertaining you with gentle tales of love. These are pretty dreams and very apt to enter into the heads of lovers when they think of a connection without the advantages of fortune. But they must not be indulged. You must apply your situation to real life, and think how you should feel in scenes of which you may find examples every day. So far My Dear Betsey as the tenderest affection can compensate for other inconveniences in making your estimate, you cannot give too large a credit for this article. My heart overflows with every thing for you, that admiration, esteem and love can inspire. *I would this moment give the world to be near you only to kiss your sweet hand.* Believe what I say to be truth and imagine what are my feelings when I say it. Let it awake your sympathy and let our hearts melt in a prayer to be soon united, never more to be separated.

Adieu loveliest of your sex
AH

[6] As a consequence of his precarious finances, Hamilton cautions Elizabeth that in marrying him she should be prepared for the possibility of a humble rather than exalted life. He contends that preparing to accept the worst would make them better appreciate any good fortune they might experience.

CONCLUSION

In spite of his meager means and questionable family background, Hamilton had proved himself to be a man of strong character and was enthusiastically accepted by both Elizabeth and her family. Although his connection to the Schuyler family served him well politically, he never relied on the wealth of his in-laws. Even when he and Elizabeth faced strained financial circumstances, Hamilton was not overly consumed by money and was determined to provide for his family through his own efforts.

Source: Collection of Mrs. John C. Hamilton, Elmsford, New York. From *The Papers of Alexander Hamilton*, vol. 2, 1779–1781, ed. Harold C. Syrett. New York: Columbia University Press, 1961, 397–400.

Letter to James Hamilton Regarding Their Father

June 22, 1785

INTRODUCTION

In 1765, James Hamilton Sr. abandoned his young sons Alexander and James, along with their mother, on the island of St. Croix and assumed no further responsibility for them. Remarkably, neither Hamilton's brother nor his absent father, who both continued to reside in the West Indies throughout their lives, exhibited much interest in Hamilton or his extraordinary achievements in America. Hamilton, nevertheless, demonstrated a continued concern for their well-being and a desire to maintain correspondence.

In the spring of 1785, Alexander received a letter from his brother requesting financial assistance. Hamilton's reply revealed that, although their relationship was clearly strained, he still harbored a strong affection for his brother and father.

My Dear Brother:

[1] In response to his brother's letter requesting financial assistance, Hamilton gently scolds him for not replying to the letter he sent six months prior and for having only written twice in several years.

[2] After admonishing his brother's failure to write, Hamilton conveys an eagerness to assist him.

I have received your letter of the 31st of May last, which, and one other, are the only letters I have received from you in many years.[1] I am a little surprised you did not receive one which I wrote to you about six months ago. The situation you describe yourself to be in gives me much pain, and nothing will make me happier than, as far as may be in my power, to contribute to your relief.[2] I will cheerfully pay your draft upon me for fifty pounds sterling, whenever it shall appear. I wish it was in my power to desire you to enlarge the sum; but though my future prospects are of the most flattering kind my present engagements would render it inconvenient to me to advance you a larger sum. My affection for you, however, will not permit me to be inattentive to your welfare, and I hope time will prove to you that I feel all the sentiment of a brother. Let me only request of you to exert your industry for a year or two more where you are, and at the end of that time I promise myself to be able to [invite you to a more] comfortable settlement [in this Country]. Allow me only to give you one caution, which is to avoid if possible getting in debt. Are you *married* or *single?*[3] If the *latter*, it is my wish for many reasons it may be agreeable to you to continue in that state.

[3] Hamilton's lack of knowledge concerning his brother's marital status demonstrates how distant the two had become.

84

But what has become of our dear father? It is an age since I have heared from him or of him, though I have written him several letters. Perhaps, alas! he is no more, and I shall not have the pleasing opportunity of contributing to render the close of his life more happy than the progress of it. My heart bleeds at the recollection of his misfortunes and embarrassments.[4] Sometimes I flatter myself his brothers have extended their support to him, and that he now enjoys tranquillity and ease. At other times I fear he is suffering in indigence. I entreat you, if you can, to relieve me from my doubts, and let me know how or where he is, if alive, if dead, how and where he died. Should he be alive inform him of my inquiries, beg him to write to me, and tell him how ready I shall be to devote myself and all I have to his accommodation and happiness.

I do not advise your coming to this country at present, for the war has also put things out of order here, and people in your business find a subsistence difficult enough. My object will be, by-and-by, to get you settled on a farm.

Believe me always your affectionate friend and brother,

Alex. Hamilton.

[4] Although Hamilton's father had clearly ignored Hamilton's attempts to reestablish correspondence, Hamilton, astoundingly, exhibits no bitterness or anger toward him. Instead, he expresses sorrow for any misfortune he might have experienced and a tender longing to help relieve his financial state.

CONCLUSION

In spite of his father's abandonment, and an apparently strained relationship with his perhaps envious brother, Hamilton continued to exhibit a deep sense of loyalty and familial responsibility. He repeatedly urged his father and brother to come to America, paid many of their debts, and even financially supported his father in his old age, yet neither his brother nor his father ever came to America to visit Hamilton, Elizabeth, or their children.

Source: *National Intelligencer*, February 17, 1859.

Letter to Elizabeth Hamilton on Being Away

September 8, 1786

INTRODUCTION

As Hamilton advanced in his political career, he was frequently called away from his wife and children for extended periods. During these times, he would write to Elizabeth, expressing angst and sorrow in their absence.

[1] Hamilton, at the time a member of the New York legislature, had left for Philadelphia and then Maryland where he was to represent New York as one of the twelve delegates to the Annapolis Convention.

[2] Hamilton lived a life perpetually torn between his unwavering ambition, which frequently led him away from home, and his desire to enjoy the pleasures of domesticity in the company of his wife and children.

I wrote to you My beloved Betsey at Philadelphia; but through mistake brought off the letter with me; which I did not discover till my arrival here.[1] I was not very well on the first part of the journey; but my health has been improved by travelling and is now as good as I could wish. Happy, however I cannot be, absent from you and my darling little ones. I feel that nothing can ever compensate for the loss of the enjoyments I leave at home, or can ever put my heart at tolerable ease. In the bosom of my family alone must my happiness be sought, and in that of my Betsey is every thing that is charming to me.[2] Would to heaven I were there! Does not your heart re-echo the wish?

In reality my attachments to home disqualify me for either business or pleasure abroad; and the prospect of a detention here for Eight or ten days perhaps a fortnight fills me with an anxiety which will best be conceived by my Betseys own impatience.

I am straitened for time & must conclude. I presume this will find you at Albany. Kiss my little ones a thousand times for me. Remember me affectionately to Your Parents, to Peggy, to all. Think of me with as much tenderness as I do of you and we cannot fail to be always happy

Adieu My beloved
A Hamilton
Anapolis
Sepr. 8. 1786

CONCLUSION

Throughout Hamilton's political and legal career, Elizabeth not only efficiently managed the couple's growing family and household but also provided Hamilton with a consistent source of strength and support. The more embroiled Hamilton became in the nasty realities of political life, the more anxious he became in his family's absence and the more dependent he was on Elizabeth as a steady, unassuming confidante.

Source: Hamilton Papers, Library of Congress.

Letter to Angelica Schuyler Church on Her Departure

November 8, 1789

INTRODUCTION

In spite of his deep love for his wife Elizabeth, Hamilton occasionally engaged in flirtatious dalliances with other women. Throughout his adult life, he was particularly drawn to Elizabeth's oldest sister Angelica who was likewise smitten with him.

Angelica—against her family's wishes—had eloped with Englishman John Barker Church, who was rumored to have fled England following a duel with a powerful Tory. Church lived for a time in the colonies under the pseudonym John B. Carter and eventually amassed a great deal of wealth during the Revolution by selling supplies to American and French forces. Following the war, Angelica and John Church traveled back and forth to England, during which time Angelica and Hamilton engaged in frequent correspondence. In the spring of 1789, Angelica, having become quite homesick and melancholy, left her husband and four children behind and traveled to America to visit her family and ailing father. When she finally returned to England after a much extended stay, Hamilton wrote a letter expressing his and Elizabeth's bitter anguish at her departure.

My Dear Sister

[1] In spite of speculation that Alexander and Angelica were lovers, Elizabeth was distraught over her older sister's impending departure. Faced with the prospect that she might never again see her dear sister, she became almost inconsolable.

[2] Hamilton references Virgil's account of Aeneas's famous departure from his lover Dido at Carthage to relate how he, his young son Philip, and the Baron von Steuben had gone down to the Battery and wept as they watched Angelica's ship sail out of sight.

After taking leave of you on board of the Packet, I hastened home to sooth and console your sister. I found her in bitter distress;[1] though much recovered from the agony, in which she had been, by the kind cares of Mrs. Bruce and the Baron. After composing her by a flattering picture of your prospects for the voyage, and a *strong infusion* of hope, that she had not taken a last farewell of you; The Baron little Phillip and myself, with her consent, walked down to the Battery; where with aching hearts and anxious eyes we saw your vessel, in full sail, swiftly bearing our loved friend from our embraces. Imagine what we felt. We gazed, we sighed, we *wept*; and casting "many a lingering longing look behind" returned home to give scope to our sorrows, and mingle without restraint our tears and our regrets.[2] The good Baron has more than ever rivetted himself in my affection: to observe his unaffected solicitude and see his old eyes brimful of sympathy had something in it that won my whole soul and filled me with more than usual complacency for human nature. Amiable Angelica! how much you are formed to endear yourself to every good heart! How deeply you have rooted yourself in the affections of your friends on this side the Atlantic! *Some* of us are and must continue inconsolable for your absence.

Betsey and myself make you the last theme of our conversation at night and the first in the morning. We talk of you; we praise you and we pray for you.[3] We dwell with peculiar interest on the little incidents that preceded your departure. Precious and never to be forgotten scenes!

But let me check, My dear Sister, these effusions of regretful friendship. Why should I alloy the happiness that courts you in the bosom of your family by images that must wound your sensibility? It shall not be. However difficult, or little natural it is to me to suppress what the fulness of my heart would utter, the sacrifice shall be made to your ease and satisfaction.

I shall not fail to execute any commission you gave me nor neglect any of your charges. Those particularly contained in your letter by the Pilot, for which Betsey joins me in returning a thousand thanks, shall be observed in all their extent. Already have I addressed the consolation, I mentioned to you, to your Father. I have no doubt the arguments I have used with him will go far towards reconciling his mind to the unexpected step you took.[4] I hope the inclosed letters may not be such as to give you pain. They arrived the day after you set sail.

I shall commit this letter to Betsey to add whatever her little affectionate heart may dictate. Kiss your children for me. Teach them to consider me as your and their father's friend. . .

Adieu Dear Angelica! Remember us always as you ought to do—Remember us as we shall you

Your ever Affect friend & brother

A Hamilton
New York November 8th. 1789

[3] Here, Hamilton asserts his and Elizabeth's mutual adoration for Angelica. As Ron Chernow (2004) points out, "Ironically, Eliza's special attachment to Angelica gave Hamilton a cover for expressing affection for Angelica that would certainly have been forbidden with other women" (134).

[4] Having enclosed in his correspondence two letters from the elder Mr. and Mrs. Schuyler, Hamilton reassures Angelica that he had pacified her father, who was angry that Angelica had decided to remain in New York City near Hamilton when the rest of her family had returned to the Schuyler manor in Albany.

CONCLUSION

Although many have speculated that Hamilton and Angelica were lovers, Elizabeth showed no ill will toward her sister and seemed to be equally infatuated with her, a fact that gave Hamilton license to express an open fondness toward Angelica for the remainder of his life.

Source: Collection of Judge Peter B. Olney, Deep River, Connecticut. From *The Papers of Alexander Hamilton*, vol. 5, June 1788—November 1789, ed. Harold C. Syrett. New York: Columbia University Press, 1962, 501–502.

Letter to Philip Hamilton on Being at School

December 5, 1791

INTRODUCTION

Hamilton, although dismissed by his own father, was an attentive and loving father to his eight children. As a man of unwavering ambition, he undoubtedly held high expectations for his children. Nevertheless, he directed them with a patient, tender care.

Shortly after his two eldest sons Philip and Alexander Jr. had gone away to school in New Jersey for the first time, Hamilton received a letter from Philip expressing contentment with his living conditions and studies. Hamilton promptly issued a warm and instructive reply.

Philadelphia December 5
1791

I received with great pleasure My Dear Philip the letter which you wrote me last week. Your Mama and myself were very happy to learn that you are pleased with your situation and content to stay as long as shall be thought for your good. We hope and believe that nothing will happen to alter this disposition.

Your Master also informs me that you recited a lesson the first day you began, very much to his satisfaction. I expect every letter from him will give me a fresh proof of your progress. For I know that you can do a great deal, if you please, and I am sure you have too much spirit not to exert yourself, that you may make us every day more and more proud of you.[1]

Your Mama has got an Ovid for you and is looking up your Mairs introduction. If it cannot be found tomorrow another will be procured and the books with the other articles she promised to send you will be forwarded in two or three days.

You remember that I engaged to send for you next Saturday and I will do it, unless you request me to put it off. For a promise must

1 Hamilton celebrates a positive report from Philip's teacher and subtly appeals to Philip's pride to encourage further excellence.

never be broken; and I never will make you one, which I will not fulfil as far as I am able.[2] But it has occurred to me that the Christmas holidays are near at hand, and I suppose your school will then break up for some days and give you an opportunity of coming to stay with us for a longer time than if you should come on Saturday. Will it not be best for you, therefore, to put off your journey till the holidays? But determine as you like best and let me know what will be most pleasing to you.[3]

A good night to my darling son. Adieu
A Hamilton

CONCLUSION

Hamilton's children clearly adored him. His devotion to them and the tactful nature in which he consistently coached them are even more noteworthy considering his own particularly troubled and directionless childhood.

Source: George Shea. *The Life and Epoch of Alexander Hamilton: A Historical Study*. Boston: Houghton, Osgood and Company, 1880.

Letter to William Hamilton on Relations in Scotland

May 2, 1797

INTRODUCTION

Although he lived most of his adult life as a vagabond, Hamilton's father James had been born into a titled Scottish family and, as the fourth son of a Scottish laird, had been raised in a medieval castle renamed The Grange in Ayrshire, Scotland. Alexander Hamilton, throughout his life, took pride in the knowledge of this noble lineage and longed to establish contact with his paternal relatives in Scotland. Finally, shortly after he had turned forty, Hamilton received the first long-overdue correspondence. His father's brother, William Hamilton, facing financial difficulties, needed Hamilton's aid to secure a position for his son Robert as an American naval officer. Consequently, William finally sent Hamilton an account of his relatives his Scotland.

Seemingly unbothered by the self-interested nature of the unprecedented communication from his wealthy uncle, Hamilton clearly delighted in the prospect of establishing a relationship with his Scottish relatives. Although his uncle had never extended any assistance to Hamilton when he had been left orphaned and penniless as a child, Hamilton swiftly replied to William's request with a brief account of his life and a pledge to assist to the best of his ability.

Albany State of New York
May the 2d. 1797
My Dear Sir

Some days since I received with great pleasure your letter of the 10th. of March. The mark, it affords, of your kind attention, and the particular account it gives me of so many relations in Scotland are extremely gratifying to me.[1] You no doubt have understood that my fathers affairs at a very early day went to wreck; so as to have rendered his situation during the greatest part of his life far from eligible. This state of things occasionned a separation between him and me, when I was very young, and threw me upon the bounty of my mothers relations,[2] some of whom were then wealthy, though by vicissitudes to which human affairs are so liable, they have been since much reduced and broken up. Myself at about sixteen came to this

[1] While Hamilton had never previously met or interacted with his relatives in Scotland, he shows no signs of ill will but only deep gratification at finally receiving an account of them.

[2] Hamilton, reluctant to speak ill of his indolent and deficient father, attributes his father's abandonment to personal misfortune, an excuse that Hamilton never permitted to reign in his own life.

Having always had a strong propensity to literary pursuits, by a course of steady and laborious exertion, I was able, by the age of Ninteen to qualify myself for the degree of Batchelor of Arts in the College of New York, and to lay a foundation, by preparatory study, for the future profession of the law.

The American Revolution supervened. My principles led me to take part in it. At nineteen I entered into the American army as Captain of Artillery. Shortly after, I became by his invitation Aide De Camp to General Washington, in which station, I served till the commencement of that Campaign which ended with the seige of York, in Virginia, and the Capture of Cornwallis's Army. This Campaign I made at the head of a corps of light infantry, with which I was present at the seige of York and engaged in some interesting operations.[4]

At the period of the peace with Great Britain, I found myself a member of Congress by appointment of the legislature of this state.

After the peace, I settled in the City of New York in the practice of the law; and was in a very lucrative course of practice, when the derangement of our public affairs, by the feebleness of the general confederation, drew me again reluctantly into public life. I became a member of the Convention which framed the present Constitution of the U States; and having taken part in this measure, I conceived myself to be under an obligation to lend my aid towards putting the machine in some regular motion. Hence I did not hesitate to accept the offer of President Washington to undertake the office of Secretary of the Treasury.

In that office, I met with many intrinsic difficulties, and many artificial ones proceeding from passions, not very worthy, common to human nature, and which act with peculiar force in republics.[5] The object, however, was effected, of establishing public credit and introducing order into the finances.

Public Office in this Country has few attractions. The pecuniary emolument is so inconsiderable as too amount to a sacrifice to any man who can employ his time with advantage in any liberal profession. The opportunity of doing good, from the jealousy of power and the spirit of faction, is too small in any station to warrant a long continuance of private sacrifices. The enterprises of party had

[3] Hamilton proceeds to provide a brief sketch of his life and accomplishments since coming to America at sixteen. Although written in a muted and modest tone, the multi-paragraph autobiography that follows makes evident the remarkable nature of Hamilton's rise and his significant role in nearly every seminal event of the revolutionary era and the early years of the American republic.

[4] As the commander of a battalion of light infantry, Hamilton had played a critical role in the successful attack on British defenses during the Battle of Yorktown, the last major battle of the Revolutionary War.

[5] Pointing out the political difficulties he faced in successfully establishing the nation's first financial system, Hamilton observes that the passions and personal interests common to humanity have a particular force in republics. In such a system, the people are free to form into factious groups and there is no superintending force to mediate between them.

so far succeeded as materially to weaken the necessary influence and energy of the Executive Authority, and so far diminish the power of doing good in that department as greatly to take the motives which a virtuous man might have for making sacrifices. The prospect was even bad for gratifying in future the love of Fame, if that passion was to be the spring of action.[6]

The Union of these motives, with the reflections of prudence in relation to a growing family, determined me as soon as my plan had attained a certain maturity to withdraw from Office. This I did by a resignation about two years since; when I resumed the profession of the law in the City of New York under every advantage I could desire.

It is a pleasing reflection to me that since the commencement of my connection with General Washington to the present time, I have possessed a flattering share of his confidence and friendship.

Having given you a brief sketch of my political career, I proceed to some further family details.

In the year 1780 I married the second daughter of General Schuyler, a Gentleman of one of the best families of this Country; of large fortune and no less personal and public consequence. It is impossible to be happier than I am in a wife and I have five Children, four sons and a daughter, the eldest a son somewhat passed fifteen, who all promise well, as far as their years permit and yield me much satisfaction. Though I have been too much in public life to be wealthy, my situation is extremely comfortable and leaves me nothing to wish but a continuance of health. With this blessing, the profits of my profession and other prospects authorise an expectation of such addition to my resources as will render the eve of life, easy and agreeable; so far as may depend on this consideration.

It is now several months since I have heared from my father who continued at the Island of St Vincents. My anxiety at this silence would be greater than it is, were it not for the considerable interruption and precariousness of intercourse, which is produced by the War.

I have strongly pressed the old Gentleman to come to reside with me, which would afford him every enjoyment of which his advanced

[6] After accounting for his tenure as secretary of Treasury, Hamilton muses about the attractions and sacrifices of public office. He identifies three factors that draw ambitious individuals to seek office: financial gain, the opportunity to do good, and a desire for fame. Clearly, frustrated following his volatile term in the Washington administration, Hamilton seems to subtly suggest that he has already given up the hope of gratifying his own ambitious desire for fame through election to America's pinnacle office, the presidency.

8 Facing financial difficulty in his own business dealings, Hamilton's uncle, William, sought to secure work for his sons. His son Robert W. Hamilton, a sailor who was in the process of becoming a naturalized American citizen, particularly desired an appointment in the United States Navy. Hamilton pledges to assist him in this regard.

age is capable. But he has declined it on the ground that the advice of his Physicians leads him to fear that the change of Climate would be fatal to him.[7] The next thing for me is, in proportion to my means to endeavour to increase his comforts where he is.

It will give me the greatest pleasure to receive your son Robert at my house in New York and still more to be of use to him; to which end my recommendation and interest will not be wanting, and, I hope, not unavailing.[8] It is my intention to embrace the Opening which your letter affords me to extend intercourse with my relations in your Country, which will be a new source of satisfaction to me.

CONCLUSION

Overlooking the fact that his Scottish relatives were clearly exploiting his prominence, Hamilton invited his cousin Robert to stay in his home and used his influence to secure him an appointment from the Adams administration as a lieutenant on the USS *Constitution*. In gratitude, the Scottish Hamiltons hung a portrait of Alexander over the mantle at The Grange. The man they had previously dismissed when he was a child in need had now, in some regard, become their savior.

Source: Hamilton Papers, Library of Congress.

SECTION V

Legal Practice

The Phocion Letters on the Treatment of Tories
1784

INTRODUCTION

In late 1783, following preliminary agreement of the terms of the peace treaty, the British officially vacated New York. In the few years prior, the New York legislature had passed and the courts began to enforce a series of anti-Tory laws, which allowed, among other things, the confiscation of Loyalist property. Although the terms of the peace treaty forbid further confiscations and prosecutions, New Yorkers, under the leadership of anti-Loyalist crusader Governor George Clinton, became increasingly desirous of exacting revenge. Tories and Loyalists—terms broadly used to describe anyone who had directly assisted the British or who had merely remained in New York City during the British occupation—were increasingly deprived of their rights as citizens without due process of law. In March 1783, the New York legislature further violated the terms of the peace treaty by passing the Trespass Act, which allowed Patriots to seek damages against Loyalists who had used their abandoned property during British occupation.

Fear of such reprisal led thousands of Tories to flee the city. Hamilton was intensely alarmed, not only by the commercial and economic damage that would result from a mass exodus of Tory businessmen but also by the inherent injustice of depriving a class of citizens of their legal and political rights. He believed that such punitive actions directly violated the rule of law, the New York Constitution, and the authority of Congress to make treaties and consequently threatened the American experiment in self-government.

Initially alone in his willingness to stand against the public frenzy, Hamilton published two letters condemning his state's treatment of Loyalists. In his first letter, written in January 1784, Hamilton criticized the New York legislature for punishing whole classes of citizens without due process of law and for ignoring the peace treaty's prohibition of further prosecutions. In his second letter, published in April 1784, Hamilton opposed a bill under consideration in the legislature that would deprive those who had had resided in occupied territory during the war of their legal status and rights as citizens.

As in many of his writings, Hamilton chose a pseudonym based on a famous character from antiquity that reflected something about the topic at hand. In this case, he chose to write as Phocion, an Athenian general known for extending mercy to defeated enemies and for enduring popular disapproval for the sake of truth, justice, and the public good.

A Letter from Phocion to the Considerate Citizens of New York
January 1784

1 Hamilton accuses those leading the anti-Tory campaign of using New York newspapers to promote sinister doctrines that are antithetical to liberty and security.

2 Hamilton laments the fact that the upright and virtuous members of the community have done nothing to stop concerted efforts to undermine the rights of citizens under the New York Constitution and the obligations of the peace treaty. As a Revolutionary War veteran and former member of Congress, Hamilton pledges that he will not stand idly by while the fruits of independence are destroyed at the hands of unprincipled men.

3 Hamilton specifically calls out a group of Patriots, who had formed the "Whig Society," to pressure local aldermen to take punitive action against and drive out remaining Loyalists. Hamilton argues that the title of Whig, which is associated with the principles of liberty and justice that inspired the Revolution, is being used by these men to serve their own nefarious purposes. In contrast to the true spirit of Whigism—which cherishes liberty, individual rights, and due process of law—members of the Whig Society advocate exiling, disenfranchising, and depriving individual citizens of their rights without trial. They consequently embrace the very same tyrannical practices that first inspired the Revolution.

While not only every personal artifice is employed by a few heated and inconsiderate spirits, to practise upon the passions of the people, but the public papers are made the channel of the most inflammatory and pernicious doctrines, tending to the subversion of all private security and genuine liberty;[1] it would be culpable in those who understand and value the true interests of the community to be silent spectators. It is, however, a common observation, that men, bent upon mischief, are more active in the pursuit of their object, than those who aim at doing good. Hence it is in the present moment, we see the most industrious efforts to violate, the constitution of this state, to trample upon the rights of the subject, and to chicane or infringe the most solemn obligations of treaty; while dispassionate and upright men almost totally neglect the means of counteracting these dangerous attempts.[2] A sense of duty alone calls forth the observations which will be submitted to the good sense of the people in this paper, from one who has more inclination than leisure to serve them; and who has had too deep a share in the common exertions in this revolution, to be willing to see its fruits blasted by the violence of rash or unprincipled men, without at least protesting against their designs.

The persons alluded to, pretend to appeal to the spirit of Whiggism, while they endeavour to put in motion all the furious and dark passions of the human mind. The spirit of Whiggism, is generous, humane, beneficent and just. These men inculcate revenge, cruelty, persecution, and perfidy.[3] The spirit of Whiggism cherishes legal liberty, holds the rights of every individual sacred, condemns or punishes no man without regular trial and conviction of some crime declared by antecedent laws, reprobates equally the punishment of the citizen by arbitrary acts of legislature, as by the lawless combinations of unauthorised individuals: While these men are advocates for expelling a large number of their fellow-citizens unheard, untried; or if they cannot effect this, are for disfranchising them, in the face of the constitution, without the judgment of their peers, and contrary to the law of the land.

The 13th article of the constitution declares, "that no member of this state shall be *disfranchised* or *defrauded of any of the rights or privileges* sacred to the subjects of this state by the constitution, unless *by the law of the land or the judgment of his peers.*"[4] If we enquire what is meant by the law of the land, the best commentators will tell us, that it means *due process of law, that is, by indictment or presentment of good and lawful men*, and trial and conviction in consequence. . .

If there had been no treaty in the way, the legislature might, by *name*, have attainted particular persons of high treason for crimes committed during the war, but independent of the treaty it could not, and cannot, without tyranny, disfranchise or punish whole classes of citizens by general discriptions, without trial and conviction of offences known by laws previously established declaring the offence and prescribing the penalty.[5]

This is a dictate of natural justice, and a fundamental principle of law and liberty.

Nothing is more common than for a free people, in times of heat and violence, to gratify momentary passions, by letting into the government, principles and precedents which afterwards prove fatal to themselves.[6] Of this kind is the doctrine of disqualification, disfranchisement and banishment by acts of legislature. The dangerous consequences of this power are manifest. If the legislature can disfranchise any number of citizens at pleasure by general descriptions, it may soon confine all the votes to a small number of partizans, and establish an aristocracy or an oligarchy; if it may banish at discretion all those whom particular circumstances render obnoxious, without hearing or trial, no man can be safe, nor know when he may be the innocent victim of a prevailing faction.[7] The name of liberty applied to such a government would be a mockery of common sense. . .

Some imprudent Whigs among us, from resentment to those who have taken the opposite side, (and many of them from worse motives) would corrupt the principles of our government, and furnish precedents for future usurpations on the rights of the community.

Let the people beware of such Counsellors. However, a few designing men may rise in consequence, and advance their private interests by such expedients, the people, at large, are sure to be the losers in

[4] Hamilton reminds his readers that those seeking to disenfranchise and deprive a whole class of citizens of their legal rights and privileges without due process of law violate the explicit language of the New York Constitution.

[5] Article VI of the peace treaty forbids further prosecution of Loyalists or confiscation of their property. Hamilton argues that had the treaty not been ratified, New York might have justly punished individuals for treason or crimes committed during the war under procedures defined by law—but punishing whole classes of citizens without a trial that results in a conviction is a form of tyranny. The right of accused individuals to defend their innocence, according to procedures defined by law, is a fundamental requirement of liberty.

[6] According to Hamilton, history had shown that when any people, in the heat of passion, adopt principles that deprive certain members of their community of the rights accorded to others, they eventually subvert their own freedom.

[7] Allowing one class of citizens to disenfranchise and subvert the rights of other citizens through legislative decree not only removes fundamental safeguards against the abuse of power but also establishes the precedent that certain classes of citizens are entitled to more protection and privilege under the law than others. This would eventually pave the way for an oligarchic system in which no group or individual would know when they too might become victims of the arbitrary will of the prevailing faction.

the event whenever they suffer a departure from the rules of general and equal justice, or from the true principles of universal liberty.

These men, not only overleap the barriers of the constitution without remorse, but they advise us to become the scorn of nations, by violating the solemn engagements of the United States.[8] They endeavour to mould the Treaty with Great-Britain, into such form as pleases them, and to make it mean any thing or nothing as suits their views. They tell us, that all the stipulations, with respect to the Tories, are merely that Congress will recommend, and the States may comply or not as they please.

But let any man of sense and candour read the Treaty, and it will speak for itself.[9] The fifth article is indeed recommendatory; but the sixth is as positive as words can make it. "*There shall be* no future confiscations made, nor prosecutions commenced against any person or persons, for, or by reason of the part which he or they may have taken in the present war, and no person shall, on that account, suffer any future loss or damage, either in his person, liberty, or property."

As to the restoration of confiscated property which is the subject of the fifth article, the states may restore or not as they think proper, because Congress engage only to recommend; but there is not a word about recommendation in the 6th article. . .

There is a very simple and conclusive point of view in which this subject may be placed. No citizen can be deprived of any right which the citizens in general are entitled to, unless forfeited by some offence. It has been seen that the regular and constitutional mode of ascertaining whether this forfeiture has been incurred, is by legal process, trial and conviction.[10] This *ex vi termini*, supposes prosecution. Now consistent with the treaty there can be no future prosecution for any thing done on account of the war. . .

Congress, say our political jugglers, have no right to meddle with our internal police. They would be puzzled to tell what they mean by the expression. The truth is, it has no definite meaning; for it is impossible for Congress to do a single act which will not directly or indirectly affect the internal police of every state. When in order to procure privileges of commerce to the citizens of these states in foreign countries, they stipulate a reciprocity of privileges here, does not such an admission of the subjects of foreign countries to

[8] The advocates of exile and disenfranchisement not only undermine the authority of the New York Constitution but also inhibit peace and weaken the country's reputation abroad.

[9] In response to those who argue that the terms of the peace treaty are merely recommendations and that the states may comply with these terms at will, Hamilton outlines the clear legal obligations imposed by the treaty. While it is true that the treaty's fifth article only recommends restitution of the previously seized estates, properties, and rights of former Loyalists, the sixth article imposes an immediate prohibition of further prosecution, confiscation, or damages against any person based on the role the person played in the war.

[10] Hamilton reiterates that the only legitimate way a citizen may be deprived of the same rights and privileges of other citizens is through a trial and conviction—but such a conviction supposes prosecution, which the peace treaty forbids.

certain rights within these states operate, immediately upon their internal police? And were this not done, would not the power of making commercial treaties vested in Congress, become a mere nullity? In short if nothing was to be done by Congress that would affect our internal police, in the large sense in which it has been taken, would not all the powers of the confederation be annihilated and the union dissolved?. . .[11]

The men who are at the head of the party which contends for, disqualification and expulsion, endeavoured to inlist a number of people on their side by holding out motives of private advantage to them. To the trader they say, you will be overborne by the large capitals of the Tory merchants; to the Mechanic, your business will be less profitable, your wages less considerable by the interference of Tory workmen. A man, the least acquainted with trade, will indeed laugh at such suggestion.[12] He will know, that every merchant or trader has an interest in the aggregate mass of capital or stock in trade; that what he himself wants in capital, he must make up in credit; that unless there are others who possess large capitals, this credit cannot be had, and that in the diminution of the general capital of the State, commerce will decline, and his own prospects of profit will diminish.

These arguments, if they were understood, would be conclusive with the Mechanic: "There is already employment enough for all the workmen in the city, and wages are sufficiently high. If you could raise them by expelling those who have remained in the city, and whom you consider as rivals, the extravagant price of wages would have two effects; it would draw persons to settle here, not only from other parts of this State, but from the neighbouring States: Those classes of the community who are to employ you, will make a great many shifts rather than pay the exorbitant prices you demand; a man will wear his old cloaths so much longer before he gets a new suit; he will buy imported shoes cheap rather than those made here at so dear a rate: The owner of a house will defer the repairs as long as possible; he will only have those which are absolutely necessary made; he will not attend to elegant improvement, and the like will happen in other branches. These circumstances will give you less employment, and in a very little time bring back your wages to what they now are, and even sink them lower. But this is not all: You are not required merely to expel your rival mechanics, but you must drive away the rich merchants and others who are called Tories, to please your leaders, who will persuade you they are dangerous to

[11] Hamilton believed that the future of the union was at stake in the battle over the treatment of the Tories. If Congress had no power to dictate the internal affairs of the states in the realm of its delegated authority and if New York were allowed to continue to disregard the terms of the treaty with impunity, then the confederation would serve no purpose and the union would dissolve.

[12] In the argument that follows, Hamilton contends that driving out prosperous Tories will harm the state economically. Hamilton asserts that anyone acquainted with basic principles of trade will recognize the fallacy of the claim that wages will be higher and businesses will be more profitable if Tory competition is driven out of state. Driving out prosperous Tories, according to Hamilton, will only deprive the region of the capital and customer base necessary for economic growth and development. He further explains that even if the shortage of labor caused by a mass exodus of Tories leads to a temporary increase in wages, the increase would eventually either reduce demand for services or attract workers from other states—both of which would cause wages to return to their previous levels.

your liberty (though in fact they only mean their own consequence). By this conduct you will drive away the principal part of those who have the means of becoming large undertakers. The Carpenters and Masons in particular, must be content with patching up the houses already built and building little huts upon the vacant lots, instead of having profitable and durable employment in erecting large and elegant edifices."

. . . But say some, to suffer these wealthy disaffected men to remain among us, will be dangerous to our liberties; enemies to our government, they will be always endeavouring to undermine it and bring us back to the subjection of Great-Britain. The safest reliance of every government is on mens interests. This is a principle of human nature, on which all political speculation to be just, must be founded. Make it the interest of those citizens, who, during the revolution, were opposed to us to be friends to the new government, by affording them not only protection, but a participation in its privileges, and they will undoubtedly become its friends. . . . A disorderly or a violent government may disgust the best citizens, and make the body of the people tired of their Independence. . .[13]

Viewing the subject in every possible light, there is not a single interest of the community but dictates moderation rather than violence. That honesty is still the best policy; that justice and moderation are the surest supports of every government, are maxims, which however they may be called trite, at all times true, though too seldom regarded, but rarely neglected with impunity. Were the people of America, with one voice, to ask, What shall we do to perpetuate our liberties and secure our happiness? The answer would be, "govern well" and you have nothing to fear either from internal disaffection or external hostility. Abuse not the power you possess, and you need never apprehend its diminution or loss. But if you make a wanton use of it, if you furnish another example, that despotism may debase the government of the many as well as the few, you like all others that have acted the same part, will experience that licentiousness is the fore-runner to slavery.[14]

How wise was that policy of Augustus, who after conquering his enemies, when the papers of Brutus were brought to him, which would have disclosed all his secret associates, immediately ordered them to be burnt. He would not even know his enemies, that they might cease to hate when they had nothing to fear.

[13] In opposition to those who argue that remaining Tories would present a constant threat to the republic, Hamilton contends that loyalty is fostered through protection. If the Tories are represented and protected by the regime, they will have a personal stake in its perpetuation and will become devoted friends—but if they find themselves continually deprived of their civil and political rights, they would only become more hostile and willing to support any opposing force promising change. Furthermore, if the effort to exact revenge against Loyalists causes the state to abandon the rule of law and become "disorderly and violent," even the loyalty of the best citizens will be shaken.

[14] Hamilton argues that the best way to protect liberty is to perpetuate it through good government and the rule of law. When, acting out of fear or self-interest, the people debase republican government by resorting to licentious acts of despotism, they pave the way for their own eventual enslavement.

How laudable was the example of Elizabeth, who when she was transfered from the prison to the throne, fell upon her knees and thanking Heaven, for the deliverance it had granted her, from her bloody persecutors; dismissed her resentment.[15] "This act of pious gratitude says the historian, seems to have been the last circumstance in which she remembered any past injuries and hardships. With a prudence and magnanimity truly laudable, she buried all offences in oblivion, and received with affability even those, who had acted with the greatest virulence against her." She did more—she retained many of the opposite party in her councils.

The reigns of these two sovereigns, are among the most illustrious in history. Their moderation gave a stability to their government, which nothing else could have affected. This was the secret of uniting all parties.

These sentiments are delivered to you in the frankness of conscious integrity, by one who *feels* that solicitude for the good of the community which the zealots, whose opinions he encounters profess, by one who pursues not as they do, the honour or emoluments of his country, by one who, though he has had, in the course of the Revolution, a very *confidential* share in the public councils, civil and military, and has as often, at least, met danger in the common cause as any of those who now assume to be the guardians of the public liberty, asks no other reward of his countrymen, than to be heard without prejudice for their own interest.

PHOCION.
Second Letter from Phocion to the Considerate Citizens of New York

April 1784

The little hasty production, under the signature of PHOCION, has met with a more favourable reception from the public, than was expected. The force of plain truth has carried it along against the stream of prejudice; and the principles, it holds out, have gained ground, in spite of the opposition of those, who were either too angry, or too much interested to be convinced. Men of this description, have, till lately, contented themselves with virulent invectives against the Writer, without attempting to answer his arguments; but alarmed at the progress of the sentiments advocated by him, one of them has at

[15] Hamilton calls for a spirit of moderation and magnanimity in the treatment of Loyalists by appealing to the examples of two historical figures. Caesar Augustus refused to learn the names of those who had conspired with Brutus to assassinate his uncle, recognizing that such knowledge would only consume him with a desire for revenge and increase his enemies' fear and resentment. Under his leadership, Rome experienced decades of peace and prosperity. Hamilton then references Queen Elizabeth I, who following her release from prison and ascension to the throne, did not take punitive action against her former enemies but instead restored tranquility by appointing several of them to her inner council.

last come forward with an answer; with what degree of success, let those, who are most partial to his opinion, determine. . .

Mentor proposes to treat the sentiments of Phocion as a political novelty, but if he is serious, it is a proof that he is not even "tolerably well informed." They are as old as any regular notions of free government among mankind, and are to be met with, not only in every speculative Writer, on these subjects, but are interwoven in the theory and practice of that code, which constitutes the law of the land. They speak the common language of this country at the beginning of the revolution, and are essential to its future happiness and respectability.[16]

The principles of all the arguments I have used or shall use, lie within the compass of a few simple propositions, which, to be assented to, need only to be stated.

First, That no man can forfeit or be justly deprived, without his consent, of any right, to which as a member of the community he is entitled, but for some crime incurring the forfeiture.

Secondly, That no man ought to be condemned unheard, or punished for supposed offences, without having an opportunity of making his defence.

Thirdly, That a crime is *an act* committed or omitted, in violation of a public law, either forbidding or commanding it.

Fourthly, That a prosecution is in its most precise signification, an *inquiry* or *mode of ascertaining*, whether a particular person has committed, or omitted such *act*.

Fifthly, That *duties* and *rights* as applied to subjects are reciprocal; or in other words, that a man cannot be a *citizen* for the purpose of punishment, and not a *citizen* for the purpose of privilege.[17]

These propositions will hardly be controverted by any man professing to be a friend to civil liberty. The application of them will more fully appear hereafter.

By the declaration of Independence on the 4th of July, in the year 1776, acceded to by our Convention on the ninth, the late colony of

[16] Hamilton responds to an opponent, writing under the pseudonym Mentor, by reiterating that the principles of the rule of law, due process of law, and equal protection of law are not novel. Rather, they are the fundamental principles of civil liberty that inspired the Revolution and were incorporated into the country's laws. Furthermore, their maintenance is essential for the nation's future credibility and happiness.

[17] Hamilton reiterates a major tenet of social contract theory that individuals have a duty to obey the laws in exchange for the protection they receive under the law. It is unreasonable and unjust to subject citizens to the punishment of the law, while depriving them of protection under those same laws.

New-York became an independent state. All the inhabitants, who were subjects under the former government, and who did not withdraw themselves upon the change which took place, were to be considered as citizens, owing allegiance to the new government, This, at least, is the legal presumption;[18] and this was the principle, in fact, upon which all the measures of our public councils have been grounded. Duties have been exacted, and punishments inflicted according to this rule. . .

It was the policy of the revolution, to inculcate upon every citizen the obligation of renouncing his habitation, property, and every private concern for the service of his country, and many of us have scarcely yet learned to consider it as less than treason to have acted in a different manner. But it is time we should correct the exuberances of opinions propagated through policy, and embraced from enthusiasm; and while we admit, that those who did act so disinterested and noble a part, deserve the applause and, wherever they can be bestowed with propriety the rewards of their country, we should cease to impute indiscriminate guilt to those, who, submitting to the accidents of war, remained with their habitions and property.[19] We should learn, that this conduct is tolerated by the general sense of mankind; and that according to that sense, whenever the state recovers the possession of such parts as were for a time subdued, the citizens return at once to all the rights, to which they were formerly entitled.

As to the second head of forfeiture by misconduct, there is no doubt, that all such as remaining within the British lines, did not merely yield an obedience, which they could not refuse, without ruin; but took a voluntary and interested part with the enemy, in carrying on the war, became subject to the penalties of treason.[20] They could not however, by that conduct, make themselves aliens, because though they were bound to pay a temporary and qualified obedience to the conqueror, they could not transfer their eventual allegiance from the state to a foreign power. By becoming aliens too, they would have ceased to be traitors; and all the laws of the state passed during the revolution, by which they are considered and punished as subjects, would have been, by that construction, unintelligible and unjust. . .

Among the extravagancies with which these prolific times abound, we hear it often said that the constitution being the creature of the people, their sense with respect to any measure, if it even stand in opposition to the constitution, will sanctify and make it right.

[18] Hamilton argues that following the declaration of independence from Great Britain, New York assumed the rights and responsibilities of a sovereign state. Accordingly, it set up its own constitution and governing system. All subjects of the former government who remained following independence, by tacit consent, became citizens who owed allegiance to the new government and were therefore entitled to its protection.

[19] Hamilton condemns the attempt to strip citizenship rights from groups of individuals solely because they had remained in districts taken over by the British army. Although citizens were encouraged to leave occupied territories during the Revolution, Hamilton argues that those who remained had not committed a crime. They were only guilty of the misfortune of living in territories that were inadequately defended.

[20] Hamilton points out that citizens in occupied territories who had actively aided the enemy could be tried for treason, but such individuals could not be denied legal protection as citizens until they were convicted under a court of law. Nevertheless, as he states elsewhere, individual prosecutions are now forbidden by the peace treaty.

[21] In response to Hamilton's contention that attempts to disenfranchise Tories violate the New York Constitution, his adversaries had argued that any measure supported by the people should be upheld. Hamilton replies by explaining that constitutions—which require broad consensus and are implemented to protect the permanent and aggregate interests of the people—are superior to ordinary acts of legislation which merely represent the momentary will of the majority.

[22] If societies and majorities may disregard existing compacts at whim, then it would be impossible for individuals to know their civil rights and duties—as these would be continually subject to the arbitrary whim of whatever faction happens to hold power.

[23] Hamilton highlights the important responsibility that the first generation of leaders in republics have to future generations. They have the ability to establish beneficial principles and habits that extend far beyond their reign. If Americans act wisely in the early years, they will not only secure their own future happiness but also provide a worthy example for all mankind.

[24] In contrast, if out of a short-sighted desire for vengeance or temporary convenience leaders ignore constitutional safeguards against usurpation and tyranny, they will establish a precedent for the arbitrary use of power that will threaten the rights of individuals for generations to come.

Happily, for us, in this country, the position is not to be controverted; that the constitution is the creature of the people; but it does not follow that they are not bound by it, while they suffer it to continue in force; nor does it follow, that the legislature, which is, on the other hand, a creature of the constitution, can depart from it, on any presumption of the contrary sense of the people.[21]

The constitution is the compact made between the society at large and each individual. The society therefore, cannot without breach of faith and injustice, refuse to any individual, a single advantage which he derives under that compact, no more than one man can refuse to perform his agreement with another. If the community have good reasons for abrogating the old compact, and establishing a new one, it undoubtedly has a right to do it; but until the compact is dissolved with the same solemnity and certainty with which it was made, the society, as well as individuals, are bound by it. . .

The contrary doctrine serves to undermine all those rules, by which individuals can know their duties and their rights, and to convert the government into a government of *will* not of *laws*. . .[22]

I shall now with a few general reflections conclude.

Those, who are at present entrusted with power, in all these infant republics, hold the most sacred deposit that ever was confided to human hands. 'Tis with governments as with individuals, first impressions and early habits give a lasting bias to the temper and character. Our governments hitherto have no habits. How important to the happiness not of America alone, but of mankind, that they should acquire good ones.[23]

If we set out with justice, moderation, liberality, and a scrupulous regard to the constitution, the government will acquire a spirit and tone, productive of permanent blessings to the community. If on the contrary, the public councils are guided by humour, passion and prejudice; if from resentment to individuals, or a dread of partial inconveniences, the constitution is slighted or explained away, upon every frivolous pretext, the future spirit of government will be feeble, distracted and arbitrary. The rights of the subject will be the sport of every party vicissitude.[24] There will be no settled rule of conduct, but every thing will fluctuate with the alternate prevalency of contending factions.

The world has its eye upon America. The noble struggle we have made in the cause of liberty, has occasioned a kind of revolution in human sentiment. The influence of our example has penetrated the gloomy regions of despotism, and has pointed the way to inquiries, which may shake it to its deepest foundations.[25] Men begin to ask every where, who is this tyrant, that dares to build his greatness on our misery and degradation? What commission has he to sacrifice millions to the wanton appetites of himself and the few minions that surround his throne?

To ripen inquiry into action, it remains for us to justify the revolution by its fruits.

If the consequences prove, that we really have asserted the cause of human happiness, what may not be expected from so illustrious an example? In a greater or less degree, the world will bless and imitate!

But if experience, in this instance, verifies the lesson long taught by the enemies of liberty; that the bulk of mankind are not fit to govern themselves, that they must have a master, and were only made for the rein and the spur: We shall then see the final triumph of despotism over liberty. The advocates of the latter must acknowledge it to be an *ignis fatuus*, and abandon the pursuit. With the greatest advantages for promoting it, that ever a people had, we shall have betrayed the cause of human nature.

Let those in whose hands it is placed, pause for a moment, and contemplate with an eye of reverence, the vast trust committed to them. Let them retire into their own bosoms and examine the motives which there prevail. Let them ask themselves this solemn question—Is the sacrifice of a few mistaken, or criminal individuals, an object worthy of the shifts to which we are reduced to evade the constitution and the national engagements? Then let them review the arguments that have been offered with dispassionate candour; and if they even doubt the propriety of the measures, they may be about to adopt, let them remember, that in a doubtful case, the constitution ought never to be hazarded, without extreme necessity.

PHOCION

[25] Hamilton opened his Phocion letters by criticizing the shortsightedness of his fellow citizens for their failure to extend mercy, but he now appeals to their pride. Americans are in some sense a chosen people, in that they were the first to fight a revolution based on the universal principles of equal rights, liberty, and consent. If the American experiment in self-government succeeds, it will be a shining example of liberty and an impediment to worldwide tyranny, but if the principles of the revolution are frittered away by momentary passions, Americans will have deprived themselves and mankind of a valuable example.

Lamentably, Hamilton's writings as Phocion failed to halt legislative retaliation against Loyalists and temporarily tarnished his reputation as a war hero. Hamilton was publically charged with sacrificing his revolutionary credentials and his political prospects in pursuit of Loyalist money. Because his willingness to publically take up the Loyalist cause brought—in Hamilton's own words—"a plentiful harvest to us lawyers," he struggled to defend himself against such accusations of pecuniary self-interest. There is little evidence, however, that Hamilton was motivated by a desire for wealth in his choice of causes or clients. Although frequently in high demand, he often charged lower-than-average fees and took on many cases pro bono. Furthermore, his Phocion letters were consistent with his larger effort to establish a strong national identity rooted in the rule of law and tempered liberty.

Source: *A Letter from Phocion to the Considerate Citizens of New York on the Politics of the Day* and *A Second Letter from Phocion to the Considerate Citizens of New York. Containing Remarks on Mentor's Reply.* New York: Printed by Samuel Loudon, 1784.

Rutgers v. Waddington, Brief No. 6
1784

Around the time he published his second Phocion letter, Hamilton also began providing legal counsel to beleaguered Tories. His first and one of his best-known cases, *Rutgers v. Waddington*, involved an eighty-year-old widow, Elizabeth Rutgers, who had fled New York leaving behind her brewery and alehouse when the city was captured by the British in 1776. Under military orders, British merchant Benjamin Waddington and a partner took over and operated Rutgers's abandoned brewery. Although Waddington did not pay rent from 1778 to 1780, he did pay to refurbish the dilapidated brewery. Then, from 1780 to 1783, according to the dictate of General Henry Clinton, he paid rent to the Trinity Church Vestry for the Poor until the property was destroyed by a fire shortly before the end of the British occupation.

On her return to New York, Mrs. Rutgers brought suit under New York's Trespass Act against Joseph Waddington (Benjamin Waddington's uncle and acting agent), seeking restitution for damages and back rent for the entire period of British occupation. Because the Trespass Act allowed cases to be heard by any inferior court within the state, Rutgers's counsel brought suit before the Mayor's Court of New York City, where local magistrates would be congenial to aggrieved Patriots.

As Waddington's defense lawyer, Hamilton faced a difficult task—the plaintiff, a widow who had loyally supported the Patriot cause, was a sympathetic figure. Furthermore, the facts of the case were indisputable, and the language of the Trespass Act, which prohibited the use of military orders as a defense for occupation, was clearly applicable. Thus, rather than disputing the application of the relevant law to the litigation at hand, Hamilton questioned the validity of the law itself. Appealing to general principles of law and government, a method he would use throughout his law career, Hamilton challenged the legitimacy of the Trespass Act under international laws of war, the New York Constitution, and the treaty-making authority of Congress.

In the case of *Rutgers v. Waddington*, the defense team prepared a series of trial briefs, likely used as notes for the argument presented to the court. While the author of the first legal brief is unknown, Hamilton is the known author of briefs two through six. These briefs, which include tersely stated points, are the only record of Hamilton's argument before the court. Brief No. 6—a few selections of which are included here—appears to be the brief Hamilton used on petition for appeal following the Mayor's Court judgment (Goebel 1964). Although the appeal was never heard, the brief provides a good summary of Hamilton's main arguments in the case.

1 Hamilton opens by emphasizing the importance of the case at hand. Its outcome will affect the nation's good faith with other countries, the strength and safety of the Confederation, and the quality of future jurisprudence. He further observes that an "injurious" or mistaken judgment, which allows the states to continue to violate the terms of the peace treaty, would destroy the peace and provide the British with a "good cause of war."

2 Referring to the authority of renowned international law theorist Emmerich de Vattel's treatise, *The Law of Nations*, Hamilton explains that nations are governed by two types of moral obligations, those pertaining to themselves and those pertaining to other nations. The necessary or internal law refers to a nation's application of the law of nature to its own citizens. The voluntary or external law refers to the law of nature applied to the relationship between nations. The law of nature, according to Vattel, is based on the principle that each nation "remains absolutely free and independent with respect to all other men, and all *other* Nations, as long as it has not voluntarily submitted to them."

3 While individual governments are obligated by the Necessary Law to strictly uphold the principles of justice imposed by the law of nature in relation to their own citizens, the same rules cannot be enforced in the context of sovereign nations. Sovereign nations are free and independent from one another's authority, and since there is no commonly acknowledged superior to judge disputes between them, each nation maintains an equal right to regulate its own actions and to determine the just causes of war with other nations. Thus, in any mutually agreed-upon war, each side possesses an equal right to use the property acquired in battle.

4 Hamilton contends that the war between Great Britain and America was a solemn, or mutually agreed-upon, war—one in which both sides formally declared war and authorized hostilities. Thus, the laws of nations regarding the acquisition of property in war apply.

Introduction on the Importance of the cause

Affects national character—national faith—confederation treaty—Immediate safety of the STATE. FRONTIER POSTS character of our Jurisprudence—

INJURIOUS JUDGEMENT—a good cause of war. . .[1]

QUESTION now is whether a judgement already given in an Inferior Court consonant with our bests Interests shall be reversed in a superior Court. . .

NATIONS are under two sorts of Obligations

I The INTERNAL
II The EXTERNAL

The first founded on Necessary or Internal law of nations the second on external or voluntary law of Nations. . .[2]

BY THE VOLUNTARY both parties have equal rights, having no COMMON JUDGE

AND THE EFFECTS of the war on both sides are the same—

THESE EFFECTS are principally *impunity* and the *acquisition of property!!!*. . .[3]

OBJECTION This is not a solemn war; consequently the effects not the same—

ANSWER This by the best opinions and authorities makes no difference—

AND THE APPROVED practices of nations is against the OBJECTION. . .

But the war between G B & America was a solemn War. . .[4]

The Act of Parliament authorizing certain hostilities was a Legislative declaration of War

Declaration of Independence speaks of an open war existing—

Congress by a formal resolution authorised citizens of the United Colonies to cruise against British. . .

It has been said and it may be said again that the state of New York has no common law of nations

THE ANSWER is

1 That it results from the relations of Universal society

2 That our constitution adopts the common law of which the *law of nations is a part*[5]

3dly The United States are the Directors of our Intercourse with foreign nations And

They have expressly become parties to the law of nations—

The INQUIRY then is What are these effects of War?[6]

The general PROPOSITION OF the *jus belli* is that . . . Moveable goods belong to the Captor forever as soon as the *battle is over* & The fruits of immoveable goods while they are in possession. . .

The Common law carries the rights of war so far as to give property in a prisoner & an action of Trespass for taking him away

Brooke gives the property of one subject taken in War to a fellow subject recaptor, if fresh persuit & claim be not made the same day before the setting sun.

And this doctrine is applied to real property as well as personal

Hence we see the common law not only adopts the law of nation in its full extent as a general doctrine but particular adjudications recognize the operation of capture.

The last adjudication excludes all idea of question about the justice of war; for

[5] Hamilton argues that the New York Constitution of 1777 incorporated the customs and judicial precedents of English common law, which includes the law of nations. Under the law of nations, Waddington was entitled to use Rutgers's abandoned property since he was acting under military authority. Consequently, awarding Rutgers damages under the Trespass Act would violate the law of nations and, by implication, the English common law and the New York Constitution.

[6] Citing various legal authorities, Hamilton discusses the rights of property during periods of war. He concludes that an occupying army has a right to use any real property under military control. Thus, Mrs. Rutgers had no grounds for seeking compensation.

THE CIVIL law of every state must presume its own SOVER-EIGN in *the right*

OBJECTION But it may be said THESE Adjudications relate only to moveable goods—What is the law respecting real goods?—

The best Writers will tell us—The FRUITS *during the possession* belong to the Conqueror. . .

We find that moveables once taken are *booty* and gone forever, immoveables when recovered return Postliminy to their Original owners—

It will be proper to settle accurate Ideas of Postliminium Vatel defines it "That right in virtue of which *persons & things taken by the enemy* are restored to their former state when *coming again* under the power of the nation to which they belonged."

It is plainly a rule which regulates only the *internal rights of a nation within itself* and has no operation either with respect to the adverse party or to neutral nations—

Hence it has nothing to do with the Idea of a claim of damages from the adverse nation. . .

CONSEQUENCE—The enemy having a right to the use of the Plaintiffs property & having exercised their right through the Defendant & for valuable consideration he cannot be made answerable to another without injustice and a violation of the law of Universal society.

Further It cannot be done without violation of the Treaty of peace. . .[7]

Objections

1st It may be said Congress had no right to bind us Tis meddling with our *Internal Police.*

Answer

Then the Confederation is the shadow of a shade![8]

But CONGRESS had an unquestionable right

[7] Hamilton's second major argument was that the Trespass Act, and thus the *Rutgers* case, additionally violated the terms of the peace treaty agreed to by Congress, which prohibited further punitive suits for action taken during the war.

[8] In response to the claim that New York, as a sovereign state, was not bound by the terms of the treaty, Hamilton asserts that if Congress does not have the authority to speak for the nation in making treaties, then the Confederation is purposeless.

Our Sovereignty and Independence began by a FOEDERAL ACT

OUR EXTERNAL SOVEREIGNTY is only known in the UNION.

FOREIGN NATIONS only recognize it in the UNION.

BY THE DECLARATION OF INDEPENDENCE which is the fundamental constitution of every state, the UNITED STATES assert their power to levy war conclude peace and contract alliances all which is acceded to by

THE NEW YORK CONVENTION who do not pretend to authenticate the act, but only to give their approbation to it

Congress had then complete Sovereignty!!!

THE UNION is known and legalized in the Constitution previous to the Confederation and the first act of our government adopts it as a fundamental law

THESE REFLECTIONS teach us to respect the Sovereignty of the Union & to consider its constitutional powers as not controulable by any state!

The Confederation is an abridgement of those Powers—

. . . [I]t leaves Congress the full and exclusive powers of WAR PEACE & TREATY

The Power of making PEACE is the power of determining the Conditions of it[9]

It is a rule of reason & law *that to whomsoever* anything is granted that also is granted without which it cannot exist. . .

IF CONGRESS have not a power to adjust an equivalent for damages sustained and remit the rest, they have no power to make peace. . .

BUT IT MAY BE ASKED

[9] Hamilton contends that Congress derived the constitutional power to wage war, negotiate peace, and forge alliances with other nations on behalf of the states in their collective capacity, first under the Declaration of Independence and then under the Articles of Confederation—both of which were approved by the people of New York. Congress, in addition, possessed by clear implication the power to determine the reasonable conditions of peace. Because Article VI of the Treaty forbid further confiscations or prosecutions for injuries or damages caused by either side during the war, Waddington should have legally been absolved of any liability for his occupation of Rutgers's brewery.

How could they give away the rights of the Citizens of New York?

The answer is two fold

First the Citizens of New York gave them power to do it for their own safety—

And Secondly—The power results from this principle of all Governments—

That the property of all the Individuals of a state is the property of the sate itself in regard to other nations.

Hence an injury from the Government gives a right to take in war the property of its innocent subjects

Hence also the claim of damages for injuries done is in the public who may agree for an equivalent release the claim without it.

Our EXTERNAL sovereignty existing in the Union the property of all citizens in regard to foreign states belongs to the United States. . .

The power of Congress in making Treaties is of a Legislative kind

Their proclamation enjoining the observance of it is a law.

And a law Paramount to that of any particular state. . .[10]

HERE let us examine some important Questions

It is said the sovereign Authority may for *reasons of state* violate its treaties and the laws in violation bind its own subjects—

This however goes on bold ground to wit that the Legislature intended to violate the treaty—

But in our Constitution it is not true that the sovereignty of any one state has legally this power—

Each State has delegated all powers of this kind to Congress.

[10] Under the terms of the confederation, Congress was vested with the authority to ratify treaties on behalf of the union. The terms of the treaty, being legislative in nature, have the force of law and are therefore obligatory and superior to any conflicting state law.

They are equally to judge of the necessity of breaking as the propriety of making treaties—

The legislature of any one state has nothing to do with what are called *reasons of state*—

We might as well say a particular County has a right to alter the Laws of the state as a particular state the laws of the Confederation—

It has been and it may be said again that the Legislature may alter the laws of Nations—

This is not true in theory. . .

Nor is it constitutional in our government; for Congress have the exclusive direction of our foreign affairs & of all matters relating to the Laws of Nations.

No single state has any legal jurisdiction to alter them.

It may be again said that the accession to the Confederation was an act of our Legislature Why may not another act alter or dissolve it?

Answer It is not true; for the Union is known in our constitution as pre-existing—The act of Confederation is a modification & abridgment of Foederal authority by the original compact

But if this were not the case, the reasoning would not apply—

For this Government in acceding to the Confederation is to be considered not as a sovereign *enacting a law* but as a party to a contract; as a member of a more extensive community agreeing to a constitution of government[11]

It is absurd to say, One of the parties to a contract may at pleasure alter it without the consent of the others—

It will not be denied that a part of an empire may in certain cases dismember itself from the rest

But this supposes a dissolution of the Original contract

[11] Hamilton rebuffs the claim that the New York legislature—having originally granted legislative authority to the confederation—might repeal such a delegation of power with subsequent legislation. Hamilton points out that the original compact of union, under which independence from Great Britain was declared and the war was waged, existed prior to adoption of the New York Constitution. The Articles of Confederation simply modified this already-existing federal authority. Thus, any alteration of Congress's delegated authority would require an agreement of all parties to the original contract of union.

While the Confederation exists a law of a particular state derogating from its constitutional authority *is no law.*[12]

But how are the judges to decide—They are servants of the state?

Answer. The CONFEDERATION vesting no judicial powers in Congress excepting in prize causes—In all other matters

The judges of each state must of necessity be judges of the United States—[13]

And they must take notice of the law of Congress as part of the law of the land—

Though it should be admitted that they would be absolutely concluded by a law of the state in respect to its own citizens in respect to foreigners they must judge according to that law which alone the constitution knows as regulating their concerns.

It must not be conceded that the Legislature of one state cannot repeal a law of the United States—

It is a rule of law that where there are two laws, one not repeating the other expressly or virtually, the Judges must construe them so as to make them stand together—

Here that golden rule of the Roman Orator may be applied. . . . "When two or more laws clash that which relates to the most important concerns ought to prevail."[14]

CONCLUSION

After nearly two months of deliberation, New York mayor James Duane delivered the opinion of the court. Handing down a somewhat ambiguous judgment, Duane stopped short of establishing either the supremacy of the state legislature or the supremacy of the law of nations and the national treaty. Instead, he determined that Waddington owed rent to Rutgers for the period, between 1778 and 1780, when he had not paid rent to anyone, but that he was not liable for the period in which he had paid rent under British orders to the Vestry for the Poor. Duane argued that the treaty protected Waddington during the time that he was acting under the direct authority of the British commander in chief; therefore, the Trespass Act did not apply in this particular instance.

Although Duane ultimately concluded that the court did not have the power to invalidate the Trespass Act in its entirety, his decision to grant Waddington partial amnesty under the terms of the treaty infuriated the public and only increased the growing animosity toward Hamilton. Hamilton was viciously attacked in the press as a monarchist and lackey for the British and was even threatened with assassination. Nevertheless, as Chernow (2004) observes, Hamilton's willingness to endure intense public disapproval following the *Rutgers* case demonstrates that "he was not a politician seeking popularity but a statesman determined to change minds" (197). Ultimately, Hamilton's fortitude bore fruit. A few years later as sentiment toward the Tories began to change, Hamilton successfully convinced the New York legislature to repeal major pieces of anti-Tory legislation, including the Trespass Act, the Confiscation Act, and the Citation Act. In addition, the *Rutgers* case provided a public forum for Hamilton to introduce the principles of national supremacy and judicial review, concepts he would continue to articulate and defend throughout his career.

Source: Special Collections, Hamilton College Library, Clinton, New York.

Speech in the Case of *People v. Croswell*

1804

INTRODUCTION

In one of the last and most celebrated cases of his legal career, Hamilton represented newspaper editor Harry Croswell, who had been indicted for seditious libel against President Jefferson. In his weekly paper *The Wasp*, Croswell wrote that Jefferson had paid notorious journalist James T. Callender "for calling Washington a traitor, a robber, and a perjurer; for calling Adams a hoary-headed incendiary; and for most grossly slandering the private characters of men who he well knew were virtuous."

Although Jefferson was a long-time proponent of freedom of the press and had pardoned editors jailed under the Sedition Act, his stance began to change when he experienced an onslaught of negative coverage by Federalist newspapers toward the end of his first term. Complaining that the newspapers had "abandoned prostitution to falsehood," Jefferson expressed a desire for a "few wholesome prosecutions" of Federalist journalists. New York attorney general Ambrose Spencer, a recent convert to the Jeffersonian Republicans and a frequent target of *The Wasp*, initiated such a prosecution against Harry Croswell in Hudson, New York.

Although Croswell's allegations were presumably true and had been previously asserted by other sources, the prosecution charged that Croswell's statements had injured Jefferson's reputation and consequently undermined his authority as head of state. Therefore, regardless of whether his statements were true or not, Croswell had committed seditious libel.

A grand jury indicted Croswell in early 1803, and his case was heard by a circuit court in Calverack, New York, later that year. Under English common law, seditious libel consisted of any written statement that injured a government official's reputation, even if it were true. Thus, the presiding judge instructed jurors that they only needed to determine whether or not Croswell had published defamatory statements. On these grounds, the jury had no choice but to find Croswell guilty.

Hamilton, who had previously been consumed by other cases, agreed to represent Croswell pro bono in his motion for appeal. In February 1804, speaking before the New York Supreme Court in Albany, Hamilton passionately stressed the importance of maintaining a free press by allowing truth as a defense in libel suits.

May it please the Court:

In rising to address your honors at so late a period of the day, and after your attention has been so much fatigued, and the cause has been so ably handled, I may say, so exhausted, I feel a degree of embarrassment which it is with difficulty I can surmount. I fear lest it should not be possible for me to interest the attention of the court on the subject on which I have to speak. Nevertheless, I have a duty to perform, of which I cannot acquit myself, but by its execution. I have, however, this consolation, that though I may fail in the attempt, I shall be justified by the importance of the question. I feel that it is of the utmost magnitude; of the highest importance viewed in every light. First, as it regards the character of the head of our nation; for, if indeed the truth can be given in evidence, and that truth can, as stated in the indictment, be established, it will be a serious truth, the effect of which it will be impossible to foresee. It is important also as it regards the boundaries of power between the constituent parts of our constitutional tribunals, to which we are, for the law and the fact, to resort—our judges and our juries. It is important, as it regards settling the right principles that may be applied to the case, in giving to either the one or the other the authority destined to it by the spirit and letter of our law. It is important on account of the influence it must have on the rights of our citizens.[1] Viewing it, therefore, in these lights, I hope I shall, in the arduous attempt, be supported by its importance, and if any doubt hangs on the mind of the court, I shall, I trust, be able to satisfy them that a new trial ought to be had. . .

After these preliminary observations, and before I advance to the full discussion of this question, it may be necessary for the safety and accuracy of investigation, a little to define what this liberty of the press is, for which we contend, and which the present doctrines of those opposed to us, are, in our opinions, calculated to destroy.

The liberty of the press consists, in my idea, in publishing the truth, from good motives and for justifiable ends, though it reflect on the government, on magistrates, or individuals.[2] If it be not allowed, it excludes the privilege of canvassing men, and our rulers. It is in vain to say, you may canvass measures. This is impossible without the right of looking to men.[3] To say that measures can be discussed, and that there shall be no bearing on those who are the authors of those

[1] Hamilton stresses that the question of whether truth should be admitted as a defense in libel cases is of fundamental importance for a variety of reasons. First, since the defamatory statement in question involves the president, it is impossible to foresee what effect the truth might have on the well-being of the nation and its future stability. Second, the question is important because it will determine the level of authority given to judges and juries to exercise deference in libel suits. It is additionally important because it will determine the principles used to decide the outcome of the case at hand. Finally, it is important because it will influence the rights of citizens generally to speak the truth.

[2] Hamilton contends that the liberty of the press ultimately consists in the ability of individuals to publish with impunity what is true, as long as they are acting out of good motives for justifiable ends.

[3] Hamilton argues that it is fruitless to give individuals a right to criticize the actions of government, if they don't also have the right to criticize officials responsible for those actions. A critique of measures inevitably involves a corresponding critique of the persons answerable for them.

4 Furthermore, the maintenance of free and elective government depends on the people's ability to identify and remove from office those who abuse power or execute deleterious measures. Without this ability, the people will be unable to thwart corruption and tyranny.

5 Although advocating for freedom of the press, Hamilton emphasizes that there are just limits to freedom and that the press should not be completely unfettered.

6 Hamilton—having himself been the frequent victim of slander—laments the degree to which repeated falsehoods harm the reputation of even the finest characters. Referring to Jefferson's slander against George Washington, Hamilton states that "drops of water, in long and continued succession, will wear out adamant." In other words, repeated slander, even if untrue, will eventually negatively affect the public perception and reputation of any man, even one as admirable as Washington.

7 Although someone who uses the truth wantonly should be criminally liable and punished, restrictions on legitimate statements should not be defined a priori but should be based on a judgment of motives by the courts.

measures, cannot be done. The very end and reason of discussion would be destroyed. Of what consequence to show its object? Why is it to be thus demonstrated, if not to show, too, who is the author? It is essential to say, not only that the measure is bad and deleterious, but to hold up to the people who is the author, that, in this our free and elective government, he may be removed from the seat of power. If this be not to be done, then in vain will the voice of the people be raised against the inroads of tyranny.4 For, let a party but get into power, they may go on from step to step, and, in spite of canvassing their measures, fix themselves firmly in their seats, especially as they are never to be reproached for what they have done. This abstract mode, in practice, can never be carried into effect. But if, under the qualifications I have mentioned, the power be allowed, the liberty for which I contend will operate as a salutary check. In speaking thus for the freedom of the press, I do not say there ought to be an unbridled license;5 or that the characters of men who are good will naturally tend eternally to support themselves. I do not stand here to say that no shackles are to be laid on this license.

I consider this spirit of abuse and calumny as the pest of society. I know the best of men are not exempt from the attacks of slander. Though it pleased God to bless us with the first of characters, and though it has pleased God to take him from us and this band of calumniators, I say that falsehood eternally repeated would have affected even his name. Drops of water, in long and continued succession, will wear out adamant.6 This, therefore, cannot be endured. It would be to put the best and the worst on the same level.

I contend for the liberty of publishing truth, with good motives and for justifiable ends, even though it reflect on government, magistrates, or private persons. I contend for it under the restraint of our tribunals. When this is exceeded, let them interpose and punish.7 From this will follow none of those consequences so ably depicted. When, however, we do look at consequences, let me ask whether it is right that a permanent body of men, appointed by the executive, and, in some degree, always connected with it, should exclusively have the power of deciding on what shall constitute a libel on our rulers, or that they shall share it, united with a changeable body of men chosen by the people. Let our juries still be selected, as they now are, by lot. But it cannot be denied, that every body of men is, more or less, liable to be influenced by the spirit of the existing administration;

that such a body may be liable to corruption, and that they may be inclined to lean over towards party modes. No man can think more highly of our judges, and I may say personally so of those who now preside, than myself; but I must forget what human nature is, and how her history has taught us that permanent bodies may be so corrupted, before I can venture to assert that it cannot be. As then it may be, I do not think it safe thus to compromise our independence. For though, as individuals, the judges may be interested in the general welfare, yet, if once they enter into these views of government, their power may be converted into the engine of oppression. It is in vain to say that allowing them this exclusive right to declare the law, on what the jury has found, can work no ill; for, by this privilege, they can assume and modify the fact, so as to make the most innocent publication libellous. It is therefore not a security to say, that this exclusive power will but follow the law. It must be with the jury to decide on the intent; they must in certain cases be permitted to judge of the law, and pronounce on the combined matter of law and of fact. . .[8]

Some observations have, however, been made in opposition to these principles. It is said, that as no man rises at once high into office, every opportunity of canvassing his qualities and qualifications is afforded, without recourse to the press; that his first election ought to stamp the seal of merit on his name. This, however, is to forget how often the hypocrite goes from stage to stage of public fame, under false array, and how often, when men obtain the last object of their wishes, they change from that which they seemed to be; that men, the most zealous reverers of the people's rights, have, when placed on the highest seat of power, become their most deadly oppressors. It becomes, therefore, necessary to observe the actual conduct of those who are thus raised up.[9]

I have already shown that, though libelling shall continue to be a crime, it ought to be so only when under a restraint, in which the court and the jury shall co-operate. What is a libel that it should be otherwise? . . .

My definition of a libel is, and I give it with all diffidence after the words of Lord Camden—my definition, then, is this: I would call it a slanderous or ridiculous writing, picture, or sign, with a malicious or mischievous design or intent, towards government, magistrates,

[8] Government officials are more likely to be influenced by the spirit of the existing administration than fluctuating bodies chosen by lot; therefore, juries, rather than appointed judges, should be granted discretion to weigh the truth and intent of defamatory statements and to determine liability based on the particular facts of each case.

[9] In response to the argument that those elected to office have already proven that they merit the people's trust and should thus be shielded from further criticism, Hamilton counters that individuals frequently secure election under false pretenses. In a subtle reference to Jefferson, Hamilton contends that those who fervently identify themselves as the champions of the people often become their greatest oppressors once in office. A free press is thereby necessary to hold those elected to high office accountable for their use of power.

or individuals.[10] If this definition does not embrace all that may be so called, does it not cover enough for every beneficial purpose of justice? If it have a good intent, it ought not to be a libel, for it then is an innocent transaction; and it ought to have this intent, against which the jury have, in their discretion, to pronounce. It shows itself to us as a sentence of fact. Crime is a matter of fact by the code of our jurisprudence. In my opinion, every specific case is a matter of fact, for the law gives the definition. It is some act in violation of law. When we come to investigate, every crime includes an intent. Murder consists in killing a man with malice prepense. Manslaughter, in doing it without malice, and at the moment of an impulse of passion. Killing may even be justifiable, if not praiseworthy, as in defence of chastity about to be violated. In these cases the crime is defined, and the intent is always the necessary ingredient. The crime is matter of law, as far as definition is concerned; fact, as far as we are to determine its existence. . .

I do not deny this doctrine of the immateriality of the truth as a universal negative to a publication's being libellous, though true. But still I do say, that in no case may you not show the intent; for, whether the truth be a justification will depend on the motives with which it was published.

Personal defects can be made public only to make a man disliked. Here, then, it will not be excused; it might, however, be given in evidence to show the libellous degree. Still, however, it is a subject of inquiry. There may be a fair and honest exposure. But if he uses the weapon of truth wantonly; if for the purpose of disturbing the peace of families; if for relating that which does not appertain to official conduct, so far we say the doctrine of our opponents is correct.[11] If their expressions are, that libellers may be punished though the matter contained in the libel be true, in these I agree. I confess that the truth is not material as a broad proposition respecting libels. But that the truth cannot be material in any respect, is contrary to the nature of things. No tribunal, no codes, no systems can repeal or impair this law of God, for by his eternal laws it is inherent in the nature of things. . .[12]

11 While Hamilton suggests that the truth of a statement indicates a lack of malevolent intent, he concedes that even the truth can be used maliciously. Thus, those who use the truth for the sole purpose of injuring an official outside of their public capacity, such as to disturb the peace of families, should be criminally liable.

12 Although the licentious publication of truth should be punished, restricting the truth altogether violates the eternal laws of God and nature, which Hamilton identifies as the source of truth.

I never did think the truth was a crime; I am glad the day is come in which it is to be decided, for my soul has ever abhorred the thought that a free man dared not speak the truth; I have forever rejoiced when this question has been brought forward. . .

Thus, then, stands the matter, on English conduct, and on English precedent. Let us see if any thing in the annals of America will further the argument. Zenger's case has been mentioned as an authority. A decision in a factitious period, and reprobated at the very time. . . . To pursue the precedents more emphatically our own, let us advert to the sedition law, branded indeed with epithets the most odious, but which will one day be pronounced a valuable feature in our national character. In this we find not only the intent but the truth may be submitted to the jury, and that even in a justificatory manner.[13] This, I affirm, was on common-law principles. It would, however, be a long detail to investigate the applicability of the common law to the Constitution of the United States. It is evident, however, that parts of it use a language which refers to former principles. The *habeas corpus* is mentioned, and as treason, it adopts the very words of the common law. Not even the Legislature of the Union can change it. Congress itself cannot make constructive or new treasons. Such is the general tenor of the Constitution of the United States, that it evidently looks to antecedent law. What is, on this point, the great body of the common law? Natural law and natural reason applied to the purposes of society. What are the English courts now doing but adopting natural law?

What have the court done here? Applied moral law to constitutional principles, and thus the judges have confirmed this construction of the common law; and therefore, I say, by our Constitution it is said the truth may be given in evidence. In vain it is to be replied that some committee met, and in their report gave it the name of amendment. For when the act says declared, I say the highest legislative bodies in this country have declared that the common law is, that the truth shall be given in evidence; and this I urge as a proof of what that common law is. On this point a fatal doctrine would be introduced if we were to deny the common law to be in force according to our federal Constitution. Some circumstances have doubtless weakened my position. Impeachments of an extraordinary nature have echoed through the land, charging as crimes things unknown, and although our judges, according to that Constitution, must appeal to the definitions of the common law for treasons, crimes, and misdemeanors, this, no doubt, was that no vague words might be used. If, then, we discharge all evidence of the common law, they may be pronounced guilty *ad libitum*, and the crime and offence being at once their will, there would be an end of that Constitution.

[13] After surveying inconsistencies in English common law, Hamilton identifies American precedents for using truth as a defense. He cites the case of John Peter Zenger, who was acquitted by a jury in 1733 after publishing defamatory statements against the royal governor of New York. Hamilton further notes that even the much-maligned Sedition Act made truth admissible as a defense in libel suits.

14 The freedom of press is even more essential given the spirit of faction pervading the country. Without a free press, those in power could use libel laws to stifle or silence the views of their political opponents and thereby secure their permanent rule. This would undermine the spirit of constitutional government.

15 Hamilton warns that tyranny will never be introduced into the country by the force of arms but rather slowly creeps in when judicial tribunals, acting under the pretense of law, degrade the people's liberties and deprive them of substance. The freedom to publish what is true, within justified limits, is therefore a salutary check against the abuse of power and a bulwark of liberty.

By analogy a similar construction may be made of our own Constitution, and our judges thus got rid of. This may be of the most dangerous consequences. It admonishes us to use with caution these arguments against the common law; to take care how we throw down this barrier which may secure the men we have placed in power; to guard against a spirit of faction, that great bane to our community, that mortal poison to our land. It is considered by all great men as the natural disease of our form of government, and therefore we ought to be careful to restrain that spirit. We have been careful that when one party comes in it shall not be able to break down and bear away the others. If this be not so, in vain have we made constitutions;[14] for if it be not so, then we must go into anarchy, and from thence to despotism and to a master. Against this I know there is an almost insurmountable obstacle in the spirit of the people. They would not submit to be thus enslaved. Every tongue, every arm would be uplifted against it; they would resist, and resist, and resist, till they hurled from their seats those who dared make the attempt. To watch the progress of such endeavors is the office of a free press—to give us early alarm, and put us on our guard against the encroachments of power. This, then, is a right of the utmost importance; one for which, instead of yielding it up, we ought rather to spill our blood. Going on, however, to precedents, I find another in the words of Chief-Justice Jay, when pronouncing the law on this subject. The jury are, in the passage already cited, told the law, and the fact is for their determination; I find him telling them that it is their right. This admits of no qualification. The little, miserable conduct of the judge in Zenger's case, when set against this, will kick the beam; and it will be seen that even the twelve judges do not set up, with deference, however, to their known ability, that system now insisted on. If the doctrine for which we contend is true in regard to treason and murder, it is equally true in respect to libel. For there is the great danger. Never can tyranny be introduced into this country by arms; these can never get rid of a popular spirit of inquiry; the only way to crush it down is by a servile tribunal. It is only by the abuse of the forms of justice that we can be enslaved. An army never can do it. For ages it can never be attempted. The spirit of the country, with arms in their hands, and disciplined as a militia, would render it impossible. Every pretence that liberty can be thus invaded is idle declamation. It is not to be endangered by a few thousand of miserable, pitiful military. It is not thus that the liberty of this country is to be destroyed. It is to be subverted only by a pretence of adhering to all the forms of law, and yet by breaking down the substance of our liberties; by devoting a wretched but honest man as the victim of a nominal trial.[15]

Those who heard Hamilton's speech in defense of Croswell, including many members of the New York Senate and Assembly, reported that it was one of the finest of his entire career. Even Attorney General Ambrose Spencer, who had initially brought charges against Croswell, reported that Hamilton was "the greatest man this country has ever produced."

In spite of the awe he inspired in his audience, Hamilton was unable to convince the court. The four judges were split two to two, and Croswell's conviction was left standing. Nevertheless, Hamilton's eloquent plea greatly impacted those who heard it. Although Hamilton did not live to witness it, the New York legislature enacted legislation making truth a defense the following year. Other states followed suit, and the doctrine was eventually embraced as the standard for libel cases throughout the republic.

Source: Henry Cabot Lodge, ed. *The Works of Alexander Hamilton*. Federal Edition, vol. 8. New York: G.P. Putnam's Sons, 1904.

SECTION VI

Creating and Defending the Constitution

Address to the Annapolis Convention

September 14, 1786

INTRODUCTION

Following the Revolution, the thrill of victory and newly acquired independence was over-shadowed by the persistent failures of the Articles of Confederation and the inability of Congress to maintain order and stability within and among the states.

Among its more problematic defects, Congress was unable to issue and enforce uniform policies concerning interstate and foreign trade. Consequently, the individual states began to impose tariffs and trade barriers against one another, which led to intense interstate hostility. Hoping to strengthen the union and prevent civil war, James Madison urged the Virginia legislature to call for a general meeting of commissioners from each state to "consider how far a uniform system in their commercial regulations may be necessary to their common interest and their permanent harmony" (Knott and Williams 2015, 134). The Virginia legislature complied, and the meeting convened in Annapolis, Maryland, in early September 1786.

To Madison's disappointment, the Annapolis Convention was poorly attended, with only five states sending commissioners. With so few states represented, the delegates lacked the authority to determine an appropriate response to the interstate commercial crisis. Nevertheless, they agreed that the Articles of Confederation were fundamentally flawed and needed serious revision. Hamilton, who was serving as a delegate from New York, recognized a long-awaited opportunity to advance the cause of nationalism. He issued a resolution on behalf of the present commissioners calling for a convention with broad authority to amend the Articles of Confederation and make it "adequate to the exigencies of union" (Hamilton 1962, vol. 3, 690). This report was unanimously approved by the commissioners at Annapolis on September 14, 1786.

To the Honorable the Legislatures of Virginia, Delaware Pennsylvania, New Jersey, and New York.[1]

The Commissioners from the said states, respectively assembled at Annapolis, humbly beg leave to report.

That, pursuant to their several appointments, they met, at Annapolis in the State of Maryland, on the eleventh day of September. . .,

[1] Commissioners from the five listed states were present during the proceedings at Annapolis.

[2] Hamilton summarizes the decision-making authority granted to the commissioners by their respective states.

and having proceeded to a Communication of their powers; they found, that[2] the States of New York, Pennsylvania and Virginia had, in substance, and nearly in the same terms, authorised their respective Commissioners "to meet such commissioners as were, or might be, appointed by the other States in the Union, at such time and place, as should be agreed upon by the said Commissioners to take into consideration the trade and Commerce of the United States, to consider how far an uniform system in their commercial intercourse and regulations might be necessary to their common interest and permanent harmony, and to report to the several States, such an Act, relative to this great object, as when unanimously ratified by them would enable the United States in Congress assembled effectually to provide for the same."

That the State of Delaware, had given similar powers to their Commissioners, with this difference only that the Act to be framed in virtue of those powers, is required to be reported "to the United States in Congress Assembled, to be agreed to by them, and confirmed by the Legislatures of every State."

[3] Unlike the commissioners of previously mentioned states, whose decision-making authority was limited to commercial regulations, New Jersey had granted its commissioners the authority to consider "other important matters" as well. Hamilton appeals to this extended authority to justify a more comprehensive convention later in his report.

That the State of New Jersey had enlarged the object of their Appointment, empowering their Commissioners, "to consider how far an uniform system in their commercial regulations and *other important matters*, might be necessary to the common interest and permanent harmony of the several States,"[3] and to report such an Act on the subject, as when ratified by them "would enable the United States in Congress Assembled, effectually to provide for the exigencies of the Union."

That appointments of Commissioners have also been made by the States of New Hampshire, Massachusetts, Rhode Island, and North Carolina, none of whom however have attended; but that no information has been received by your Commissioners of any appointments having been made by the States of Connecticut, Maryland, South Carolina, or Georgia.

That the express terms of the powers to your Commissioners supposing a deputation from all the States, and having for object the Trade and Commerce of the United States, Your Commissioners did not conceive it advisable to proceed on the business of their mission, under the Circumstance of so partial and defective a representation.

Deeply impressed however with the magnitude and importance of the object confided to them on this occasion, your Commissioners cannot forbear to indulge an expression of their earnest and unanimous wish, that speedy measures may be taken, to effect a general meeting, of the States, in a future Convention, for the same and such other purposes, as the situation of public affairs, may be found to require.[4]

If in expressing this wish, or in intimating any other sentiment, your Commissioners should seem to exceed the strict bounds of their appointment, they entertain a full confidence, that a conduct, dictated by an anxiety for the welfare, of the United States, will not fail to receive an indulgent construction.

In this persuasion your Commissioners submit an opinion, that the Idea of extending the powers of their Deputies, to other objects, than those of Commerce, which has been adopted by the State of New Jersey, was an improvement on the original plan, and will deserve to be incorporated into that of a future Convention; they are the more naturally led to this conclusion, as in the course of their reflections on the subject, they have been induced to think, that the power of regulating trade is of such comprehensive extent, and will enter so far into the general System of the foederal government, that to give it efficacy, and to obviate questions and doubts concerning its precise nature and limits, may require a correspondent adjustment of other parts of the Foederal System. . .[5]

Your Commissioners decline an enumeration of those national circumstances on which their opinion respecting the propriety of a future Convention with more enlarged powers, is founded; as it would be an useless intrusion of facts and observations, most of which have been frequently the subject of public discussion, and none of which can have escaped the penetration of those to whom they would in this instance be addressed. They are however of a nature so serious, as, in the view of your Commissioners to render the Situation of the United States delicate and critical, calling for an exertion of the united virtue and wisdom of all the members of the Confederacy.

Under this impression, Your Commissioners, with the most respectful deference, beg leave to suggest their unanimous conviction, that it may essentially tend to advance the interests of the union, if the

[4] Although the commissioners concluded that they lacked a quorum necessary to proceed with the business at hand, they agreed that a future convention would be necessary to address commercial disputes as well as other flaws inherent in the Articles of Confederation.

[5] Hamilton references the broad mandate granted to the commissioners of New Jersey in order to justify a new convention endowed with the authority to consider comprehensive reform. He explains that, after reflecting on commercial matters, the present commissioners had concluded that the defects of the Articles of Confederation were greater than they had thought and that addressing such defects would require major modifications to the current federal system.

[6] The commissioners unanimously agreed to recommend a convention in Philadelphia to their respective states and to seek the concurrence of the other states as well. In a previous version of this address, Hamilton had called for a convention that would "cement the bond of union." After Madison warned him that such strong nationalist wording would never be acceptable to the states, Hamilton softened the language. Nevertheless, Hamilton's charge that the convention would be endowed with the authority to adopt "provisions . . . necessary to render the constitution of the Federal Government adequate to the exigencies of union" left open the possibility that the delegates in Philadelphia might go beyond merely revising the Articles. Thus, Hamilton subtly paved the way for the adoption of an entirely new political system.

States, by whom they have been respectively delegated, would themselves concur, and use their endeavours to procure the concurrence of the other States, in the appointment of Commissioners, to meet at Philadelphia on the second Monday in May next, to take into consideration the situation of the United States, to devise such further provisions as shall appear to them necessary to render the constitution of the Fœderal Government adequate to the exigencies of the Union;[6] and to report such an Act for that purpose to the United States in Congress Assembled, as when agreed to, by them, and afterwards confirmed by the Legislatures of every State will effectually provide for the same.

Though your Commissioners could not with propriety address these observations and sentiments to any but the States they have the honor to Represent, they have nevertheless concluded from motives of respect, to transmit Copies of this report to the United States in Congress assembled, and to the executives of the other States.

By order of the Commissioners

Dated at Annapolis

September 14.1776

Resolved that the Chairman sign the aforegoing Report in behalf of the Commissioners

Then adjourned. . .
NEW YORK

Egbt: Benson
Alexander Hamilton
NEW JERSEY

Abra: Clark
Wm Chls Houston
Js. Schureman
PENNSYLVANIA

Tench Coxe
DELAWARE

Geo: Read
John Dickinson
Richard Bassett
VIRGINIA
Edmund Randolph
Js. Madison Jr.
St. George Tucker

In the months following the Annapolis Convention, the fate of the American union became even more precarious as the federal government teetered on the brink of bankruptcy and debt from the war threatened to overwhelm the economies of individual states. In response to crushing taxes and land seizures in Massachusetts, a group of indebted farmers led by Daniel Shays openly rebelled, shutting down county courthouses and attempting to take over the federal arsenal in Springfield. While the national government's response to the crisis was too weak, the state's response was overly draconian. Thus, Shays' Rebellion gave new vigor and credibility to those calling for a stronger national government to maintain order, stability, and liberty. By late February 1787, Congress approved the call for a convention in Philadelphia, and all of the states, except Rhode Island, eventually agreed to send delegates.

Source: Papers of the Continental Congress, National Archives.

Speech in the Constitutional Convention on a Plan of Government

June 18, 1787

INTRODUCTION

Despite his pivotal role in bringing about the Constitutional Convention, Hamilton did not play a particularly active role in the convention itself. He had succeeded in being appointed as one of New York's three delegates, but the other two delegates, Robert Yates and John Lansing, were staunch opponents of a stronger federal system having been chosen at the behest of anti-nationalist governor George Clinton. Since each state voted as a single delegation, Hamilton recognized that his vote would ultimately be nullified by his fellow delegates and his influence consequently stifled.

One notable exception to Hamilton's largely passive role in the convention occurred following the introduction of the Virginia and New Jersey Plans. The Virginia Plan, drafted by James Madison and introduced by Virginia governor Edmund Randolph, significantly diminished state power and established a national government consisting of bicameral legislature (with representation in both houses based on population), a single executive, and a national judiciary. In contrast to the sweeping reform proposed by the Virginia Plan, the New Jersey Plan largely retained the existing confederation but enhanced Congress's power to tax and regulate foreign and interstate commerce. The small states, concerned about the scheme of representation under the Virginia Plan, particularly favored the call of the New Jersey Plan for equal representation of the states in Congress.

As the convention split between factions supporting the opposing plans, Hamilton intervened to introduce a more radical plan of his own. Although there are no written transcripts of Hamilton's speech, several members of the convention took copious notes. James Madison's carefully recorded account is included here.

18 June 1787

Mr. Hamilton, had been hitherto silent on the business before the Convention, partly from respect to others whose superior abilities age & experience rendered him unwilling to bring forward ideas dissimilar to theirs, and partly from his delicate situation with respect to his own State, to whose sentiments as expressed by his Colleagues, he could by no means accede. The crisis however which now marked our affairs, was too serious to permit any scruples whatever to prevail over the duty imposed on every man to contribute his efforts for the public safety & happiness.[1] He was obliged therefore to declare himself unfriendly to both plans. He was particularly opposed to that from N. Jersey, being fully convinced, that no amendment of the confederation, leaving the States in possession of their sovereignty could possibly answer the purpose. . .[2]—As to the powers of the Convention, he thought the doubts started on that subject had arisen from distinctions & reasonings too subtle. . . . He agreed moreover with the Honbl. gentleman from Va. (Mr. R.) that we owed it to our Country, to do on this emergency whatever we should deem essential to its happiness. The States sent us here to provide for the exigences of the Union. To rely on & propose any plan not adequate to these exigences, merely because it was not clearly within our powers, would be to sacrifice the means to the end. . .[3]

What then is to be done? Here he was embarrassed. The extent of the Country to be governed, discouraged him. The expence of a general Govt. was also formidable; unless there were such a diminution of expence on the side of the State Govts. as the case would admit. If they were extinguished, he was persuaded that great oeconomy might be obtained by substituting a general Govt. He did not mean however to shock the public opinion by proposing such a measure. On the other hand he saw no *other* necessity for declining it. They are not necessary for any of the great purposes of commerce, revenue, or agriculture. Subordinate authorities he was aware would be necessary. There must be district tribunals: corporations for local purposes. . .[4] The only difficulty of a serious nature which occurred to him, was that of drawing representatives from the extremes to the center of the Community.[5] What inducements can be offered that will suffice? The moderate wages for the 1st. branch, would only be a bait to little demagogues. Three dollars or thereabouts he supposed would be the Utmost. The Senate he feared from a similar cause, would be filled by certain undertakers who wish for particular offices under the Govt. This view of the subject almost led him to despair that a Republican Govt. could be established over so great an extent. He was sensible at the same time that it would be unwise to propose one of any other form. In his private opinion he had no scruple in declaring, supported as he was by the opinions of so many of the

[1] Recognizing that progress had stalled and that the convention was in danger of collapsing due to parochial squabbles over schemes of representation in Congress, Hamilton intervened to once again elevate deliberation to a discussion of what would be necessary for the happiness of the nation as a whole. According to Madison's account, Hamilton maintains that he had previously hesitated to express his ideas, partly because he was reticent to publically discount the views of other well-respected delegates and partly because his own delegation lacked consensus. Nevertheless, he concludes that, as the crisis in national affairs had reached a critical state, he was obligated to contribute his own views concerning what might promote "public safety and happiness."

[2] Although Hamilton effectively lays the groundwork for compromise by declaring opposition to both of the previously introduced plans, he specifically criticizes the New Jersey Plan, which—aside from vesting Congress with increased powers over revenue and trade—left the loose confederation of sovereign states under the Articles of Confederation intact. Hamilton argues that as long as states retain ultimate sovereignty, no amendment of the Articles of Confederation would achieve the convention's objective "to provide for the exigencies of Union."

[3] In an attempt to convince the convention of the necessity of an entirely new political system, Hamilton reiterates Virginia governor Edmund Randolph's argument that the convention should not reject a plan of government simply because it exceeds the convention's defined authority to revise the Articles of Confederation. For, as Hamilton argues, to do anything less than what would be essential for the nation's future happiness, simply because it was "not within our powers," would "be to sacrifice the means to the end."

[4] Hamilton had believed for some time that only a true national government possessing coercive authority over citizens, without the intervention of states, would maintain

the union and secure its future prosperity. Here, he makes a more extreme argument than anything he had ever before or would ever after suggest. Though he says that he would refrain from shocking public opinion by calling for the abolition of the states, he radically asserts that the states are financially burdensome and unnecessary and that local affairs might be better directed by district tribunals or counties.

5 After calling for a virtual eradication of the state governments, Hamilton says that the only challenge to such a proposal that still concerns him is attracting qualified representatives. He worries that the great travel distance from geographic extremes to the seat of the national government might discourage good men from running for office and that the miniscule salary of a national representative would attract only petty demagogues or those with no other worthwhile pursuits. Thus, he despairs over whether a republican government would be possible in a country of such great extent, but he also recognizes that no other form of government would be acceptable in America.

6 Hamilton then makes an inflammatory claim that would haunt him for the rest of his life, stating that, in his own private opinion, the British government—with its House of Commons, House of Lords, and a king—was the best designed in the world. Robert Hendrickson (1981) points out, however, that Madison may have exaggerated Hamilton's praise of the British since, according to other accounts of Hamilton's speech (including those of Robert Yates, John Lansing, and Rufus King), Hamilton had merely argued that the British government provided a viable model of a strong executive limited by a bicameral legislature.

7 Recognizing that his praise of British constitutional monarchy might shock a convention consisting of those who had signed the Declaration of Independence and fought in the Revolutionary War, Hamilton encourages his fellow delegates to consider the evolution of their own views. Even the most tenacious defenders of republicanism,

wise & good, that the British Govt. was the best in the world: and that he doubted much whether any thing short of it would do in America.[6] He hoped Gentlemen of different opinions would bear with him in this, and begged them to recollect the change of opinion on this subject which had taken place and was still going on. It was once thought that the power of Congs was amply sufficient to secure the end of their institution. The error was now seen by every one. The members most tenacious of republicanism, he observed, were as loud as any in declaiming agst. the vices of democracy. This progress of the public mind led him to anticipate the time, when others as well as himself would join in the praise bestowed by Mr. Neckar on the British Constitution, namely, that it is the only Govt. in the world "which unites public strength with individual security."[7]—In every community where industry is encouraged, there will be a division of it into the few & the many. Hence separate interests will arise. There will be debtors & Creditors &c. Give all power to the many, they will oppress the few. Give all power to the few they will oppress the many. Both therefore ought to have power, that each may defend itself agst. the other. To the want of this check we owe our paper money—instalment laws &c To the proper adjustment of it the British owe the excellence of their Constitution. . .[8]

What is the inference from all these observations? That we ought to go as far in order to attain stability and permanency, as republican principles will admit. Let one branch of the Legislature hold their places for life or at least during good-behaviour. Let the Executive also be for life.[9] He appealed to the feelings of the members present whether a term of seven years, would induce the sacrifices of private affairs which an acceptance of public trust would require, so as to ensure the services of the best Citizens. On this plan we should have in the Senate a permanent will, a weighty interest, which would answer essential purposes. But is this a Republican Govt. it will be asked? Yes, if all the Magistrates are appointed, and vacancies are filled, by the people, or a process of election originating with the people. . .[10]

Having made these observations he would read to the Committee a sketch of a plan which he shd. prefer to either of those under consideration. He was aware that it went beyond the ideas of most members. But will such a plan be adopted out of doors? In return he would ask will the people adopt the other plan? At present they will adopt neither. But he sees the Union dissolving or already dissolved—he sees evils operating in the States which must soon cure the people of their fondness for democracies—he sees that a great progress has been already made & is still going on in the public mind.[11] He thinks therefore that the people will in time be unshackled from their prejudices; and whenever that happens, they will themselves not be satisfied at stopping where the plan of Mr. R. wd. place them, but be ready to go as far at least as he proposes. He did not mean to offer the paper he had sketched as a proposition to the Committee. It was meant only to give a more correct view of his ideas. . .

He read his sketch in the words following. . .[12]

I.   The Supreme Legislative power of the United States of America to be vested in two different bodies of men; the one to be called the Assembly, the other the Senate who together shall form the Legislature of the United States with power to pass all laws whatsoever subject to the Negative hereafter mentioned.

II.   The Assembly to consist of persons elected by the people to serve for three years.

III. The Senate to consist of persons elected to serve during good behaviour; their election to be made by electors chosen for that purpose by the people: in order to this the States to be divided into election districts. On the death, removal or resignation of any Senator his place to be filled out of the district from which he came.

IV.   The supreme Executive authority of the United States to be vested in a Governour to be elected to serve during good behaviour—the election to be made by Electors chosen by the people in the Election Districts aforesaid—The authorities & functions of the Executive to be as follows: to have a negative on all laws about to be passed, and the execution of all laws passed, to have the direction of war when authorized or begun; to have with the advice and approbation of the Senate the power of making all treaties; to have the sole appointment of the heads or chief officers of the departments of Finance, War and Foreign Affairs; to have the nomination of all other officers (Ambassadors to foreign Nations included) subject to the approbation or rejection of the Senate; to have the power of pardoning all offences except Treason; which he shall not pardon without the approbation of the Senate.

having witnessed the failures and ineffectiveness of Congress, now acknowledged the vices of democracy. Thus, he anticipated a time when his colleagues would join in agreement with French finance minister Jacques Necker, who had praised the British system as the only one in the world that had successfully combined "public strength" and "individual security."

[8] Every society in which people are encouraged to engage freely in industry would culminate in an unequal distribution of wealth and a division of interest between the few and the many, such as the division that had arisen between debtors and creditors. The few, if in power, would seek to oppress the many, and the many, if in power, would seek to oppress the few. The passage of harmful and inflationary paper money laws in the states was one such example. Hamilton implies that the key to the stability and strength of the British system was rooted in its separation of powers and checks and balances based on competing class interests. Hamilton meant to propose a uniquely republican system for America that would promote these same traits.

[9] While many of his adversaries accused him of supporting aristocracy, and even monarchy, Hamilton, first and foremost, strove to promote a republican system that would avoid the volatility and fragility that had plagued the union under the Articles of Confederation. Thus, he sought a republican adaptation of Britain's division of powers between the different social classes. On these grounds, Hamilton proposed that an independent executive and one branch of the legislature be elected for a life term. This would allow the people to select a permanent and stable will, which could counteract the fleeting tides of majority opinion that would be represented in the more democratic branch of the legislature.

[10] According to Hamilton a government remained republican in form so long as no person held a hereditary right to power or privilege and all ruling offices were filled by a process originating either directly or indirectly from popular election.

[11] Although Hamilton admits that his plan had no chance of success, and he later alleges that he offered it only to give a more correct view of his ideas, it is unclear how seriously he hoped the Committee of the Whole, and eventually the public at large, would take his proposals. He points out that none of the plans currently under consideration would have any immediate chance of acceptance outside of the convention's walls, yet the crisis in government was profoundly reshaping public opinion. Consequently, Hamilton conjectures that by the time the choice is put before the people they would be willing to accept even his more radical proposals.

[12] Hamilton concludes his speech by reading aloud a draft of his proposed plan of government. The plan consisted of a national government, with exclusive authority over military and foreign affairs, governed by a president and a senate chosen by electors selected by the people for lifetime appointments, but subject to impeachment; an assembly selected through direct popular election for three-year terms; and a national judiciary, consisting of judges serving lifetime terms during good behavior.

V.   On the death resignation or removal of the Governour his authorities to be exercised by the President of the Senate till a Successor be appointed.

VI.   The Senate to have the sole power of declaring war, the power of advising and approving all Treaties, the power of approving or rejecting all appointments of officers except the heads or chiefs of the departments of Finance War and foreign affairs.

VII.   The Supreme Judicial authority to be vested in Judges to hold their offices during good behaviour with adequate and permanent salaries. This Court to have original jurisdiction in all causes of capture, and an appellative jurisdiction in all causes in which the revenues of the general Government or the citizens of foreign nations are concerned.

VIII.   The Legislature of the United States to have power to institute Courts in each State for the determination of all matters of general concern.

IX.   The Governour Senators and all officers of the United States to be liable to impeachment for mal—and corrupt conduct; and upon conviction to be removed from office, & disqualified for holding any place of trust or profit—all impeachments to be tried by a Court to consist of the Chief or Judge of the Superior Court of Law of each State, provided such Judge shall hold his place during good behavior, and have a permanent salary.

X.   All laws of the particular States contrary to the Constitution or laws of the United States to be utterly void; and the better to prevent such laws being passed, the Governour or president of each state shall be appointed by the General Government and shall have a negative upon the laws about to be passed in the State of which he is Governour or President.

XI.   No State to have any forces land or Naval; and the Militia of all the States to be under the sole and exclusive direction of the United States, the officers of which to be appointed and commissioned by them.

On these several articles he entered into explanatory observations corresponding with the principles of his introductory reasoning.

Committee rose & the House adjourned.

Hamilton's plan of government had very little direct impact on the convention, as it was largely ignored. Following Hamilton's speech, delegate William Samuel Johnson reported that Hamilton had been "praised by everybody, [but] supported by none" (Chernow 2004, 233). Since Hamilton had acknowledged that his plan had virtually no chance of acceptance and later backtracked on his call for extinguishing the sovereignty of the states, many scholars have suggested that Hamilton may have introduced an extreme nationalist plan in order to make a reformed version of the Virginia Plan seem more moderate in comparison and thereby break the standstill and foster compromise. Others, such as Karl Walling (1999), have suggested that Hamilton may have been trying to spur delegates to pay greater attention to the institutions the people would need rather than limiting their focus to what they believed the people would be willing to accept.

One thing is certain: the ideas Hamilton espoused during his controversial convention speech—whether correctly or incorrectly viewed—persisted to taint his reputation for the rest of his life. Although Hamilton continuously emphasized merit as the just basis for promotion and political power, and although he never advocated hereditary titles or any of the other arbitrary privileges that characterized the European class system, he was unable to shake the accusation that he had abandoned the democratic principles of the Revolution in favor of government by aristocratic elites.

Although Hamilton never again advocated lifetime appointments in the executive or legislative branches, he did not waver in his commitment to endow the institutions under the Constitution with the strength and stability that had made Great Britain the most free, secure, and powerful nation in the known world.

Source: Max Farrand, ed. *The Records of the Federal Convention of 1787*. Rev. ed., 4 vols. New Haven, CT: Yale University Press, 1937, 1: 282–293.

Letter to George Washington on the Constitutional Convention

July 3, 1787

INTRODUCTION

By the end of June, the convention had reached a complete stalemate in deliberations arising from disputes between the large and small states. After briefly delivering remarks on the importance of strength and stability in making the country respectable in the eyes of other nations, Hamilton left the convention to attend to personal business at home. During his absence, he wrote George Washington, the convention's presiding officer, to express his sincere hope that the delegates would adopt necessary measures for preventing "disunion, anarchy, and misery."

---

[1] Hamilton explains that his interactions and observations as he traveled through New Jersey on his way to New York only reinforced his conviction that a strong union was necessary and that the convention's unique opportunity to establish such a system must not be squandered.

[2] In attempt to encourage fortitude among the delegates, Hamilton maintains that his conversations with community leaders and learned men outside of the convention had put him in a better position to judge public sentiment. He contends that although state officials, such as New York governor George Clinton, continued to play into the people's fear of centralized power, public sentiment was becoming more and more amenable to the idea of a robust union. Thus, the delegates should not be inhibited by a supposed repugnancy of the people in their efforts to construct an efficient constitution.

[3] He admitted that although the people were not ready to accept the particular plan he had proposed, they would be likely favorable to one "equally energetic."

Dr. Sir.

In my passage through the Jerseys and since my arrival here I have taken particular pains to discover the public sentiment and I am more and more convinced that this is the critical opportunity for establishing the prosperity of this country on a solid foundation.[1] I have conversed with men of information not only of this City but from different parts of the state; and they agree that there has been an astonishing revolution for the better in the minds of the people. The prevailing apprehension among thinking men is that the Convention, from a fear of shocking the popular opinion, will not go far enough. They seem to be convinced that a strong well mounted government will better suit the popular palate than one of a different complexion. Men in office are indeed taking all possible pains to give an unfavourable impression of the Convention; but the current seems to be running strongly the other way. . .[2]

These appearances though they will not warrant a conclusion that the people are yet ripe for such a plan as I advocate, yet serve to prove that there is no reason to despair of their adopting one equally energetic, if the Convention should think proper to propose it.[3]

They serve to prove that we ought not to allow too much weight to objections drawn from the supposed repugnancy of the people to an efficient constitution. I confess I am more and more inclined to believe that former habits of thinking are regaining their influence with more rapidity than is generally imagined.

Not having compared ideas with you, Sir, I cannot judge how far our sentiments agree; but as I persuade myself the genuineness of my representations will receive credit with you, my anxiety for the event of the deliberations of the Convention induces me to make this communication of what appears to be the tendency of the public mind. I own to you Sir that I am seriously and deeply distressed at the aspect of the Councils which prevailed when I left Philadelphia. I fear that we shall let slip the golden opportunity of rescuing the American empire from disunion anarchy and misery.[4] No motley or feeble measure can answer the end or will finally receive the public support. Decision is true wisdom and will be not less reputable to the Convention than salutary to the community.

I shall of necessity remain here ten or twelve days; if I have reason to believe that my attendance at Philadelphia will not be mere waste of time, I shall after that period rejoin the Convention.

I remain with sincere esteem Dr Sir Yr. Obed serv
A Hamilton

[4] Hamilton expresses his distress that the opportunity to preserve the American empire might slip away. Thus, he reiterates the importance of fearlessly setting the union on a firm foundation, arguing that a "motley or feeble measure" would neither achieve the purpose of the convention nor the support of the public.

On receiving Hamilton's letter, Washington immediately responded that he, too, was pessimistic that the convention might disintegrate or fail to produce a workable plan. These concerns were heightened by the fact that Hamilton's fellow state delegates, Yates and Lansing, had left the convention in disgust, never to return. By mid-July, however, the delegates agreed to the Connecticut Compromise, which divided Congress into two houses: a Senate, where all states would have equal representation, and a House of Representatives, where representation would be based on a state's population. This broke the deadlock between the small and large states and paved the way for further deliberation.

Since the convention required the presence of at least two delegates for a state to retain its voting rights, Hamilton remained largely on the sidelines, traveling back and forth from New York to Philadelphia. Hamilton entered into debate only a few times: once in opposition to a provision restricting membership in Congress to native-born Americans, other times in favor of a presidential selection process independent from Congress, and in opposition to state legislative selection of senators.

Despite his misgivings on the final plan that emerged, Hamilton was committed to see it brought to fruition. On September 8, he joined the Committee on Style, which arranged the articles and revised the prose; and on September 17, 1787, he urged the thirty-nine state delegates still present to sign the charter, stating that "no man's ideas were more remote from the plan than his were known to be; but is it possible to deliberate between anarchy and Convulsion on one side, and the chance of good to be expected from the plan on the other?" Since Lansing and Yates refused to return, Hamilton was restricted from signing the U.S. Constitution on behalf of his state. Still, wanting to express his clear support, he signed the document as an individual.

Source: George Washington Papers, Library of Congress.

The Federalist

1787–1788

Instead of sending the recently signed U.S. Constitution to the state legislatures for ratification, the convention delegates specified that the proposed Constitution would go into effect once it was approved by at least nine autonomous state conventions—made up of delegates selected directly by the people. In this way, the state governments would be unable to thwart popular support, and the new government would derive its authority directly from the people.

As the state conventions began to assemble, intense and hostile debate broke out between those who favored the proposed union, known as Federalists, and the Anti-Federalists, who believed that the new system undermined freedom and the sovereignty of the states. Nowhere was the debate over ratification more intense than in New York, where the Anti-Federalists had established a particularly strong foothold. Ever since the Annapolis Convention, they had worked under the leadership of Governor George Clinton to obstruct reform. Within days of the Constitution's signing, they began to wage a battle against ratification in the New York press, criticizing the convention as illegitimate for going beyond its congressional mandate to revise the Articles of Confederation. Governor Clinton personally authored a series of essays, under the pseudonyms "Cato" and "Inspector." In these essays, Clinton attacked both the substance of the Constitution and Hamilton personally, by highlighting his foreign birth, illegitimacy, and alleged love of monarchy.

Increasingly concerned that the opposition might prevail, Hamilton found recourse by turning to the press himself. In early October 1787, he devised a bold plan to encourage the election of Federalist-minded delegates to the New York Ratifying Convention, which was scheduled to take place the following June. Hamilton enlisted the aid of well-respected Federalists, New Yorker John Jay and Virginian James Madison, to join him in authoring a series of anonymous essays designed to provide a comprehensive defense of the various characteristics and provisions of the proposed Constitution.

The essays, which were published intermittently in New York newspapers between October 1787 and April 1788, were eventually compiled into a single edition that was sent to help with ratification in other battleground states. The final project, known as *The Federalist*, totaled eighty-five essays written collectively under the pseudonym Publius, after Publius Valerius Publicola who had helped found the Roman republic. Jay wrote a few of the early essays pertaining to foreign relations before he was incapacitated by illness. Madison's writing focused primarily on the failures of ancient and modern republics and confederacies, the need for essential safeguards against the abuse of power, and the design and operation of Congress. Hamilton, who wrote the bulk of the essays, focused more on the connection between energetic government and civil and political liberty. His major contributions ranged in topics from the importance of union to the failures of the previous confederacy and the necessity of an energetic national government vested with requisite power. His essays culminated in a call for a stronger executive, an independent judiciary endowed with judicial review, and an opposition to the Bill of Rights.

An annotated selection of several of Hamilton's major contributions are included here.

Federalist No. 1
October 17, 1787

To the People of the State of New York:

AFTER an unequivocal experience of the inefficiency of the subsisting federal government, you are called upon to deliberate on a new Constitution for the United States of America. The subject speaks its own importance; comprehending in its consequences nothing less than the existence of the UNION, the safety and welfare of the parts of which it is composed, the fate of an empire in many respects the most interesting in the world.[1] It has been frequently remarked that it seems to have been reserved to the people of this country, by their conduct and example, to decide the important question, whether societies of men are really capable or not of establishing good government from reflection and choice, or whether they are forever destined to depend for their political constitutions on accident and force.[2] If there be any truth in the remark, the crisis at which we are arrived may with propriety be regarded as the era in which that decision is to be made; and a wrong election of the part we shall act may, in this view, deserve to be considered as the general misfortune of mankind. This idea will add the inducements of philanthropy to those of patriotism, to heighten the solicitude which all considerate and good men must feel for the event. Happy will it be if our choice should be directed by a judicious estimate of our true interests, unperplexed and unbiased by considerations not connected with the public good. But this is a thing more ardently to be wished than seriously to be expected. The plan offered to our deliberations affects too many particular interests, innovates upon

[1] Hamilton opens the first essay of *The Federalist* by connecting the fate of the union and the safety and success of its parts with the fate of the proposed Constitution. As he had done in his earlier Phocion letters, Hamilton emphasizes the global implications of the success or failure of the American experiment.

[2] Hamilton identifies the unprecedented situation in which the country finds itself. Americans, he says, are in the unique position of being able to reflect on their circumstances and to frame a government on the basis of reason and choice rather than chance. Throughout history, governments had been imposed either by accident of history or by military force. Never before had a people gathered together in times of peace to deliberate about the governing institutions under which they would live. If successful, the American experiment would provide mankind with a valuable model of self-government. Thus, Hamilton emphasizes that moral obligation as well as patriotism should impel interest in the debate at hand.

too many local institutions, not to involve in its discussion a variety of objects foreign to its merits, and of views, passions and prejudices little favorable to the discovery of truth.[3]

Among the most formidable of the obstacles which the new Constitution will have to encounter may readily be distinguished the obvious interest of a certain class of men in every State to resist all changes which may hazard a diminution of the power, emolument, and consequence of the offices they hold under the State establishments; and the perverted ambition of another class of men, who will either hope to aggrandize themselves by the confusions of their country, or will flatter themselves with fairer prospects of elevation from the subdivision of the empire into several partial confederacies than from its union under one government.[4]

It is not, however, my design to dwell upon observations of this nature. I am well aware that it would be disingenuous to resolve indiscriminately the opposition of any set of men (merely because their situations might subject them to suspicion) into interested or ambitious views. . . . And a further reason for caution, in this respect, might be drawn from the reflection that we are not always sure that those who advocate the truth are influenced by purer principles than their antagonists. Ambition, avarice, personal animosity, party opposition, and many other motives not more laudable than these, are apt to operate as well upon those who support as those who oppose the right side of a question.[5] Were there not even these inducements to moderation, nothing could be more ill-judged than that intolerant spirit which has, at all times, characterized political parties. For in politics, as in religion, it is equally absurd to aim at making proselytes by fire and sword. Heresies in either can rarely be cured by persecution.[6]

And yet, however just these sentiments will be allowed to be, we have already sufficient indications that it will happen in this as in all former cases of great national discussion. A torrent of angry and malignant passions will be let loose. . . . An enlightened zeal for the energy and efficiency of government will be stigmatized as the offspring of a temper fond of despotic power and hostile to the principles of liberty. An over-scrupulous jealousy of danger to the rights of the people, which is more commonly the fault of the head than of the heart, will be represented as mere pretense and artifice, the stale bait for popularity at the expense of the public good.[7] It will be

[3] Hamilton expresses the wish that deliberation over the proposed Constitution be based on an unbiased and sincere desire to promote the public good and the cause of truth. He laments, however, that such an expectation ignores human nature and the uncertain role of motives in politics. The founding of a new political order would inevitably affect a variety of parties, and the acceptance or rejection of the proposed plan is bound to benefit certain interests at the expense of others. Thus, it is important to take into consideration the fact that those making arguments might be motivated by a cause other than truth.

[4] Without giving specific names, Hamilton identifies two types of leaders whose opposition to the proposed government might be motivated by sinister intentions: state politicians who fear a diminishing of their own political privileges and power and demagogues hoping to take advantage of chaos and division to promote their own ambitions.

[5] After identifying that powerful interests and ambition might encourage opposition to ratification, Hamilton concedes that further discussion of motives would be counterproductive since self-interest and upright intentions likely exist on both sides of the issue. Thus, he implies that it is best to concentrate solely on the merits of the plan itself.

[6] Advocating a spirit of toleration and reasoned debate, Hamilton argues that extreme partisanship like religious zealotry is ineffective. In politics, as in religion, real converts are won through persuasion.

[7] In spite of his appeal for moderation, Hamilton warns that, because so much is at stake, the debate will be characterized by the most vicious passions and accusations. Those who favor energy and efficiency in government will be stigmatized as "hostile to the principles of liberty." This supposed zeal for the rights and liberties of the people, however, is misguided and disingenuous.

forgotten, on the one hand, that jealousy is the usual concomitant of love, and that the noble enthusiasm of liberty is apt to be infected with a spirit of narrow and illiberal distrust. On the other hand, it will be equally forgotten that the vigor of government is essential to the security of liberty; that, in the contemplation of a sound and well-informed judgment, their interest can never be separated; and that a dangerous ambition more often lurks behind the specious mask of zeal for the rights of the people than under the forbidden appearance of zeal for the firmness and efficiency of government.[8] History will teach us that the former has been found a much more certain road to the introduction of despotism than the latter, and that of those men who have overturned the liberties of republics, the greatest number have begun their career by paying an obsequious court to the people; commencing demagogues, and ending tyrants.

In the course of the preceding observations, I have had an eye, my fellow-citizens, to putting you upon your guard against all attempts, from whatever quarter, to influence your decision in a matter of the utmost moment to your welfare, by any impressions other than those which may result from the evidence of truth. You will, no doubt, at the same time, have collected from the general scope of them, that they proceed from a source not unfriendly to the new Constitution. Yes, my countrymen, I own to you that, after having given it an attentive consideration, I am clearly of opinion it is your interest to adopt it. I am convinced that this is the safest course for your liberty, your dignity, and your happiness. . . . My motives must remain in the depository of my own breast. My arguments will be open to all, and may be judged of by all. They shall at least be offered in a spirit which will not disgrace the cause of truth.[9]

I propose, in a series of papers, to discuss the following interesting particulars:[10]

THE UTILITY OF THE UNION TO YOUR POLITICAL PROSPERITY THE INSUFFICIENCY OF THE PRESENT CONFEDERATION TO PRESERVE THAT UNION THE NECESSITY OF A GOVERNMENT AT LEAST EQUALLY ENERGETIC WITH THE ONE PROPOSED, TO THE ATTAINMENT OF THIS OBJECT THE CONFORMITY OF THE PROPOSED CONSTITUTION TO THE TRUE PRINCIPLES OF REPUBLICAN GOVERNMENT ITS ANALOGY TO YOUR OWN STATE CONSTITUTION

9 Hamilton emphasizes that his goal is to promote the cause of truth and to demonstrate why the adoption of the Constitution is essential for the country's liberty, dignity, and happiness. He then concludes by stating that, although the purity of his motives can be known only to himself, his arguments will be clearly presented for all to judge.

10 Hamilton outlines the plan for the ensuing series of essays as follows: the necessity of maintaining a perpetual union, the insufficiency of the Articles of Confederation for securing that union, the necessity of a national government at least as powerful as the one proposed for preserving the union, the conformity of the proposed plan to republican principles, an analysis of the powers belonging to the federal government compared to those of the states, and the additional security the plan will provide for liberty and property.

and lastly, THE ADDITIONAL SECURITY WHICH ITS ADOPTION WILL AFFORD TO THE PRESERVATION OF THAT SPECIES OF GOVERNMENT, TO LIBERTY, AND TO PROPERTY.

In the progress of this discussion I shall endeavor to give a satisfactory answer to all the objections which shall have made their appearance, that may seem to have any claim to your attention.
PUBLIUS

Federalist No. 6
November 14, 1787

To the People of the State of New York:

THE three last numbers of this paper have been dedicated to an enumeration of the dangers to which we should be exposed, in a state of disunion, from the arms and arts of foreign nations. I shall now proceed to delineate dangers of a different and, perhaps, still more alarming kind—those which will in all probability flow from dissensions between the States themselves, and from domestic factions and convulsions.[11] These have been already in some instances slightly anticipated; but they deserve a more particular and more full investigation.

A man must be far gone in Utopian speculations who can seriously doubt that, if these States should either be wholly disunited, or only united in partial confederacies, the subdivisions into which they might be thrown would have frequent and violent contests with each other.[12] To presume a want of motives for such contests as an argument against their existence, would be to forget that men are ambitious, vindictive, and rapacious. To look for a continuation of harmony between a number of independent, unconnected sovereignties in the same neighborhood, would be to disregard the uniform course of human events, and to set at defiance the accumulated experience of ages.

The causes of hostility among nations are innumerable.[13] There are some which have a general and almost constant operation upon the collective bodies of society. Of this description are the love of power or the desire of pre-eminence and dominion—the jealousy of power, or the desire of equality and safety. There are others which have a

[11] In *Federalist* Nos. 3–5, John Jay outlined why the union would be necessary in terms of foreign affairs. In *Federalist* No. 6, Hamilton shifts in focus to the necessity of union for domestic tranquility and discusses the likelihood of dissension between the states if they remain disunited.

[12] Hamilton ridicules the fanciful thinking of those who believe that the states, operating as independent commercial republics, would not "have frequent and violent contests with one another." Although Hamilton was devoted to the ideals of a free and just government, he was also a notorious realist. In other words, he consistently held that the progressive improvement to the science of politics had not been accompanied by a progressive improvement in human nature. Thus, any well-designed government must account for the tendency of human beings to act in a self-interested way and to seek power or goods at the expense of others. Nowhere is Hamilton's renowned realism more apparent than in this essay, where he argues that to hope for perpetual peace between dismembered sovereign states is to ignore reason and historical experience and "to forget that men are ambitious, vindictive, and rapacious."

[13] After contending that conflicts between the states would inevitably arise in the absence of a strong union, Hamilton delineates the causes of hostilities between nations. The causes of conflict include the love of power or the desire for dominion, rivalries over commerce, and the private passions of those in positions of influence who seek their own personal aggrandizement at the expense of the community.

more circumscribed though an equally operative influence within their spheres. Such are the rivalships and competitions of commerce between commercial nations. And there are others, not less numerous than either of the former, which take their origin entirely in private passions; in the attachments, enmities, interests, hopes, and fears of leading individuals in the communities of which they are members. Men of this class, whether the favorites of a king or of a people, have in too many instances abused the confidence they possessed; and assuming the pretext of some public motive, have not scrupled to sacrifice the national tranquillity to personal advantage or personal gratification. . .

But notwithstanding the concurring testimony of experience, in this particular, there are still to be found visionary or designing men, who stand ready to advocate the paradox of perpetual peace between the States, though dismembered and alienated from each other. The genius of republics (say they) is pacific; the spirit of commerce has a tendency to soften the manners of men, and to extinguish those inflammable humors which have so often kindled into wars. Commercial republics, like ours, will never be disposed to waste themselves in ruinous contentions with each other. They will be governed by mutual interest, and will cultivate a spirit of mutual amity and concord.[14]

Is it not (we may ask these projectors in politics) the true interest of all nations to cultivate the same benevolent and philosophic spirit? If this be their true interest, have they in fact pursued it? Has it not, on the contrary, invariably been found that momentary passions, and immediate interest, have a more active and imperious control over human conduct than general or remote considerations of policy, utility or justice?[15] Have republics in practice been less addicted to war than monarchies? Are not the former administered by MEN as well as the latter? Are there not aversions, predilections, rivalships, and desires of unjust acquisitions, that affect nations as well as kings? . . . Let experience, the least fallible guide of human opinions, be appealed to for an answer to these inquiries.[16]

Sparta, Athens, Rome, and Carthage were all republics; two of them, Athens and Carthage, of the commercial kind. Yet were they as often engaged in wars, offensive and defensive, as the neighboring monarchies of the same times. . .

[14] Hamilton laments that, in spite of abundant evidence to the contrary, many still argue that commercial republics will not go to war with one another because their interdependence encourages cooperation and they have a long-term mutual interest in preserving peace.

[15] Hamilton asks a series of questions to demonstrate his contention that commercial republics are just as prone to war as other nations. Responding to the contention that people will not violate their long-term interest by going to war with a fellow commercial republic, he observes that people often have little concern for, or cannot seek, their long-term interests and are instead most frequently motivated by instant gratification, which is as likely to produce competition as cooperation.

[16] Hamilton suggests that the theory that commercial republics are likely to remain at peace can be tested in the light of historical experience. Hamilton appeals to the ancient examples of Sparta, Athens, Rome, and Carthage, and the modern example of Great Britain, to refute the idea that either republicanism or commerce will promote perpetual peace between neighboring nations.

In the government of Britain the representatives of the people compose one branch of the national legislature. Commerce has been for ages the predominant pursuit of that country. Few nations, nevertheless, have been more frequently engaged in war; and the wars in which that kingdom has been engaged have, in numerous instances, proceeded from the people. . .

From this summary of what has taken place in other countries, whose situations have borne the nearest resemblance to our own, what reason can we have to confide in those reveries which would seduce us into an expectation of peace and cordiality between the members of the present confederacy, in a state of separation? Have we not already seen enough of the fallacy and extravagance of those idle theories which have amused us with promises of an exemption from the imperfections, weaknesses and evils incident to society in every shape? Is it not time to awake from the deceitful dream of a golden age, and to adopt as a practical maxim for the direction of our political conduct that we, as well as the other inhabitants of the globe, are yet remote from the happy empire of perfect wisdom and perfect virtue?[17]

[17] Hamilton beseeches his readers to recognize the realities of political life—that the causes of conflict are rooted in human nature itself.

Let the point of extreme depression to which our national dignity and credit have sunk, let the inconveniences felt everywhere from a lax and ill administration of government, let the revolt of a part of the State of North Carolina, the late menacing disturbances in Pennsylvania, and the actual insurrections and rebellions in Massachusetts, declare—!

So far is the general sense of mankind from corresponding with the tenets of those who endeavor to lull asleep our apprehensions of discord and hostility between the States, in the event of disunion, that it has from long observation of the progress of society become a sort of axiom in politics, that vicinity or nearness of situation, constitutes nations natural enemies. An intelligent writer expresses himself on this subject to this effect: "NEIGHBORING NATIONS (says he) are naturally enemies of each other unless their common weakness forces them to league in a CONFEDERATE REPUBLIC, and their constitution prevents the differences that neighborhood occasions, extinguishing that secret jealousy which disposes all states to aggrandize themselves at the expense of their neighbors." This passage, at the same time, points out the EVIL and suggests the REMEDY.[18]

PUBLIUS

[18] After emphasizing the discord that has already occurred between the states, Hamilton concludes with a warning from French philosopher L'Abbé de Mably that neighboring nations are natural enemies and that unless they form a common league, they will always be disposed to aggrandize themselves at each other's expense. Commerce will contribute to civil harmony between the states only when they are governed by a uniform commercial policy. Vesting the power to regulate commerce in the national government would prevent the trade wars that had already arisen between the states and would help maintain a peaceful and consistent system of free trade throughout the states and with foreign nations.

[19] The general consensus at the time of the American founding was that the principles of the Revolution required a republican government—that is, government made up of representatives elected by the people, whose purpose is to protect the rights and liberties of the people and to promote the public safety and happiness of the whole. Hamilton's main task in defending the proposed Constitution was to demonstrate that it institutes a republican system superior to that which would exist under the states in its absence. Hamilton, thus, maintains that republicanism, combined with an efficient government under a firm union, would curb domestic factions and insurrection. Later, in the *Federalist* No. 10, Madison explains that a faction consists of a group of people united by a common interest or passion adverse to the rights of other individuals or to the aggregate interests of the community. Here, Hamilton explains that the danger of such faction had left the republics of Greece and Rome in a pendulum between the extremes of anarchy and tyranny.

[20] Recognizing the fact that all existing democratic governments had been destroyed at the hands of unjust popular majorities, the friends of despotism, according to Hamilton, have argued that free government is inconsistent with order in society.

[21] Hamilton contends that the American experiment provides the opportunity to prove such critics wrong.

[22] Hamilton concedes that their criticism, however, bears weight and had we not designed a republican government better in structure than previous models, the friends of liberty would have to abandon the cause of republican government as indefensible.

[23] According to Hamilton, the science of politics, like other sciences, benefits from improved knowledge. Thus, the combination of republican government and the preservation of liberty and stability is now possible—not because of a general improvement of human nature but because of an improved knowledge of how to construct governments to channel

Federalist No. 9
November 21, 1787

To the People of the State of New York:

A FIRM Union will be of the utmost moment to the peace and liberty of the States, as a barrier against domestic faction and insurrection. It is impossible to read the history of the petty republics of Greece and Italy without feeling sensations of horror and disgust at the distractions with which they were continually agitated, and at the rapid succession of revolutions by which they were kept in a state of perpetual vibration between the extremes of tyranny and anarchy.[19] If they exhibit occasional calms, these only serve as short-lived contrast to the furious storms that are to succeed. If now and then intervals of felicity open to view, we behold them with a mixture of regret, arising from the reflection that the pleasing scenes before us are soon to be overwhelmed by the tempestuous waves of sedition and party rage. . .

From the disorders that disfigure the annals of those republics the advocates of despotism have drawn arguments, not only against the forms of republican government, but against the very principles of civil liberty.[20] They have decried all free government as inconsistent with the order of society, and have indulged themselves in malicious exultation over its friends and partisans. Happily for mankind, stupendous fabrics reared on the basis of liberty, which have flourished for ages, have, in a few glorious instances, refuted their gloomy sophisms. And, I trust, America will be the broad and solid foundation of other edifices, not less magnificent, which will be equally permanent monuments of their errors.[21]

But it is not to be denied that the portraits they have sketched of republican government were too just copies of the originals from which they were taken. If it had been found impracticable to have devised models of a more perfect structure, the enlightened friends to liberty would have been obliged to abandon the cause of that species of government as indefensible.[22] The science of politics, however, like most other sciences, has received great improvement. The efficacy of various principles is now well understood, which were either not known at all, or imperfectly known to the ancients.[23] The regular distribution of power into distinct departments; the introduction of legislative balances and checks; the institution of courts composed

of judges holding their offices during good behavior; the representation of the people in the legislature by deputies of their own election: these are wholly new discoveries, or have made their principal progress towards perfection in modern times. They are means, and powerful means, by which the excellences of republican government may be retained and its imperfections lessened or avoided.[24] To this catalogue of circumstances that tend to the amelioration of popular systems of civil government, I shall venture, however novel it may appear to some, to add one more, on a principle which has been made the foundation of an objection to the new Constitution; I mean the ENLARGEMENT of the ORBIT within which such systems are to revolve, either in respect to the dimensions of a single State or to the consolidation of several smaller States into one great Confederacy.[25] The latter is that which immediately concerns the object under consideration.
PUBLIUS

Federalist No. 15
December 1, 1787

To the People of the State of New York.

IN THE course of the preceding papers, I have endeavored, my fellow-citizens, to place before you, in a clear and convincing light, the importance of Union to your political safety and happiness.[26] I have unfolded to you a complication of dangers to which you would be exposed, should you permit that sacred knot which binds the people of America together be severed or dissolved by ambition or by avarice, by jealousy or by misrepresentation. . .

In pursuance of the plan which I have laid down for the discussion of the subject, the point next in order to be examined is the "insufficiency of the present Confederation to the preservation of the Union." It may perhaps be asked what need there is of reasoning or proof to illustrate a position which is not either controverted or doubted, to which the understandings and feelings of all classes of men assent, and which in substance is admitted by the opponents as well as by the friends of the new Constitution. It must in truth be acknowledged that, however these may differ in other respects, they in general appear to harmonize in this sentiment, at least, that there are material imperfections in our national system, and that something is necessary to be done to rescue us from impending anarchy.[27]

human nature so it would best serve the public good. He lists four improvements to the science of politics that compose the major themes of *The Federalist*: separation of the functions of government into distinct departments; legislative checks and balances; an independent judiciary, or the institution of courts composed of judges holding office during good behavior; and representation by elected legislatures.

[24] These discoveries incorporated into the structure of the proposed Constitution, which were either wholly new or further perfected in modern times, were a powerful means of making republican government possible by securing its benefits, while lessoning or avoiding its imperfections.

[25] To the previous four improvements Hamilton adds a fifth: "the enlargement of the orbit" or the territorial extension of republican government. Seeking to dispel the myth that liberty could only exist in a small republic, Hamilton lays the foundation for Madison's argument in *Federalist* No. 10 that a large republic, created by the union of states, would better break and control the violence of factions.

[26] Hamilton explains that the purpose of the preceding papers was to demonstrate that a union of states is essential for the safety and happiness of the American people. He then turns to the question of the character of the national government, starting with a discussion of why the previous government under the Articles of Confederation was insufficient.

[27] Hamilton highlights the general consensus, among opponents and friends of the proposed Constitution alike, that the Articles of Confederation are flawed and that action is necessary to prevent impending anarchy.

The facts that support this opinion are no longer objects of speculation. They have forced themselves upon the sensibility of the people at large, and have at length extorted from those, whose mistaken policy has had the principal share in precipitating the extremity at which we are arrived, a reluctant confession of the reality of those defects in the scheme of our federal government, which have been long pointed out and regretted by the intelligent friends of the Union.

We may indeed with propriety be said to have reached almost the last stage of national humiliation. There is scarcely anything that can wound the pride or degrade the character of an independent nation which we do not experience.[28] Are there engagements to the performance of which we are held by every tie respectable among men? These are the subjects of constant and unblushing violation. Do we owe debts to foreigners and to our own citizens contracted in a time of imminent peril for the preservation of our political existence? These remain without any proper or satisfactory provision for their discharge. Have we valuable territories and important posts in the possession of a foreign power which, by express stipulations, ought long since to have been surrendered? These are still retained, to the prejudice of our interests, not less than of our rights. Are we in a condition to resent or to repel the aggression? We have neither troops, nor treasury, nor government. Are we even in a condition to remonstrate with dignity? The just imputations on our own faith, in respect to the same treaty, ought first to be removed. Are we entitled by nature and compact to a free participation in the navigation of the Mississippi? Spain excludes us from it. Is public credit an indispensable resource in time of public danger? We seem to have abandoned its cause as desperate and irretrievable. Is commerce of importance to national wealth? Ours is at the lowest point of declension. Is respectability in the eyes of foreign powers a safeguard against foreign encroachments? The imbecility of our government even forbids them to treat with us. Our ambassadors abroad are the mere pageants of mimic sovereignty. Is a violent and unnatural decrease in the value of land a symptom of national distress? The price of improved land in most parts of the country is much lower than can be accounted for by the quantity of waste land at market, and can only be fully explained by that want of private and public confidence, which are so alarmingly prevalent among all ranks, and which have a direct tendency to depreciate property of every kind. Is private credit the friend and patron of industry? That most useful

[28] Hamilton asserts that, instead of the promising future made possible by victory in the Revolution, the country had experienced a rapid moral decline, which culminated in a state of national humiliation. He provides a series of examples of the nation's fragility and loss of dignity both at home and abroad.

kind which relates to borrowing and lending is reduced within the narrowest limits, and this still more from an opinion of insecurity than from the scarcity of money. . .

It is true, as has been before observed that facts, too stubborn to be resisted, have produced a species of general assent to the abstract proposition that there exist material defects in our national system; but the usefulness of the concession, on the part of the old adversaries of federal measures, is destroyed by a strenuous opposition to a remedy, upon the only principles that can give it a chance of success. While they admit that the government of the United States is destitute of energy, they contend against conferring upon it those powers which are requisite to supply that energy. They seem still to aim at things repugnant and irreconcilable; at an augmentation of federal authority, without a diminution of State authority; at sovereignty in the Union, and complete independence in the members. They still, in fine, seem to cherish with blind devotion the political monster of an imperium in imperio.[29] This renders a full display of the principal defects of the Confederation necessary, in order to show that the evils we experience do not proceed from minute or partial imperfections, but from fundamental errors in the structure of the building. . .

The great and radical vice in the construction of the existing Confederation is in the principle of LEGISLATION for STATES or GOVERNMENTS, in their CORPORATE or COLLECTIVE CAPACITIES, and as contradistinguished from the INDIVIDUALS of which they consist.[30] Though this principle does not run through all the powers delegated to the Union, yet it pervades and governs those on which the efficacy of the rest depends. Except as to the rule of appointment, the United States has an indefinite discretion to make requisitions for men and money; but they have no authority to raise either, by regulations extending to the individual citizens of America. The consequence of this is, that though in theory their resolutions concerning those objects are laws, constitutionally binding on the members of the Union, yet in practice they are mere recommendations which the States observe or disregard at their option. . .[31]

There is nothing absurd or impracticable in the idea of a league or alliance between independent nations for certain defined purposes precisely stated in a treaty regulating all the details of time, place,

[29] Hamilton directly confronts those who concur, based on irrefutable evidence, that the Articles of Confederation are deficient but who oppose granting the federal government the requisite powers to overcome the deficiencies. Such adversaries, he says, wish to augment federal authority without diminishing the authority of the states. Hamilton, along with other Federalists, supports a system that divides sovereignty between the national government and the states. Yet as long as the central government lacks final sovereignty over its delegated responsibilities, the nation would suffer from the problem of *imperium in imperio*—an irreconcilable overlap in authority.

[30] After contending that the defects in the confederation stem from fundamental design errors, Hamilton asserts that its greatest flaw stems from the fact that federal law operates only on the states in their collective capacity rather than on the individual citizens who make up the states. Since the union lacked coercive authority over individuals, the states could simply refuse requisitions for men and money, and the central government had no practical ability to raise revenue or troops. For that matter, the union was unable to enforce any of its dictates—the refusal of the states to uphold the terms of the peace treaty being one major example.

[31] Without the ability to sanction recalcitrant individuals, laws are not really laws but mere recommendations that can be disregarded at will.

circumstance, and quantity; leaving nothing to future discretion; and depending for its execution on the good faith of the parties. Compacts of this kind exist among all civilized nations, subject to the usual vicissitudes of peace and war, of observance and non-observance, as the interests or passions of the contracting powers dictate...

If the particular States in this country are disposed to stand in a similar relation to each other, and to drop the project of a general DISCRETIONARY SUPERINTENDENCE, the scheme would indeed be pernicious, and would entail upon us all the mischiefs which have been enumerated under the first head; but it would have the merit of being, at least, consistent and practicable Abandoning all views towards a confederate government, this would bring us to a simple alliance offensive and defensive; and would place us in a situation to be alternate friends and enemies of each other, as our mutual jealousies and rivalships, nourished by the intrigues of foreign nations, should prescribe to us.[32]

But if we are unwilling to be placed in this perilous situation; if we still will adhere to the design of a national government, or, which is the same thing, of a superintending power, under the direction of a common council, we must resolve to incorporate into our plan those ingredients which may be considered as forming the characteristic difference between a league and a government; we must extend the authority of the Union to the persons of the citizens,—the only proper objects of government...[33]

Government implies the power of making laws. It is essential to the idea of a law, that it be attended with a sanction; or, in other words, a penalty or punishment for disobedience.
PUBLIUS

Federalist No. 23
December 18, 1787

To the People of the State of New York:

THE necessity of a Constitution, at least equally energetic with the one proposed, to the preservation of the Union, is the point at the examination of which we are now arrived.

[32] Hamilton observes that leagues or alliances between sovereign entities exist for certain defined purposes, but without the threat of coercion, such alliances depend solely on the good faith of their members and the terms of agreement are frequently violated. A mere league or alliance between states would consequently place the states in the situation of alternating between being friends and enemies.

[33] Hamilton concludes that if the states want to avoid the peril inherent in ordinary alliances, the states must give up their authority over individuals in certain areas, so that federal government is empowered to operate directly on individuals and to use coercion in cases of disobedience. While Hamilton has not yet discussed the three functions of government, this statement implies that the national government must be endowed with not only legislative authority but executive and judicial authority as well.

The principal purposes to be answered by union are these the common defense of the members; the preservation of the public peace as well against internal convulsions as external attacks; the regulation of commerce with other nations and between the States; the superintendence of our intercourse, political and commercial, with foreign countries.[34]

The authorities essential to the common defense are these: to raise armies; to build and equip fleets; to prescribe rules for the government of both; to direct their operations; to provide for their support. These powers ought to exist without limitation, BECAUSE IT IS IMPOSSIBLE TO FORESEE OR DEFINE THE EXTENT AND VARIETY OF NATIONAL EXIGENCIES, OR THE CORRESPONDENT EXTENT AND VARIETY OF THE MEANS WHICH MAY BE NECESSARY TO SATISFY THEM. The circumstances that endanger the safety of nations are infinite, and for this reason no constitutional shackles can wisely be imposed on the power to which the care of it is committed.[35] This power ought to be coextensive with all the possible combinations of such circumstances; and ought to be under the direction of the same councils which are appointed to preside over the common defense.

This is one of those truths which, to a correct and unprejudiced mind, carries its own evidence along with it; and may be obscured, but cannot be made plainer by argument or reasoning. It rests upon axioms as simple as they are universal; the MEANS ought to be proportioned to the END; the persons, from whose agency the attainment of any END is expected, ought to possess the MEANS by which it is to be attained.[36]

Whether there ought to be a federal government intrusted with the care of the common defense, is a question in the first instance, open for discussion; but the moment it is decided in the affirmative, it will follow, that that government ought to be clothed with all the powers requisite to complete execution of its trust.[37] And unless it can be shown that the circumstances which may affect the public safety are reducible within certain determinate limits; unless the contrary of this position can be fairly and rationally disputed, it must be admitted, as a necessary consequence, that there can be no limitation of that authority which is to provide for the defense and protection of the community, in any matter essential to its efficacy that is, in any

[34] Hamilton begins his defense of the power vested in the national government under the proposed Constitution by identifying the principal objectives of the union. These objectives include the common defense of the country against domestic insurrection and foreign attack, the regulation of foreign and interstate commerce, and general diplomacy. Interestingly, the authority to regulate commerce is the only power that Congress did not already possess under the Articles of Confederation—and, by that time, most of the states favored an amendment to the articles granting such authority. Thus, as James Stoner (2003) observes, "The center of [Hamilton's] defense of the Constitution's innovated substitute for the confederate republic is his argument that Union must be strengthened not so much by the addition of enumerated powers as by a complete restructuring that will make it effective in achieving its ends" (232).

[35] Focusing specifically on common defense, Hamilton identifies a variety of powers necessary to achieve such a broad objective. He argues that because the threats to the common defense of nations are infinite, and because necessity cannot always be predicted in advance, these discretionary powers must exist without limit. The same applies to commerce and every other matter over which the government of the union is granted jurisdiction. Once an objective is defined, the national government must be empowered to pass all laws and make all regulations related to it.

[36] Hamilton defends this argument by appealing to the self-evident axiom that the means must be requisite to the ends. If the government is going to exercise its responsibilities effectively, it must by default possess control over certain means. It is more realistic to define ends with precision than it is to define necessary means, which change based on unpredictable exigencies. Consequently, the proper way to limit the scope of government power is to limit its objectives.

[37] While debate over which objectives properly belong to the different levels of government is appropriate, once an objective

is granted it must by implication include whatever discretionary powers are essential for its exercise.

[38] Hamilton contends that even the framers of the failing confederacy had recognized the truth that unfettered discretion is necessary to carry out allocated duties. Under the Articles of Confederation, Congress was given unrestricted power to collect revenue and to build and direct the military. The defect in the confederacy, thus, lay not so much in the powers allocated to it, but in the way those powers were exercised. The proposed Constitution improves on the confederation, not because it allocates additional formal power, but because it restructures the way power is exercised so that it will be effective.

[39] Reiterating his argument from *Federalist* No. 15, Hamilton asserts that energy and effectiveness depend on the ability of the federal government to derive its authority for its limited objectives directly from the people and to legislate directly on them rather than on the states in their collective capacities. This inevitably implies a major change in the governing institutions compared to what existed under the Articles of Confederation.

[40] After presenting an expansive view of the discretionary powers granted to the federal government, Hamilton contends that such authority is more safely exercised in a republican government. The benefit of being republican is that the people can appoint someone to use discretion for them, but they can also hold that person responsible for any abuses of power, after the fact, by refusing to return them to power. Any allocation of power that does not conform to these principles of representation ought to be rejected.

matter essential to the FORMATION, DIRECTION, or SUPPORT of the NATIONAL FORCES.

Defective as the present Confederation has been proved to be, this principle appears to have been fully recognized by the framers of it; though they have not made proper or adequate provision for its exercise. Congress have an unlimited discretion to make requisitions of men and money; to govern the army and navy; to direct their operations.[38] As their requisitions are made constitutionally binding upon the States, who are in fact under the most solemn obligations to furnish the supplies required of them, the intention evidently was that the United States should command whatever resources were by them judged requisite to the "common defense and general welfare." It was presumed that a sense of their true interests, and a regard to the dictates of good faith, would be found sufficient pledges for the punctual performance of the duty of the members to the federal head.

The experiment has, however, demonstrated that this expectation was ill-founded and illusory; and the observations, made under the last head, will, I imagine, have sufficed to convince the impartial and discerning, that there is an absolute necessity for an entire change in the first principles of the system; that if we are in earnest about giving the Union energy and duration, we must abandon the vain project of legislating upon the States in their collective capacities; we must extend the laws of the federal government to the individual citizens of America;[39] we must discard the fallacious scheme of quotas and requisitions, as equally impracticable and unjust. The result from all this is that the Union ought to be invested with full power to levy troops; to build and equip fleets; and to raise the revenues which will be required for the formation and support of an army and navy, in the customary and ordinary modes practiced in other governments. . .

Every view we may take of the subject, as candid inquirers after truth, will serve to convince us, that it is both unwise and dangerous to deny the federal government an unconfined authority, as to all those objects which are intrusted to its management. It will indeed deserve the most vigilant and careful attention of the people, to see that it be modeled in such a manner as to admit of its being safely vested with the requisite powers. If any plan which has been, or may be, offered to our consideration, should not, upon a dispassionate inspection, be found to answer this description, it ought to be rejected.[40] A government, the constitution of which renders it unfit

to be trusted with all the powers which a free people OUGHT TO DELEGATE TO ANY GOVERNMENT, would be an unsafe and improper depositary of the NATIONAL INTERESTS. Wherever THESE can with propriety be confided, the coincident powers may safely accompany them.
PUBLIUS

Federalist No. 70
March 15, 1788

To the People of the State of New York:

THERE is an idea, which is not without its advocates, that a vigorous Executive is inconsistent with the genius of republican government.[41] The enlightened well-wishers to this species of government must at least hope that the supposition is destitute of foundation; since they can never admit its truth, without at the same time admitting the condemnation of their own principles. Energy in the Executive is a leading character in the definition of good government.[42] It is essential to the protection of the community against foreign attacks; it is not less essential to the steady administration of the laws; to the protection of property against those irregular and high-handed combinations which sometimes interrupt the ordinary course of justice; to the security of liberty against the enterprises and assaults of ambition, of faction, and of anarchy. Every man the least conversant in Roman story, knows how often that republic was obliged to take refuge in the absolute power of a single man, under the formidable title of Dictator, as well against the intrigues of ambitious individuals who aspired to the tyranny, and the seditions of whole classes of the community whose conduct threatened the existence of all government, as against the invasions of external enemies who menaced the conquest and destruction of Rome.[43]

There can be no need, however, to multiply arguments or examples on this head. A feeble Executive implies a feeble execution of the government. A feeble execution is but another phrase for a bad execution; and a government ill executed, whatever it may be in theory, must be, in practice, a bad government.[44]

Taking it for granted, therefore, that all men of sense will agree in the necessity of an energetic Executive, it will only remain to inquire, what are the ingredients which constitute this energy? How far can

[41] The proposed Constitution was the first in history to institute a republic with a single-headed, or unitary, executive. Thus, in the very first sentence, of *Federalist* No. 70, Hamilton acknowledges the long-standing, but inaccurate, assumption that there is an inconsistency between republicanism and a strong executive. He asserts sarcastically that such "enlightened well-wishers" ought to hope that their assumption is erroneous because, without vigor and consistency in execution, republicanism is perpetually doomed to fail.

[42] In contrast to his critics, Hamilton emphatically declares that energy, or strength and vitality, in the executive is the defining attribute of good government. It is necessary for the consistent administration of the laws, for the protection of the nation against foreign attack, and for the security of property and liberty against faction and anarchy.

[43] In an effort to demonstrate that republican governments are not exempt from the necessity facing all governments, Hamilton references the ancient Roman republic, which was forced in times of crisis to submit to the dictatorship of a single individual.

[44] In claiming that it is unnecessary to enumerate examples of feeble execution resulting in a bad government, Hamilton likely believed that the weak executives of the state constitutions and the nonexistent executive under the Articles of Confederation were obvious to his readers.

[45] Energy, as referenced here, relates to the vigor and efficacy with which power is exercised. Hamilton identifies four qualities that contribute to such energy in the executive: unity, or the vesting of executive power in a single person; duration, giving the executive a substantial term of office to encourage firmness in the employment of power and an opportunity to demonstrate merit; adequate measure of support, an adequate salary not subject to diminution at the hands of legislators; and competent powers, constitutionally defined powers appropriate for effectively discharging the duties of the office.

[46] Although Americans had witnessed the failures of Congress under the Articles of Confederation and the weak executives instituted by the states, the association of energetic executive power with monarchy still loomed large and was aggravated by frequent comparisons of the American president and the British king during the ratification debates. Thus, Hamilton emphasizes the importance of safety and responsibility in addition to energy, as unique qualities of a republican executive. While subsequent essays address various aspects of energy, Hamilton seeks to demonstrate here why vesting executive power in a single president is essential for both energy and responsibility.

[47] Focusing first on the importance of unity for energy, Hamilton contends that a single individual will be better able to act quickly, decisively, and covertly—which is essential given the executive duty to vigorously enforce the law and protect the nation from domestic insurrection and foreign threats.

they be combined with those other ingredients which constitute safety in the republican sense? And how far does this combination characterize the plan which has been reported by the convention?

The ingredients which constitute energy in the Executive are, first, unity; secondly, duration; thirdly, an adequate provision for its support; fourthly, competent powers.[45]

The ingredients which constitute safety in the republican sense are, first, a due dependence on the people, secondly, a due responsibility. . .[46]

That unity is conducive to energy will not be disputed. Decision, activity, secrecy, and despatch will generally characterize the proceedings of one man in a much more eminent degree than the proceedings of any greater number;[47] and in proportion as the number is increased, these qualities will be diminished.

This unity may be destroyed in two ways: either by vesting the power in two or more magistrates of equal dignity and authority; or by vesting it ostensibly in one man, subject, in whole or in part, to the control and co-operation of others, in the capacity of counsellors to him. . .

Wherever two or more persons are engaged in any common enterprise or pursuit, there is always danger of difference of opinion. If it be a public trust or office, in which they are clothed with equal dignity and authority, there is peculiar danger of personal emulation and even animosity. From either, and especially from all these causes, the most bitter dissensions are apt to spring. Whenever these happen, they lessen the respectability, weaken the authority, and distract the plans and operation of those whom they divide. If they should unfortunately assail the supreme executive magistracy of a country, consisting of a plurality of persons, they might impede or frustrate the most important measures of the government, in the most critical emergencies of the state. And what is still worse, they might split the community into the most violent and irreconcilable factions, adhering differently to the different individuals who composed the magistracy.

Men often oppose a thing, merely because they have had no agency in planning it, or because it may have been planned by those whom they dislike. But if they have been consulted, and have happened to disapprove, opposition then becomes, in their estimation, an indispensable duty of self-love. They seem to think themselves bound in honor, and by all the motives of personal infallibility, to defeat the success of what has been resolved upon contrary to their sentiments. Men of upright, benevolent tempers have too many opportunities of remarking, with horror, to what desperate lengths this disposition is sometimes carried, and how often the great interests of society are sacrificed to the vanity, to the conceit, and to the obstinacy of individuals, who have credit enough to make their passions and their caprices interesting to mankind. Perhaps the question now before the public may, in its consequences, afford melancholy proofs of the effects of this despicable frailty, or rather detestable vice, in the human character.

Upon the principles of a free government, inconveniences from the source just mentioned must necessarily be submitted to in the formation of the legislature; but it is unnecessary, and therefore unwise, to introduce them into the constitution of the Executive.[48] It is here too that they may be most pernicious. In the legislature, promptitude of decision is oftener an evil than a benefit. The differences of opinion, and the jarrings of parties in that department of the government, though they may sometimes obstruct salutary plans, yet often promote deliberation and circumspection, and serve to check excesses in the majority. When a resolution too is once taken, the opposition must be at an end. That resolution is a law, and resistance to it punishable. But no favorable circumstances palliate or atone for the disadvantages of dissension in the executive department. Here, they are pure and unmixed. There is no point at which they cease to operate. They serve to embarrass and weaken the execution of the plan or measure to which they relate, from the first step to the final conclusion of it. They constantly counteract those qualities in the Executive which are the most necessary ingredients in its composition, vigor and expedition, and this without any counterbalancing good. In the conduct of war, in which the energy of the Executive is the bulwark of the national security, every thing would be to be apprehended from its plurality. . .

But one of the weightiest objections to a plurality in the Executive, and which lies as much against the last as the first plan, is, that it tends to conceal faults and destroy responsibility.[49] Responsibility is of two kinds to censure and to punishment. The first is the more

[48] After describing in detail why plurality in the executive would lead to dissension and thereby weaken execution, Hamilton draws a sharp contrast between the virtues involved in legislating and those required for effective execution. Whereas the process of legislating benefits from the deliberation and circumspection promoted by a plurality of views, executive functions—particularly in times of war—require promptitude of decision.

[49] Hamilton, in addition, objects to plurality in the executive because it destroys republican responsibility by depriving the people of the opportunity to censure the misconduct of the persons they have entrusted with power and to remove them from office if necessary. While the nature of executive power requires discretionary judgment, safety requires that the executive be accountable for the use and misuse of that trust. Dividing executive power weakens such accountability by making it difficult for the people to discover faults and assign responsibility.

important of the two, especially in an elective office. Man, in public trust, will much oftener act in such a manner as to render him unworthy of being any longer trusted, than in such a manner as to make him obnoxious to legal punishment. But the multiplication of the Executive adds to the difficulty of detection in either case. It often becomes impossible, amidst mutual accusations, to determine on whom the blame or the punishment of a pernicious measure, or series of pernicious measures, ought really to fall. It is shifted from one to another with so much dexterity, and under such plausible appearances, that the public opinion is left in suspense about the real author. The circumstances which may have led to any national miscarriage or misfortune are sometimes so complicated that, where there are a number of actors who may have had different degrees and kinds of agency, though we may clearly see upon the whole that there has been mismanagement, yet it may be impracticable to pronounce to whose account the evil which may have been incurred is truly chargeable. "I was overruled by my council. The council were so divided in their opinions that it was impossible to obtain any better resolution on the point." These and similar pretexts are constantly at hand, whether true or false. And who is there that will either take the trouble or incur the odium, of a strict scrutiny into the secret springs of the transaction? Should there be found a citizen zealous enough to undertake the unpromising task, if there happen to be collusion between the parties concerned, how easy it is to clothe the circumstances with so much ambiguity, as to render it uncertain what was the precise conduct of any of those parties? . . .

It is evident from these considerations, that the plurality of the Executive tends to deprive the people of the two greatest securities they can have for the faithful exercise of any delegated power, first, the restraints of public opinion, which lose their efficacy, as well on account of the division of the censure attendant on bad measures among a number, as on account of the uncertainty on whom it ought to fall; and, secondly, the opportunity of discovering with facility and clearness the misconduct of the persons they trust, in order either to their removal from office or to their actual punishment in cases which admit of it.

In England, the king is a perpetual magistrate; and it is a maxim which has obtained for the sake of the public peace, that he is unaccountable for his administration, and his person sacred. Nothing, therefore, can be wiser in that kingdom, than to annex to the king a constitutional council, who may be responsible to the nation for the advice they give.[50] Without this, there would be no responsibility whatever in the executive department an idea inadmissible in a free government. But even there the king is not bound by the resolutions of his council, though they are answerable for the advice they give. He is the absolute master of his own conduct in the exercise of his office, and may observe or disregard the counsel given to him at his sole discretion.

But in a republic, where every magistrate ought to be personally responsible for his behavior in office the reason which in the British Constitution dictates the propriety of a council, not only ceases to apply, but turns against the institution. In the monarchy of Great Britain, it furnishes a substitute for the prohibited responsibility of the chief magistrate, which serves in some degree as a hostage to the national justice for his good behavior. In the American republic, it would serve to destroy, or would greatly diminish, the intended and necessary responsibility of the Chief Magistrate himself. . .

When power, therefore, is placed in the hands of so small a number of men, as to admit of their interests and views being easily combined in a common enterprise, by an artful leader, it becomes more liable to abuse, and more dangerous when abused, than if it be lodged in the hands of one man; who, from the very circumstance of his being alone, will be more narrowly watched and more readily suspected, and who cannot unite so great a mass of influence as when he is associated with others.
PUBLIUS

Federalist No. 78
May 28, 1788

To the People of the State of New York:

WE PROCEED now to an examination of the judiciary department of the proposed government.[51]

In unfolding the defects of the existing Confederation, the utility and necessity of a federal judicature have been clearly pointed out. It is the less necessary to recapitulate the considerations there urged, as the propriety of the institution in the abstract is not disputed; the

[50] Hamilton concludes by contrasting the nature of a republican executive with that of a monarch. In England, dividing executive power between a council and a king promotes security because, while the people might know when the king has abused power, they have no electoral means of holding the king accountable. In a republic, however, where the people are the final judge, power is more safely exercised by a single individual, who can be more narrowly watched by the public at large.

[51] In *Federalist* No. 22 Hamilton asserts that one of the major defects of the Articles of Confederation is the lack of a federal judiciary "to expound and define [the] true meaning and operation of laws." In this essay, Hamilton discusses why an independent federal judiciary, consisting of indirectly appointed judges serving a life tenure, will contribute to effective constitutional republicanism.

only questions which have been raised being relative to the manner of constituting it, and to its extent. To these points, therefore, our observations shall be confined. . .

First. As to the mode of appointing the judges; this is the same with that of appointing the officers of the Union in general, and has been so fully discussed in the two last numbers, that nothing can be said here which would not be useless repetition.

Second. As to the tenure by which the judges are to hold their places; this chiefly concerns their duration in office; the provisions for their support; the precautions for their responsibility.

According to the plan of the convention, all judges who may be appointed by the United States are to hold their offices DURING GOOD BEHAVIOR; which is conformable to the most approved of the State constitutions and among the rest, to that of this State. . . . The standard of good behavior for the continuance in office of the judicial magistracy, is certainly one of the most valuable of the modern improvements in the practice of government.[52] In a monarchy it is an excellent barrier to the despotism of the prince; in a republic it is a no less excellent barrier to the encroachments and oppressions of the representative body. And it is the best expedient which can be devised in any government, to secure a steady, upright, and impartial administration of the laws.

Whoever attentively considers the different departments of power must perceive, that, in a government in which they are separated from each other, the judiciary, from the nature of its functions, will always be the least dangerous to the political rights of the Constitution; because it will be least in a capacity to annoy or injure them.[53] The Executive not only dispenses the honors, but holds the sword of the community. The legislature not only commands the purse, but prescribes the rules by which the duties and rights of every citizen are to be regulated. The judiciary, on the contrary, has no influence over either the sword or the purse; no direction either of the strength or of the wealth of the society; and can take no active resolution whatever. It may truly be said to have neither FORCE nor WILL, but merely judgment;[54] and must ultimately depend upon the aid of the executive arm even for the efficacy of its judgments. . .

[52] Hamilton contends that life tenure of federal judges during good behavior is "one of the most valuable" innovations in the science of politics. It gives judges the fortitude to resist the repressive actions of the prince in a monarchy and the intemperance of the legislature in a republic. In all governments it contributes to the maintenance of individual rights and the rule of law.

[53] Sensitive to concerns that indirect appointment and life tenure will negatively affect republicanism, Hamilton contends that the judiciary will be the least dangerous branch to the political rights of the other branches because it has no direct control over the purse or the sword.

[54] Although Hamilton states here that the judicial branch has neither force nor will and that it completely depends on the other branches to give its decisions efficacy, he later argues that permanent tenure will give judges the independence and strength necessary to uphold the Constitution against encroachments by the other branches and the temporary delusions or passions of the multitude.

The complete independence of the courts of justice is peculiarly essential in a limited Constitution. By a limited Constitution, I understand one which contains certain specified exceptions to the legislative authority; such, for instance, as that it shall pass no bills of attainder, no ex-post-facto laws, and the like. Limitations of this kind can be preserved in practice no other way than through the medium of courts of justice, whose duty it must be to declare all acts contrary to the manifest tenor of the Constitution void.[55] Without this, all the reservations of particular rights or privileges would amount to nothing.

Some perplexity respecting the rights of the courts to pronounce legislative acts void, because contrary to the Constitution, has arisen from an imagination that the doctrine would imply a superiority of the judiciary to the legislative power. It is urged that the authority which can declare the acts of another void, must necessarily be superior to the one whose acts may be declared void. As this doctrine is of great importance in all the American constitutions, a brief discussion of the ground on which it rests cannot be unacceptable.

There is no position which depends on clearer principles, than that every act of a delegated authority, contrary to the tenor of the commission under which it is exercised, is void. No legislative act, therefore, contrary to the Constitution, can be valid. To deny this, would be to affirm, that the deputy is greater than his principal; that the servant is above his master; that the representatives of the people are superior to the people themselves; that men acting by virtue of powers, may do not only what their powers do not authorize, but what they forbid.[56]

If it be said that the legislative body are themselves the constitutional judges of their own powers, and that the construction they put upon them is conclusive upon the other departments, it may be answered, that this cannot be the natural presumption, where it is not to be collected from any particular provisions in the Constitution. It is not otherwise to be supposed, that the Constitution could intend to enable the representatives of the people to substitute their WILL to that of their constituents. It is far more rational to suppose, that the courts were designed to be an intermediate body between the people and the legislature, in order, among other things, to keep the latter within the limits assigned to their authority. The interpretation of the laws is the proper and peculiar province of the courts.

[55] While the bulk of judicial power is spent applying existing law to particular cases and judging between disputing parties, Hamilton argues that the judiciary also serves an important role in maintaining limited government. After explaining that the Constitution limits the scope of government power, particularly its legislative powers, Hamilton boldly claims that the judiciary needs to give force to these limitations. Unless the courts exercise judicial review—the power to strike down executive or congressional actions that violate the terms of the Constitution—the constitutional limitations on the scope and exercise of power are meaningless.

[56] While the power of judicial review is not explicitly mentioned in the text of the Constitution, Hamilton argues that it is logically mandated by the nature of the Constitution itself. Hamilton, thus, distinguishes between constitutions, which are permanent acts of the people meant to limit the scope of government power for the permanent and aggregate interests of the whole, and ordinary acts of legislation, which are passed by temporary and fleeting majorities in the legislature. Because the Constitution is superior to ordinary acts of legislation, the courts have a duty to uphold it.

A constitution is, in fact, and must be regarded by the judges, as a fundamental law. It therefore belongs to them to ascertain its meaning, as well as the meaning of any particular act proceeding from the legislative body. If there should happen to be an irreconcilable variance between the two, that which has the superior obligation and validity ought, of course, to be preferred; or, in other words, the Constitution ought to be preferred to the statute, the intention of the people to the intention of their agents.

Nor does this conclusion by any means suppose a superiority of the judicial to the legislative power. It only supposes that the power of the people is superior to both; and that where the will of the legislature, declared in its statutes, stands in opposition to that of the people, declared in the Constitution, the judges ought to be governed by the latter rather than the former.[57] They ought to regulate their decisions by the fundamental laws, rather than by those which are not fundamental. . .

It can be of no weight to say that the courts, on the pretense of a repugnancy, may substitute their own pleasure to the constitutional intentions of the legislature.[58] This might as well happen in the case of two contradictory statutes; or it might as well happen in every adjudication upon any single statute. The courts must declare the sense of the law; and if they should be disposed to exercise WILL instead of JUDGMENT, the consequence would equally be the substitution of their pleasure to that of the legislative body. The observation, if it prove any thing, would prove that there ought to be no judges distinct from that body.

If, then, the courts of justice are to be considered as the bulwarks of a limited Constitution against legislative encroachments, this consideration will afford a strong argument for the permanent tenure of judicial offices, since nothing will contribute so much as this to that independent spirit in the judges which must be essential to the faithful performance of so arduous a duty.

This independence of the judges is equally requisite to guard the Constitution and the rights of individuals from the effects of those ill humors, which the arts of designing men, or the influence of particular conjunctures, sometimes disseminate among the people themselves, and which, though they speedily give place to better

[57] Hamilton emphasizes that he is not claiming that the judiciary is superior to the legislature. Rather, he is affirming that the fundamental law of the people is superior to ordinary acts of legislation. Whenever two laws conflict, it is obvious that the courts ought to comply with whichever law is higher in authority.

[58] Hamilton cautions that judicial review does not give judges license merely to substitute their own particular will or preferences for those of Congress. They are solely to interpret acts of coordinate branches in light of the Constitution.

information, and more deliberate reflection, have a tendency, in the meantime, to occasion dangerous innovations in the government, and serious oppressions of the minor party in the community. Though I trust the friends of the proposed Constitution will never concur with its enemies, in questioning that fundamental principle of republican government, which admits the right of the people to alter or abolish the established Constitution, whenever they find it inconsistent with their happiness, yet it is not to be inferred from this principle, that the representatives of the people, whenever a momentary inclination happens to lay hold of a majority of their constituents, incompatible with the provisions in the existing Constitution, would, on that account, be justifiable in a violation of those provisions; or that the courts would be under a greater obligation to connive at infractions in this shape, than when they had proceeded wholly from the cabals of the representative body. Until the people have, by some solemn and authoritative act, annulled or changed the established form, it is binding upon themselves collectively, as well as individually; and no presumption, or even knowledge, of their sentiments, can warrant their representatives in a departure from it, prior to such an act. But it is easy to see, that it would require an uncommon portion of fortitude in the judges to do their duty as faithful guardians of the Constitution, where legislative invasions of it had been instigated by the major voice of the community.[59]

But it is not with a view to infractions of the Constitution only, that the independence of the judges may be an essential safeguard against the effects of occasional ill humors in the society. These sometimes extend no farther than to the injury of the private rights of particular classes of citizens, by unjust and partial laws. Here also the firmness of the judicial magistracy is of vast importance in mitigating the severity and confining the operation of such laws.[60] It not only serves to moderate the immediate mischiefs of those which may have been passed, but it operates as a check upon the legislative body in passing them; who, perceiving that obstacles to the success of iniquitous intention are to be expected from the scruples of the courts, are in a manner compelled, by the very motives of the injustice they meditate, to qualify their attempts. This is a circumstance calculated to have more influence upon the character of our governments, than but few may be aware of. . .

[59] While the people always retain a right to alter or abolish the Constitution if they find that it is inconsistent with their happiness, this does not mean that the representatives of the people on the basis of a momentary inclination are justified in violating the Constitution, or that the Courts are obliged to uphold such violations by subordinate legislation. Until the people have amended or annulled the Constitution, it is binding on them. Hamilton recognizes that opposing popular majorities in the legislature is going to require "an uncommon portion of fortitude" on the part of judges. Thus, he again emphasizes the need for independence and life tenure.

[60] Hamilton maintains that judicial review will be additionally useful for upholding the rights of private citizens against infringement by majority factions. As he had stood against unjust legal oppression of former Tories in the case of *Rutgers v. Waddington*, Hamilton now argues that the courts have a duty to strike down unjust or impartial laws that favor one class of citizens at the expense of another.

That inflexible and uniform adherence to the rights of the Constitution, and of individuals, which we perceive to be indispensable in the courts of justice, can certainly not be expected from judges who hold their offices by a temporary commission. Periodical appointments, however regulated, or by whomsoever made, would, in some way or other, be fatal to their necessary independence. If the power of making them was committed either to the Executive or legislature, there would be danger of an improper complaisance to the branch which possessed it; if to both, there would be an unwillingness to hazard the displeasure of either; if to the people, or to persons chosen by them for the special purpose, there would be too great a disposition to consult popularity, to justify a reliance that nothing would be consulted but the Constitution and the laws.

There is yet a further and a weightier reason for the permanency of the judicial offices, which is deducible from the nature of the qualifications they require.[61] It has been frequently remarked, with great propriety, that a voluminous code of laws is one of the inconveniences necessarily connected with the advantages of a free government. To avoid an arbitrary discretion in the courts, it is indispensable that they should be bound down by strict rules and precedents, which serve to define and point out their duty in every particular case that comes before them; and it will readily be conceived from the variety of controversies which grow out of the folly and wickedness of mankind, that the records of those precedents must unavoidably swell to a very considerable bulk, and must demand long and laborious study to acquire a competent knowledge of them. Hence it is, that there can be but few men in the society who will have sufficient skill in the laws to qualify them for the stations of judges. And making the proper deductions for the ordinary depravity of human nature, the number must be still smaller of those who unite the requisite integrity with the requisite knowledge. These considerations apprise us, that the government can have no great option between fit character; and that a temporary duration in office, which would naturally discourage such characters from quitting a lucrative line of practice to accept a seat on the bench, would have a tendency to throw the administration of justice into hands less able, and less well qualified, to conduct it with utility and dignity. In the present circumstances of this country, and in those in which it is likely to be for a long time to come, the disadvantages on this score would be greater than they may at first sight appear; but it must be confessed, that they are far

[61] Hamilton concludes with an additional defense of permanent tenure, arguing that it is necessary to attract high-caliber federal judges with talent, intelligence, and stability of character to master the law and uphold legal precedents.

inferior to those which present themselves under the other aspects of the subject.

Upon the whole, there can be no room to doubt that the convention acted wisely in copying from the models of those constitutions which have established GOOD BEHAVIOR as the tenure of their judicial offices, in point of duration; and that so far from being blamable on this account, their plan would have been inexcusably defective, if it had wanted this important feature of good government.
PUBLIUS

Federalist No. 84
May 28, 1788

To the People of the State of New York:

IN THE course of the foregoing review of the Constitution, I have taken notice of, and endeavored to answer most of the objections which have appeared against it. . . . The most considerable of the remaining objections is that the plan of the convention contains no bill of rights.[62] Among other answers given to this, it has been upon different occasions remarked that the constitutions of several of the States are in a similar predicament. I add that New York is of the number. And yet the opposers of the new system, in this State, who profess an unlimited admiration for its constitution, are among the most intemperate partisans of a bill of rights. To justify their zeal in this matter, they allege two things: one is that, though the constitution of New York has no bill of rights prefixed to it, yet it contains, in the body of it, various provisions in favor of particular privileges and rights, which, in substance amount to the same thing; the other is, that the Constitution adopts, in their full extent, the common and statute law of Great Britain, by which many other rights, not expressed in it, are equally secured.

To the first I answer, that the Constitution proposed by the convention contains, as well as the constitution of this State, a number of such provisions.[63]

Independent of those which relate to the structure of the government, we find the following:[64] Article 1, section 3, clause 7 "Judgment in cases of impeachment shall not extend further than to removal from office, and disqualification to hold and enjoy any office of

[62] One of the most enduring critiques of the proposed Constitution by members of the state ratifying conventions was that it contained no Bill of Rights. In this essay, Hamilton explains his rationale for opposing a formal listing of rights.

[63] New York critics had responded to Hamilton's observation that the state constitution itself lacked a formal Bill of Rights by contending that rights and privileges of citizens were guaranteed in the body of state constitution and by the state's adoption of British common law. Hamilton points out that the text of the U.S. Constitution likewise contains substantial provisions protecting rights from federal and state actions.

[64] Hamilton strongly believed that the structure of government, which separates power and curbs its abuse through elections and internal checks and balances, offers a more substantial protection of rights than any explicit enumeration. Nevertheless, he points out here that the Constitution includes protections independent of its structure. He first mentions the constitutional requirement that impeachment convictions extend no further than removal from office. Any additional punishment must be imposed by the courts of justice, thereby protecting individuals from being convicted of crimes by their political opponents. Hamilton then refers to several rights of criminal defendants and the Constitution's prohibition of titles of nobility.

honor, trust, or profit under the United States; but the party convicted shall, nevertheless, be liable and subject to indictment, trial, judgment, and punishment according to law." Section 9, of the same article, clause 2 "The privilege of the writ of habeas corpus shall not be suspended, unless when in cases of rebellion or invasion the public safety may require it." Clause 3 "No bill of attainder or ex-post-facto law shall be passed." Clause 7 "No title of nobility shall be granted by the United States; and no person holding any office of profit or trust under them, shall, without the consent of the Congress, accept of any present, emolument, office, or title of any kind whatever, from any king, prince, or foreign state." Article 3, section 2, clause 3 "The trial of all crimes, except in cases of impeachment, shall be by jury; and such trial shall be held in the State where the said crimes shall have been committed; but when not committed within any State, the trial shall be at such place or places as the Congress may by law have directed." Section 3, of the same article "Treason against the United States shall consist only in levying war against them, or in adhering to their enemies, giving them aid and comfort. No person shall be convicted of treason, unless on the testimony of two witnesses to the same overt act, or on confession in open court." And clause 3, of the same section "The Congress shall have power to declare the punishment of treason; but no attainder of treason shall work corruption of blood, or forfeiture, except during the life of the person attainted."[65]

It may well be a question, whether these are not, upon the whole, of equal importance with any which are to be found in the constitution of this State. The establishment of the writ of habeas corpus, the prohibition of ex-post-facto laws, and of TITLES OF NOBILITY, TO WHICH WE HAVE NO CORRESPONDING PROVISION IN OUR CONSTITUTION, are perhaps greater securities to liberty and republicanism than any it contains.[66] The creation of crimes after the commission of the fact, or, in other words, the subjecting of men to punishment for things which, when they were done, were breaches of no law, and the practice of arbitrary imprisonments, have been, in all ages, the favorite and most formidable instruments of tyranny. . .

Nothing need be said to illustrate the importance of the prohibition of titles of nobility. This may truly be denominated the corner-stone of republican government; for so long as they are excluded, there can

[65] Hamilton concludes his discussion of the safeguards incorporated into the body of the Constitution by identifying important limitations on the crime of treason. By clearly defining treason as "levying war" against the United States or giving "comfort and aid" to its enemies, the Constitution prohibits overbroad definitions that might be used to punish anyone critical of the regime. Furthermore, conviction of treason—which frequently results in death—requires at least two witnesses or a confession in open court and cannot be used to punish anyone other than the convicted individual. For example, the friends and family members of the accused may not be deemed guilty by association.

[66] Hamilton asserts that the Constitution safeguards republican liberty by prohibiting several common instruments of tyranny, including suspending the writ of habeas corpus (arbitrarily arresting someone without charging them with a legally defined crime), ex post facto laws (making someone criminally liable for an action which was legal at the time), and titles of nobility.

never be serious danger that the government will be any other than that of the people. . .[67]

It has been several times truly remarked that bills of rights are, in their origin, stipulations between kings and their subjects, abridgements of prerogative in favor of privilege, reservations of rights not surrendered to the prince.[68] Such was MAGNA CARTA, obtained by the barons, sword in hand, from King John. Such were the subsequent confirmations of that charter by succeeding princes. Such was the PETITION OF RIGHT assented to by Charles I, in the beginning of his reign. . . . It is evident, therefore, that, according to their primitive signification, they have no application to constitutions professedly founded upon the power of the people, and executed by their immediate representatives and servants. Here, in strictness, the people surrender nothing; and as they retain every thing they have no need of particular reservations.[69] "WE, THE PEOPLE of the United States, to secure the blessings of liberty to ourselves and our posterity, do ORDAIN and ESTABLISH this Constitution for the United States of America." Here is a better recognition of popular rights, than volumes of those aphorisms which make the principal figure in several of our State bills of rights, and which would sound much better in a treatise of ethics than in a constitution of government.

But a minute detail of particular rights is certainly far less applicable to a Constitution like that under consideration, which is merely intended to regulate the general political interests of the nation, than to a constitution which has the regulation of every species of personal and private concerns.[70] If, therefore, the loud clamors against the plan of the convention, on this score, are well founded, no epithets of reprobation will be too strong for the constitution of this State. But the truth is, that both of them contain all which, in relation to their objects, is reasonably to be desired.

I go further, and affirm that bills of rights, in the sense and to the extent in which they are contended for, are not only unnecessary in the proposed Constitution, but would even be dangerous. They would contain various exceptions to powers not granted; and, on this very account, would afford a colorable pretext to claim more than were granted.[71] For why declare that things shall not be done which there is no power to do? Why, for instance, should it be said that the

[67] The prohibition of titles of nobility thwarts the imposition of arbitrary privileges and rank embodied in the European-style class system of lords and ladies.

[68] After explaining the specific limitations on the use of delegated power incorporated into the text of Constitution, Hamilton makes the case against an additional listing of rights. He first contends that bills of rights are more appropriate for monarchies than they are for republics. In a monarchy, the king is the source of authority. Subjects must therefore specifically request civil protections. Hamilton provides the example of Magna Carta and the Petition of Right, written by Parliament and agreed to by Charles I, which imposed legal limits on the prerogative of the monarch.

[69] In republics, the people, rather than their rulers, are the source of power. The people retain whatever powers they do not specifically delegate. Thus, the preamble to the Constitution, establishing the people as the fount of authority, is a better guarantor of popular rights than any specific enumeration of such rights.

[70] Hamilton implies that a Bill of Rights would be appropriate if the Constitution had created a government with authority over every area of personal and private concern. But because the government is limited to specifically defined ends, it possesses only the authority to do what is necessary for securing those ends and no more.

[71] Hamilton expresses concern that a long list of rights implies an increase, rather than decrease, in federal power as it would forbid the government from doing things it never had the authority to do in the first place. This threat was addressed in the eventual text of the Bill of Rights by the Ninth Amendment, which states that "the enumeration in the Constitution, of certain rights, shall not be construed to deny or disparage other retained by the people," and the Tenth Amendment, which states that "the powers not delegated to the United States by the Constitution, nor prohibited by it to the states, are to be reserved to the states respectively, or to the people."

liberty of the press shall not be restrained, when no power is given by which restrictions may be imposed? I will not contend that such a provision would confer a regulating power; but it is evident that it would furnish, to men disposed to usurp, a plausible pretense for claiming that power. They might urge with a semblance of reason, that the Constitution ought not to be charged with the absurdity of providing against the abuse of an authority which was not given, and that the provision against restraining the liberty of the press afforded a clear implication, that a power to prescribe proper regulations concerning it was intended to be vested in the national government. This may serve as a specimen of the numerous handles which would be given to the doctrine of constructive powers, by the indulgence of an injudicious zeal for bills of rights.

On the subject of the liberty of the press, as much as has been said, I cannot forbear adding a remark or two: in the first place, I observe, that there is not a syllable concerning it in the constitution of this State; in the next, I contend, that whatever has been said about it in that of any other State, amounts to nothing. What signifies a declaration, that "the liberty of the press shall be inviolably preserved"? What is the liberty of the press? Who can give it any definition which would not leave the utmost latitude for evasion? I hold it to be impracticable; and from this I infer, that its security, whatever fine declarations may be inserted in any constitution respecting it, must altogether depend on public opinion, and on the general spirit of the people and of the government.[72] And here, after all, as is intimated upon another occasion, must we seek for the only solid basis of all our rights.

There remains but one other view of this matter to conclude the point. The truth is, after all the declamations we have heard, that the Constitution is itself, in every rational sense, and to every useful purpose, A BILL OF RIGHTS.[73] The several bills of rights in Great Britain form its Constitution, and conversely the constitution of each State is its bill of rights. And the proposed Constitution, if adopted, will be the bill of rights of the Union.
PUBLIUS

[72] Using freedom of press as an example, Hamilton points out the difficulty of precisely defining rights. The degree to which rights are protected is dependent on public opinion and the spirit of the regime. Without a citizenry and governing structure that supports a broad understanding of free exercise of religion or liberty of the press, for example, rights might be defined and restricted into oblivion. Thus, as Hamilton earlier observes, abstract statements of rights are more appropriate "in a treatise of ethics than in a constitution of government."

[73] The debate over the Bill of Rights demonstrated a fundamental difference in the perception of how rights are protected. The Anti-Federalists and those calling for a Bill of Rights believed that the best way to protect the people's liberty is to make explicit prohibitions on the exercise of power. Hamilton adopts the contrasting view that the best way to secure rights is to channel and organize the power of government, so it is likely to be exercised effectively but not oppressively.

By the time the New York Ratifying Convention convened in June 1788 in Poughkeepsie, Hamilton faced one of his most challenging battles yet. Although eight states had already ratified, delegates elected to the New York convention opposed ratification by a margin of at least two to one. Relying on many of the arguments he had first developed in *The Federalist*, Hamilton remained the central figure in the debate. Following favorable news of ratification in New Hampshire and Virginia, he was eventually able to win over several leaders of the Anti-Federalist movement, and the convention approved the Constitution by the narrowest of margins. On July 23 in anticipation of ratification, triumphant Federalists celebrated in the streets of New York, parading down Broadway behind a horse-drawn federal ship, dubbed the *Hamilton*.

In spite of the reticence of Hamilton and others to including a Bill of Rights in the new Constitution, supporters of the proposed government eventually recognized that the lack of a Bill of Rights remained the most significant barrier to ratification. Thus, they promised that the first Congress under the new government would propose a series of amendments including a Bill of Rights. This pledge was enough to secure ratification in many states, and when the Bill of Rights was added as the first ten amendments to the Constitution in 1791, organized opposition to the new government dissipated.

In the end, no one—with the possible exception of James Madison—did more than Hamilton to secure the passage and implementation of the Constitution. Of all the literature produced during the ratification period, *The Federalist* alone has endured as the most authoritative source for understanding the Constitution and its defense, and also as a practical manual on political power, human nature, and republican government.

Source: *The Federalist: A Collection of Essays, Written in Favour of the New Constitution, as Agreed upon by the Federal Convention, September 17, 1787, in Two Volumes.* New York: Printed and sold by J. and A. M'Lean, 1788.

Letter to George Washington on the Office of the President

September 1788

INTRODUCTION

Once the Constitution was ratified, its supporters universally agreed that George Washington would help legitimize the new government and the controversial office of the president by serving as the nation's first chief executive. Washington, however, eager to retire to the tranquility of private life, was hesitant to pursue the presidency. Hamilton responded to Washington's expressed reluctance by fervently appealing to his sense of honor and patriotic duty.

New York September 1788

Dear Sir

. . . I should be deeply pained my Dear Sir if your scruples in regard to a certain station should be matured into a resolution to decline it; though I am neither surprised at their existence nor can I but agree in opinion that the caution you observe in deferring an ultimate determination is prudent. I have however reflected maturely on the subject and have come to a conclusion, (in which I feel no hesitation) that every public and personal consideration will demand from you an acquiescence in what will *certainly* be the unanimous wish of your country.[1] The absolute retreat which you meditated at the close of the late war was natural and proper. Had the government produced by the revolution gone on in a *tolerable* train, it would have been most adviseable to have persisted in that retreat. But I am clearly of opinion that the crisis which brought you again into public view left you no alternative but to comply—and I am equally clear in the opinion that you are by that act *pledged* to take a part in the execution of the government.[2] I am not less convinced that the impression of this necessity of your filling the station in question is so universal that you run no risk of any uncandid imputation, by submitting to it. But even if this were not the case, a regard to your

[1] Hamilton maintains that patriotism and private interest alike should induce Washington to seek the presidency and emphasizes the universal support for his candidacy.

[2] Hamilton reminds Washington that after the failure of the confederation he had returned to the public arena to help secure the adoption of a new government. Now he must lend his assistance to ensure the successful implementation of that government.

own reputation as well as to the public good, calls upon you in the strongest manner to run that risk.

It cannot be considered as a compliment to say that on your acceptance of the office of President the success of the new government in its commencement may materially depend. Your agency and influence will be not less important in preserving it from the future attacks of its enemies than they have been in recommending it in the first instance to the adoption of the people. Independent of all considerations drawn from this source the point of light in which you stand at home and abroad will make an infinite difference in the respectability with which the government will begin its operations in the alternative of your being or not being at the head of it.[3] I forbear to urge considerations which might have a more personal application. What I have said will suffice for the inferences I mean to draw.

First—In a matter so essential to the well being of society as the prosperity of a newly instituted government a citizen of so much consequence as yourself to its success has no option but to lend his services if called for. Permit me to say it would be inglorious in such a situation not to hazard the glory however great, which he might have previously acquired.[4]

Secondly. Your signature to the proposed system pledges your judgment for its being such an one as upon the whole was worthy of the public approbation. If it should miscarry (as men commonly decide from success or the want of it) the blame will in all probability be laid on the system itself. And the framers of it will have to encounter the disrepute of having brought about a revolution in government, without substituting any thing that was worthy of the effort. They pulled down one Utopia, it will be said, to build up another. This view of the subject, if I mistake not my dear Sir will suggest to your mind greater hazard to that fame, which must be and ought to be dear to you, in refusing your future aid to the system than in affording it.[5] I will only add that in my estimate of the matter that aid is indispensable.

I have taken the liberty to express these sentiments to lay before you my view of the subject. I doubt not the considerations mentioned have fully occurred to you, and I trust they will finally produce in your mind the same result, which exists in mine. I flatter myself the

[3] Hamilton stresses that Washington's reputation for unwavering integrity both at home and abroad would eventually translate into respect for the new government and its executive office.

[4] With remarkable candor, Hamilton argues that because Washington's support is essential to the viability and well-being of the new system, his refusal to serve would be a dereliction of duty.

[5] Hamilton warns Washington that in signing the Constitution in Philadelphia, he, along with the other framers, had tied their own reputations to its future success and that he would endanger his own fame by failing to lend his indispensable support.

frankness with which I have delivered myself will not be displeasing to you. It has been prompted by motives which you would not disapprove.

I remain My Dear Sir With the sincerest respect and regard Your Obd & hum serv

A Hamilton

CONCLUSION

Washington, eventually acknowledging his important role in the successful launch of the new government, dutifully accepted candidacy for chief executive and was shortly later unanimously elected president.

Although Washington likely would have accepted the presidency even in the absence of Hamilton's letter, he acknowledged in a letter of reply that he greatly appreciated Hamilton's forthrightness and would continue to rely on his counsel. He stated, "The same manly tone of intercourse will always be more than barely welcome. Indeed, it will be highly acceptable to me."

Source: George Washington Papers, Library of Congress.

SECTION VII

Secretary of the Treasury

Report Relative to a Provision for the Support of Public Credit

January 14, 1790

INTRODUCTION

Soon after the new government under the U.S. Constitution went into effect, Congress drafted legislation creating the first four executive cabinet positions—secretary of Treasury, secretary of state, secretary of war, and attorney general—to assist the president in meeting his responsibilities over finance, foreign relations, and war.

On September 11, 1789, nine days after signing the cabinet into law, Washington appointed Hamilton to head the prestigious Department of Treasury. As secretary of Treasury, Hamilton faced the herculean task of addressing the massive debt inherited from the Revolution. Shortly after his appointment, Congress directed Hamilton to put together a plan for restoring the public credit that had so badly deteriorated under the Articles of Confederation. Hamilton, believing that the nation's good faith and credit were essential to its long-term prosperity, independence, and security, worked tirelessly in the following months on a comprehensive proposal to effectively finance the debt. Hamilton presented his report to the House of Representatives on January 14, 1790.

[To the Speaker of the House of Representatives]

The Secretary of the Treasury, in obedience to the resolution of the House of Representatives, of the twenty-first day of September last, has, during the recess of Congress, applied himself to the consideration of a proper plan for the support of the Public Credit, with all the attention which was due to the authority of the House, and to the magnitude of the object.

In the discharge of this duty, he has felt, in no small degree, the anxieties which naturally flow from a just estimate of the difficulty of the task, from a well-founded diffidence of his own qualifications for executing it with success, and from a deep and solemn conviction of the momentous nature of the truth contained in the resolution under which his investigations have been conducted, "That

[1] Hamilton commends the House of Representatives for recognizing that the nation's public credit would contribute not only to its prosperity but also to its esteem in the eyes of its citizenry and of foreign nations. Hamilton, thus, reveals his conviction that a well-managed public debt is essential for political strength and stability.

[2] Hamilton emphasizes that the nation's security depends on its ability to fund unforeseen public dangers or exigencies, such as war. The capacity to quickly secure loans ensures that a nation always has the means to swiftly and energetically respond to inevitable crises that will threaten the lives, liberties, and properties of citizens.

[3] Since the capacity to borrow is an essential safeguard for all nations, it is important for nations to maintain the ability to borrow money on good terms. Nations that neglect their public credit and default on their obligations will have a difficult time obtaining necessary funds or will be charged higher interest rates to compensate for the greater risk, which will increase the overall cost of maintaining a government and the corresponding tax burden.

an *adequate* provision for the support of the Public Credit, is a matter of high importance to the honor and prosperity of the United States." . . .[1]

In the opinion of the Secretary, the wisdom of the House, in giving their explicit sanction to the proposition which has been stated, cannot but be applauded by all, who will seriously consider, and trace through their obvious consequences, these plain and undeniable truths.

That exigencies are to be expected to occur, in the affairs of nations, in which there will be a necessity for borrowing.[2]

That loans in times of public danger, especially from foreign war, are found an indispensable resource, even to the wealthiest of them.

And that in a country, which, like this, is possessed of little active wealth, or in other words, little monied capital, the necessity for that resource, must, in such emergencies, be proportionably urgent.

And as on the one hand, the necessity for borrowing in particular emergencies cannot be doubted, so on the other, it is equally evident, that to be able to borrow upon *good terms*, it is essential that the credit of a nation should be well established.[3]

For when the credit of a country is in any degree questionable, it never fails to give an extravagant premium, in one shape or another, upon all the loans it has occasion to make. Nor does the evil end here; the same disadvantage must be sustained upon whatever is to be bought on terms of future payment.

From this constant necessity of *borrowing* and *buying dear*, it is easy to conceive how immensely the expences of a nation, in a course of time, will be augmented by an unsound state of the public credit.

To attempt to enumerate the complicated variety of mischiefs in the whole system of the social œconomy, which proceed from a neglect of the maxims that uphold public credit, and justify the solicitude manifested by the House on this point, would be an improper intrusion on their time and patience.

In so strong a light nevertheless do they appear to the Secretary, that on their due observance at the present critical juncture, materially depends, in his judgment, the individual and aggregate prosperity of the citizens of the United States; their relief from the embarrassments they now experience; their character as a People; the cause of good government.[4]

If the maintenance of public credit, then, be truly so important, the next enquiry which suggests itself is, by what means it is to be effected? The ready answer to which question is, by good faith, by a punctual performance of contracts. States, like individuals, who observe their engagements, are respected and trusted: while the reverse is the fate of those, who pursue an opposite conduct.[5]

Every breach of the public engagements, whether from choice or necessity, is in different degrees hurtful to public credit.[6] When such a necessity does truly exist, the evils of it are only to be palliated by a scrupulous attention, on the part of the government, to carry the violation no farther than the necessity absolutely requires, and to manifest, if the nature of the case admits of it, a sincere disposition to make reparation, whenever circumstances shall permit. . .

While the observance of that good faith, which is the basis of public credit, is recommended by the strongest inducements of political expediency, it is enforced by considerations of still greater authority. There are arguments for it, which rest on the immutable principles of moral obligation.[7] And in proportion as the mind is disposed to contemplate, in the order of Providence, an intimate connection between public virtue and public happiness, will be its repugnancy to a violation of those principles.

This reflection derives additional strength from the nature of the debt of the United States. It was the price of liberty.[8] The faith of America has been repeatedly pledged for it, and with solemnities, that give peculiar force to the obligation. There is indeed reason to regret that it has not hitherto been kept; that the necessities of the war, conspiring with inexperience in the subjects of finance, produced direct infractions; and that the subsequent period has been a continued scene of negative violation, or non-compliance. But a diminution of this regret arises from the reflection, that the last seven years have exhibited an earnest and uniform effort, on the part of the government of the union, to retrieve the national credit, by doing justice to the creditors of the nation; and that the embarrassments of a defective constitution, which defeated this laudable effort, have ceased.

[4] Hamilton emphasizes that sound credit is essential for restoring the nation's badly degraded reputation. Thus, as Carson Holloway (2015) points out, Hamilton views his *Report on Public Credit* "as an effort . . . to complete the establishment of the government formed by the Constitution" (15).

[5] Hamilton emphasizes that a country's good faith and credit are established and maintained when it promptly honors its contracts. States—like private individuals—he asserts, will be better trusted if they keep their word and fulfill their obligations.

[6] Hamilton identifies two reasons why the government might break its faith by failing to repay its debts. The first occurs when those in power willfully violate their agreements out of pure self-interest; the second occurs when a country is unable to pay due to insufficient funds. Breaking faith for either reason will inevitably damage public credit. Nevertheless, governments burdened by necessity should still make every attempt to restore faith with their creditors, even if it requires renegotiating the terms of their contracts.

[7] Although Hamilton first defends the restoration of public credit for pragmatic reasons, he now argues that nations also have a moral obligation to honor their agreements. Hamilton, thus, distinguishes himself from Machiavelli, to whom he is often compared, by declaring that moral obligations are of "greater authority" than considerations of "political expediency." In other words, justice—not mere self-interest—ultimately governs the obligations that individuals and nations have to one another.

[8] The United States' moral duty to honor its debts is augmented by the fact that the money borrowed to fund the Revolution made the achievement of its liberty possible. Regretfully, however, the necessities of war, along with the financial and political incompetence of the previous system, resulted in frequent infractions of its obligations. Nevertheless, Hamilton celebrates the fact that the new system has overcome the political deficiencies that previously prevented earnest efforts to restore good faith and credit.

From this evidence of a favorable disposition, given by the former government, the institution of a new one, cloathed with powers competent to calling forth the resources of the community, has excited correspondent expectations.[9] A general belief, accordingly, prevails, that the credit of the United States will quickly be established on the firm foundation of an effectual provision for the existing debt. . .

It cannot but merit particular attention, that among ourselves the most enlightened friends of good government are those, whose expectations are the highest.

To justify and preserve their confidence; to promote the encreasing respectability of the American name; to answer the calls of justice; to restore landed property to its due value; to furnish new resources both to agriculture and commerce; to cement more closely the union of the states; to add to their security against foreign attack; to establish public order on the basis of an upright and liberal policy. These are the great and invaluable ends to be secured, by a proper and adequate provision, at the present period, for the support of public credit. . .[10]

Having now taken a concise view of the inducements to a proper provision for the public debt, the next enquiry which presents itself is, what ought to be the nature of such a provision? This requires some preliminary discussions.[11]

It is agreed on all hands, that that part of the debt which has been contracted abroad, and is denominated the foreign debt, ought to be provided for, according to the precise terms of the contracts relating to it. The discussions, which can arise, therefore, will have reference essentially to the domestic part of it, or to that which has been contracted at home. It is to be regretted, that there is not the same unanimity of sentiment on this part, as on the other.

The Secretary has too much deference for the opinions of every part of the community, not to have observed one, which has, more than once, made its appearance in the public prints, and which is occasionally to be met with in conversation. It involves this question, whether a discrimination ought not to be made between original holders of the public securities, and present possessors, by purchase.[12] Those who advocate a discrimination are for making a full provision for the securities of the former, at their nominal value; but contend, that the latter ought to receive no more than the cost to them, and the interest: And the idea is sometimes suggested of making good the difference to the primitive possessor.[13]

In favor of this scheme, it is alledged, that it would be unreasonable to pay twenty shillings in the pound, to one who had not given more for it than three or four. And it is added, that it would be hard to aggravate the misfortune of the first owner, who, probably through necessity, parted with his property at so great a loss, by obliging him to contribute to the profit of the person, who had speculated on his distresses.

The Secretary, after the most mature reflection on the force of this argument, is induced to reject the doctrine it contains, as equally unjust and impolitic, as highly injurious, even to the original holders of public securities; as ruinous to public credit.[14]

It is inconsistent with justice, because in the first place, it is a breach of contract; in violation of the rights of a fair purchaser.[15]

The nature of the contract in its origin, is, that the public will pay the sum expressed in the security, to the first holder, or his *assignee*. The *intent*, in making the security assignable, is, that the proprietor may be able to make use of his property, by selling it for as much as it *may be worth in the market*, and that the buyer may be *safe* in the purchase.

Every buyer therefore stands exactly in the place of the seller, has the same right with him to the identical sum expressed in the security, and having acquired that right, by fair purchase, and in conformity to the original *agreement* and *intention* of the government, his claim cannot be disputed, without manifest injustice.[16]

That he is to be considered as a fair purchaser, results from this: Whatever necessity the seller may have been under, was occasioned by the government, in not making a proper provision for its debts. The buyer had no agency in it, and therefore ought not to suffer. He is not even chargeable with having taken an undue advantage. He paid what the commodity was worth in the market, and took the risks of reimbursement upon himself. He of course gave a fair equivalent, and ought to reap the benefit of his hazard; a hazard which

[13] Hamilton summarizes the argument for discrimination between the different holders of debt, which James Madison would later present on the floor of the House in opposition to Hamilton's plan. According to this view, current title holders should not be payed the full value of their securities. Instead, the government should pay secondhand buyers no more than their original purchase price with interest, while reserving the remaining amount to compensate the original security holders for their losses.

[14] Hamilton rejects calls for discrimination between the current and original security holders as both unjust and unwise. He believes that allowing the government to retroactively change the terms of legally binding contracts would set a dangerous precedent, which would ultimately harm the property rights of even the original debt holders.

[15] Hamilton first argues that a discriminatory policy would be unjust because it would violate the sacred right of contract between seller and buyer. The original sale was carried out under the explicit terms that the government would "pay the sum expressed in the security" to any subsequent buyer of that security.

[16] Since the government-issued securities were designed as transferable property, the buyer, on purchase, acquired rightful possession of the amount "expressed in the security" and legally assumed not only the right to all future profits but also the risk of loss. The terms of this original agreement, Hamilton concludes, cannot be terminated "without manifest injustice."

[17] Hamilton subtly concedes that the terms of legally binding contracts might be justly altered in cases where buyers took "undue advantage," but he contends that such is not the case in the circumstance at hand. By failing to properly fund its debts, the government, not the buyers, had created the circumstances in which original security holders willingly sold their property on unfavorable terms. The buyers purchased the securities at fair market value and assumed the risk of losing their initial investment in the event that the government failed to meet its obligations.

[18] After sympathizing with those who parted with their securities below value out of economic necessity, Hamilton counteracts the narrative created by supporters of discrimination that the sales were inevitably exploitative in nature. He explains that the circumstances surrounding the sale of securities were complex and that calculations, other than economic duress, likely influenced a large percentage of transactions. For example, some sellers may have sold because they were unwilling to risk a lower profit in the future; others may have used the money from sales to invest in other more profitable enterprises; others, still, might have made up for their original loss by repurchasing securities at a later date.

was far from inconsiderable, and which, perhaps, turned on little less than a revolution in government.[17]

That the case of those, who parted with their securities from necessity, is a hard one, cannot be denied. But whatever complaint of injury, or claim of redress, they may have, respects the government solely. They have not only nothing to object to the persons who relieved their necessities, by giving them the current price of their property, but they are even under an implied condition to contribute to the reimbursement of those persons. They knew, that by the terms of the contract with themselves, the public were bound to pay to those, to whom they should convey their title, the sums stipulated to be paid to them; and, that as citizens of the United States, they were to bear their proportion of the contribution for that purpose. This, by the act of assignment, they tacitly engage to do; and if they had an option, they could not, with integrity or good faith, refuse to do it, without the consent of those to whom they sold.

But though many of the original holders sold from necessity, it does not follow, that this was the case with all of them.[18] It may well be supposed, that some of them did it either through want of confidence in an eventual provision, or from the allurements of some profitable speculation. How shall these different classes be discriminated from each other? How shall it be ascertained, in any case, that the money, which the original holder obtained for his security, was not more beneficial to him, than if he had held it to the present time, to avail himself of the provision which shall be made? How shall it be known, whether if the purchaser had employed his money in some other way, he would not be in a better situation, than by having applied it in the purchase of securities, though he should now receive their full amount? And if neither of these things can be known, how shall it be determined whether a discrimination, independent of the breach of contract, would not do a real injury to purchasers; and if it included a compensation to the primitive proprietors, would not give them an advantage, to which they had no equitable pretension.

It may well be imagined, also, that there are not wanting instances, in which individuals, urged by a present necessity, parted with the securities received by them from the public, and shortly after replaced them with others, as an indemnity for their first loss. Shall they be deprived of the indemnity which they have endeavoured to secure by so provident an arrangement?

Questions of this sort, on a close inspection, multiply themselves without end, and demonstrate the injustice of a discrimination, even on the most subtle calculations of equity, abstracted from the obligation of contract. . .

The impolicy of a discrimination results from two considerations;[19] one, that it proceeds upon a principle destructive of that *quality* of the public debt, or the stock of the nation, which is essential to its capacity for answering the purposes of money—that is the *security* of *transfer*; the other, that as well on this account, as because it includes a breach of faith, it renders property in the funds less valuable; consequently induces lenders to demand a higher premium for what they lend, and produces every other inconvenience of a bad state of public credit.

It will be perceived at first sight, that the transferable quality of stock is essential to its operation as money, and that this depends on the idea of complete security to the transferree, and a firm persuasion, that no distinction can in any circumstances be made between him and the original proprietor. . .

It is equally unnecessary to add any thing to what has been already said to demonstrate the fatal influence, which the principle of discrimination would have on the public credit.

But there is still a point in view in which it will appear perhaps even more exceptionable, than in either of the former. It would be repugnant to an express provision of the Constitution of the United States.[20] This provision is, that "all debts contracted and engagements entered into before the adoption of that Constitution shall be as valid against the United States under it, as under the confederation," which amounts to a constitutional ratification of the contracts respecting the debt, in the state in which they existed under the confederation. And resorting to that standard, there can be no doubt, that the rights of assignees and original holders, must be considered as equal. . .

The Secretary concluding, that a discrimination, between the different classes of creditors of the United States, cannot with propriety be *made*, proceeds to examine whether a difference ought to be permitted to *remain* between them, and another description of public creditors—Those of the states individually.

[19] In addition to being unjust, Hamilton contends that discrimination would be imprudent. Reiterating his earlier argument on the importance of public credit, Hamilton explains that allowing the government to retroactively diminish or alter the value of securities for subsequent buyers would undermine the good faith of the United States and would lessen the future value of government securities, leading to higher interest rates and less accessible loans.

[20] Hamilton concludes his argument against discrimination by pointing out that the language of the Constitution forbids it. By altering the terms of sale, discrimination violates the explicit constitutional protection for all contracts or agreements negotiated under the previous confederation.

[21] As a significant portion of the war debt was held by the various state governments, Hamilton next turns to the question of who should be responsible for financing the outstanding debt. Here, Hamilton contends that the state debts should be consolidated into the federal debt. This plan was politically problematic because, although each of the states had equally benefited from the independence secured by the Revolution, they had varied in their financial contributions to the war and in their efforts to pay off their debts. Nevertheless, Hamilton strongly urges assumption, believing it would contribute to "an orderly, stable and satisfactory arrangement of the national finances."

[22] Hamilton warns that if the different levels of government simultaneously attempt to extinguish their debt, they will compete for the finite resources. This would lead to "collusion and confusion" between the different governments, which would consequently divide and weaken the union.

[23] Hamilton concludes by reiterating that a properly administered debt is a "national blessing," but he cautions against frivolous borrowing and advises the country to always maintain a feasible plan for repayment.

The Secretary, after mature reflection on this point, entertains a full conviction, that an assumption of the debts of the particular states by the union, and a like provision for them, as for those of the union, will be a measure of sound policy and substantial justice.[21]

It would, in the opinion of the Secretary, contribute, in an eminent degree, to an orderly, stable and satisfactory arrangement of the national finances. . .

The principal question then must be, whether such a provision cannot be more conveniently and effectually made, by one general plan issuing from one authority, than by different plans originating in different authorities.

In the first case there can be no competition for resources; in the last, there must be such a competition. The consequences of this, without the greatest caution on both sides, might be interfering regulations, and thence collision and confusion. . .[22]

Persuaded as the Secretary is, that the proper funding of the present debt, will render it a national blessing: Yet he is so far from acceding to the position, in the latitude in which it is sometimes laid down, that "public debts are public benefits," a position inviting to prodigality, and liable to dangerous abuse,—that he ardently wishes to see it incorporated, as a fundamental maxim, in the system of public credit of the United States, that the creation of debt should always be accompanied with the means of extinguishment.[23] This he regards as the true secret for rendering public credit immortal. And he presumes, that it is difficult to conceive a situation, in which there may not be an adherence to the maxim. At least he feels an unfeigned solicitude, that this may be attempted by the United States, and that they may commence their measures for the establishment of credit, with the observance of it.

Alexander Hamilton, *Secretary of the Treasury*.

Although Hamilton's *Report on the Public Credit* was fairly well received by the House of Representatives, its delivery revealed the first signs of a fractured political alliance between Hamilton and his former *Federalist* coauthor, James Madison. As de facto leader of the House, Madison publically rallied in favor of discrimination between present and original security holders and in opposition to federal assumption of the revolutionary debt of the several states.

On the basis of Hamilton's argument, the House overwhelming voted against Madison and his call for discrimination. But in mid-April, Hamilton's plan faced a crushing blow when the House struck down the other major component of his proposal, federal assumption of state debt. Many representatives feared the increased power that assumption would give to the federal government, and the Southern states were particularly concerned that giving the federal government the power over assumption would increase its ability to interfere with and regulate the institution of slavery. In the end, after a lengthy political battle over the permanent location of the nation's capital resulted in the compromise selection of a spot on the southern Potomac River, the House finally acceded to nationalize the revolutionary debt. Nevertheless, the initial division between Hamilton and Madison, first fueled by the issue of assumption, only continued to widen in the coming years as each supported different means for securing a stable, prosperous, and free America.

Source: *Journal of the House of Representatives of the United States* (Washington, 1826).

Opinion on the Constitutionality of an Act to Establish a Bank

February 23, 1791

INTRODUCTION

One of Hamilton's top policy priorities on becoming head of the Department of Treasury was to ensure the establishment of a national bank. He believed that such a bank could serve as a depository for federal taxes and a source of easily accessible government loans and would, thereby, aid the federal government in conducting its constitutionally granted powers of collecting taxes, borrowing money, regulating commerce, and raising and supporting a navy and army. In December 1790, Hamilton presented Congress with a report calling for a quasi-public bank modeled after the bank of England. The bank would be run by private individuals, with a few positions on the governing board reserved for appointed government officials, and it would be empowered to issue paper money redeemable for gold and silver coins.

In spite of James Madison's ardent opposition on the House floor, Congress overwhelmingly passed a bill to charter a bank. By the time the bank bill made it to Washington's desk, however, it faced intense opposition from within the administration itself. Secretary of State Thomas Jefferson and Attorney General Edmund Randolph both presented Washington with lengthy manifestos challenging the constitutionality of a national bank. Although Washington was disposed to comply with the wishes of Congress, the intense opposition in his own cabinet caused him to waiver. Over the course of two days, Hamilton worked furiously on a rebuttal, which he promptly presented to Washington on February 23, 1791.

The Secretary of the Treasury having perused with attention the papers containing the opinions of the Secretary of State and Attorney General concerning the constitutionality of the bill for establishing a National Bank proceeds according to the order of the President to submit the reasons which have induced him to entertain a different opinion.

It will naturally have been anticipated that, in performing this task he would feel uncommon solicitude. Personal considerations alone arising from the reflection that the measure originated with him would be sufficient to produce it: The sense which he has manifested of the great importance of such an institution to the successful administration of the department under his particular care; and an expectation of serious ill consequences to result from a failure of the measure, do not permit him to be without anxiety on public accounts. But the chief solicitude arises from a firm persuasion, that principles of construction like those espoused by the Secretary of State and the Attorney General would be fatal to the just & indispensible authority of the United States.[1]

In entering upon the argument it ought to be premised, that the objections of the Secretary of State and Attorney General are founded on a general denial of the authority of the United States to erect corporations. . .

Now it appears to the Secretary of the Treasury, that this *general principle* is *inherent* in the very *definition* of *Government* and *essential* to every step of the progress to be made by that of the United States; namely—that every power vested in a Government is in its nature *sovereign*, and includes by *force* of the *term*, a right to employ all the *means* requisite, and fairly *applicable* to the attainment of the *ends* of such power; and which are not precluded by restrictions & exceptions specified in the constitution; or not immoral, or not contrary to the essential ends of political society.[2]

This principle in its application to Government in general would be admitted as an axiom. And it will be incumbent upon those, who may incline to deny it, to *prove* a distinction; and to shew that a rule which in the general system of things is essential to the preservation of the social order is inapplicable to the United States.

The circumstances that the powers of sovereignty are in this country divided between the National and State Governments, does not afford the distinction required. It does not follow from this, that each of the *portions* of powers delegated to the one or to the other is not sovereign *with regard to its proper objects*. It will only *follow* from it, that each has sovereign power as to *certain things*, and not as to *other things*.[3] To deny that the Government of the United States has sovereign power as to its declared purposes & trusts, because its power does not extend to all cases, would be equally to deny, that the State Governments have sovereign power in any case; because

[1] Hamilton explains that he desires to defend the bank against the charges levied by Secretary of State Thomas Jefferson and Attorney General Edmund Randolph, not only because of his authorship of the bank and his belief that it would contribute to the successful administration of the Treasury department but also because of his firm conviction that the logic of Jefferson's argument would fatally fetter the exercise of federal power. Thus, whereas Jefferson and other opponents believed that approval of the bank would lead to the unconstrained abuse of power, Hamilton believed that denying the federal government the authority to create a bank would inhibit its ability to effectually carry out its delegated powers.

[2] In response to Jefferson's claim that the Constitution does not grant the federal government the power to charter a bank, or any kind of corporation, Hamilton appeals to the fundamental character of the government itself. Inherent in the nature of the government, Hamilton argues, is the idea that it possesses sovereignty over the objects entrusted to its care and correspondingly possesses the right to exercise requisite means for the attainment of those objects. Although Hamilton, thus, infers that the federal government possesses power beyond those explicitly enumerated in the Constitution, he is careful to clarify here that he does not argue for the unlimited exercise of federal power as Jefferson fears. On the contrary, he explains that both the Constitution and universal principles of morality and justice limit not only the objects of the state's authority but also the means that can be used for attaining those ends. The Constitution and the Bill of Rights explicitly forbid certain means (e.g., the passage of the ex post facto laws or the infringement of freedom of press), and the essential objectives of political society (i.e., the protection of life, liberty, and property and the promotion of public happiness) forbid others.

Hamilton explains that division of sovereignty between the state governments and the federal government means only that each level of government is limited in its sovereignty to the objects entrusted to its care. His opponents' argument that the division of state and federal authority prohibits federal sovereignty over necessary or useful means is a fallacy rooted in the illogical belief that political society can exist without power or that a people can be governed without a ruling authority.

4 After concluding that the power to erect corporations is a logical implication of the constitutional responsibilities granted to the federal government, Hamilton proceeds to examine the specific arguments Jefferson and others make in opposition to such power.

5 Appealing to the Tenth Amendment, Jefferson had argued that since the power to erect corporations was not explicitly delegated in the Constitution it fell outside the scope of federal authority. While Hamilton concedes that the only legitimate powers are those delegated by the people, he contends that the nature and scope of delegated powers are open to rational deliberation, guided by the general theory and purposes of government.

6 In response to the fact that the Constitution does not explicitly mention the power to erect a bank, Hamilton emphasizes the generally accepted notion that *implied* powers are inherent in the idea of *express* powers. In other words, if the government is given certain *expressed* duties, it logically possesses the *implied* authority to engage in means necessary for carrying out those duties. This notion, he later explains, is incorporated in Article I, Section 8, Clause 18, of the Constitution, which reads, "The Congress shall have Power . . . To make all Laws which shall be necessary and proper for carrying into Execution the foregoing Powers, and all other Powers vested by this Constitution in the Government of the United States, or in any Department or Officer thereof." Interestingly, even James Madison, one of Jefferson's strongest allies in his

their power does not extend to every case. The tenth section of the first article of the constitution exhibits a long list of very important things which they may not do. And thus the United States would furnish the singular spectacle of a *political society* without *sovereignty*, or of a people *governed* without *government* . . .

Here then as far as concerns the reasonings of the Secretary of State & the Attorney General, the affirmative of the constitutionality of the bill might be permitted to rest. It will occur to the President that the principle here advanced has been untouched by either of them.

For a more complete elucidation of the point nevertheless, the arguments which they have used against the power of the government to erect corporations, however foreign they are to the great & fundamental rule which has been stated, shall be particularly examined.4 And after shewing that they do not tend to impair its force, it shall also be shewn, that the power of incorporation incident to the government in certain cases, does fairly extend to the particular case which is the object of the bill.

The first of these arguments is, that the foundation of the constitution is laid on this ground "that all powers not delegated to the United States by the Constitution nor prohibited to it by the States are reserved to the States or to the people," whence it is meant to be inferred, that congress can in no case exercise any power not included in those enumerated in the constitution. And it is affirmed that the power of erecting a corporation is not included in any of the enumerated powers.

The main proposition here laid down, in its true signification is not to be questioned. It is nothing more than a consequence of this republican maxim, that all government is a delegation of power. But how much is delegated in each case, is a question of fact to be made out by fair reasoning & construction upon the particular provisions of the constitution—taking as guides the general principles & general ends of government.5

It is not denied, that there are *implied*, as well as *express* powers, and that the former are as effectually delegated as the latter. . .6

Then it follows, that as a power of erecting a corporation may as well be *implied* as any other thing; it may as well be employed as an *instrument* or *mean* of carrying into execution any of the specified powers, as any other instrument or mean whatever. The only question must be, in this as in every other case, whether the mean to be employed, or in this instance the corporation to be erected, has a natural relation to any of the acknowledged objects or lawful ends of the government.[7] Thus a corporation may not be erected by congress, for superintending the police of the city of Philadelphia because they are not authorised to *regulate* the *police* of that city; but one may be erected in relation to the collection of the taxes, or to the trade with foreign countries, or to the trade between the States, or with the Indian Tribes, because it is the province of the fœderal government to regulate those objects & because it is incident to a general *sovereign* or *legislative power* to *regulate* a thing, to employ all the means which relate to its regulation to the *best* & *greatest advantage*.

A strange fallacy seems to have crept into the manner of thinking & reasoning upon the subject. Imagination appears to have been unusually busy concerning it. An incorporation seems to have been regarded as some great, independent, substantive thing—as a political end of peculiar magnitude & moment; whereas it is truly to be considered as a *quality, capacity,* or *mean* to an end.[8] Thus a mercantile company is formed with a certain capital for the purpose of carrying on a particular branch of business. Here the business to be prosecuted is the *end*; the association in order to form the requisite capital is the primary mean. Suppose that an incorporation were added to this; it would only be to add a new *quality* to that association; to give it an artificial capacity by which it would be enabled to prosecute the business with more safety & convenience. . .

To this mode of reasoning respecting the right of employing all the means requisite to the execution of the specified powers of the Government, it is objected that none but *necessary* & proper means are to be employed, & the Secretary of State maintains, that no means are to be considered as *necessary*, but those without which the grant of the power would be *nugatory*. Nay so far does he go in his restrictive interpretation of the word, as even to make the case of *necessity* which shall warrant the constitutional exercise of the power to depend on *casual* & *temporary* circumstances, an idea which alone refutes the construction. The *expediency* of exercising a particular power, at a particular time, must indeed depend on *circumstances;* but the constitutional right of exercising it must be uniform & invariable—the same today, as tomorrow.[9]

fight against the bank, had earlier argued in favor of this notion of implied powers in *The Federalist.*

[7] If *implied* powers are delegated to the federal government as a way of executing *express* powers, then the question, according to Hamilton, should not be whether or not Congress has the power to create a corporation in the first place. Instead, it should be whether or not the corporation in question is an appropriate means for carrying out the legitimate objects of the government. Thus, he clarifies that the power to create a corporation might be constitutionally legitimate in one instance but not in another. For example, Congress would be within the scope of its enumerated powers if it formed a corporation related to tax collection or trade but would act outside of its constitutional authority if it formed a corporation to regulate the Philadelphia police.

[8] Here Hamilton argues that Jefferson and other opponents of the bank mistakenly view the bank as a substantive end in and of itself. In reality, corporations are merely instruments for achieving a higher objective. In this case, the bank is a useful tool for executing constitutionally delegated ends, such as raising revenue, borrowing money, and regulating commerce.

[9] Hamilton next addresses Jefferson's interpretation of the necessary and proper clause. According to Jefferson, the necessary and, therefore, legitimate powers of the federal government would fluctuate depending on particular situations or temporary circumstances. Jefferson argued that even if banks were an indispensable means of executing delegated powers, the creation of a national bank would not be "necessary" or constitutional since state banks could provide the same services. Hamilton criticizes this view for reducing constitutional principles, which ought to be "uniform and invariable," to variable questions of expediency. Hamilton concludes that although the judgment of which powers to exercise depends on the present circumstances, the "constitutional right" of exercising such powers "must be . . . the same today as tomorrow."

All the arguments therefore against the constitutionality of the bill derived from the accidental existence of certain State-banks: institutions which *happen* to exist today, & for ought that concerns the government of the United States, may disappear tomorrow, must not only be rejected as fallacious, but must be viewed as demonstrative, that there is a *radical* source of error in the reasoning.

It is essential to the being of the National government, that so erroneous a conception of the meaning of the word *necessary*, should be exploded.

It is certain, that neither the grammatical, nor popular sense of the term requires that construction. According to both, *necessary* often means no more than *needful, requisite, incidental, useful,* or *conducive to*.[10] It is a common mode of expression to say, that it is *necessary* for a government or a person to do this or that thing, when nothing more is intended or understood, than that the interests of the government or person require, or will be promoted, by the doing of this or that thing. The imagination can be at no loss for exemplifications of the use of the word in this sense.

And it is the true one in which it is to be understood as used in the constitution. The whole turn of the clause containing it, indicates, that it was the intent of the convention, by that clause to give a liberal latitude to the exercise of the specified powers. The expressions have peculiar comprehensiveness. They are—"to make *all laws*, necessary & proper for *carrying into execution* the foregoing powers & all *other powers* vested by the constitution in the *government* of the United States, or in any *department* or *officer* thereof." To understand the word as the Secretary of State does, would be to depart from its obvious & popular sense, and to give it a *restrictive* operation; an idea never before entertained. It would be to give it the same force as if the word *absolutely* or *indispensibly* had been prefixed to it.

Such a construction would beget endless uncertainty & embarassment. The cases must be palpable & extreme in which it could be pronounced with certainty, that a measure was absolutely necessary, or one without which the exercise of a given power would be nugatory.[11] There are few measures of any government, which would stand so severe a test. To insist upon it, would be to make the criterion of the exercise of any implied power a *case of extreme necessity*; which is rather a rule to justify the overleaping of the bounds of constitutional authority, than to govern the ordinary exercise of it.

[10] Hamilton further explains that Jefferson's strict interpretation of the "necessary and proper" clause as meaning absolutely or indispensably necessary is inconsistent with the popular and grammatical sense of the clause, which has always been understood to mean "needful, requisite, incidental, useful, or conducive to."

[11] Hamilton argues that Jefferson's interpretation of what is "necessary and proper" would paralyze and embarrass the federal government in the execution of its responsibilities, as there would be few instances in which an action could be proven indispensable.

It may be truly said of every government, as well as of that of the United States, that it has only a right, to pass such laws as are necessary & proper to accomplish the objects intrusted to it. For no government has a right to do *merely what it pleases*. Hence by a process of reasoning similar to that of the Secretary of State, it might be proved, that neither of the State governments has a right to incorporate a bank.[12] It might be shewn, that all the public business of the State, could be performed without a bank, and inferring thence that it was unnecessary it might be argued that it could not be done, because it is against the rule which has been just mentioned. A like mode of reasoning would prove, that there was no power to incorporate the Inhabitants of a town, with a view to a more perfect police: For it is certain, that an incorporation may be dispensed with, though it is better to have one. It is to be remembered, that there is no *express* power in any State constitution to erect corporations.

The *degree* in which a measure is necessary, can never be a test of the *legal* right to adopt it. That must ever be a matter of opinion; and can only be a test of expediency. The *relation* between the *measure* and the *end*, between the *nature* of *the mean* employed towards the execution of a power and the object of that power, must be the criterion of constitutionality not the more or less of *necessity* or *utility*.

The practice of the government is against the rule of construction advocated by the Secretary of State. Of this the act concerning light houses, beacons, buoys & public piers, is a decisive example.[13] This doubtless must be referred to the power of regulating trade, and is fairly relative to it. But it cannot be affirmed, that the exercise of that power, in this instance, was strictly necessary; or that the power itself would be *nugatory* without that of regulating establishments of this nature.

This restrictive interpretation of the word *necessary* is also contrary to this sound maxim of construction namely, that the powers contained in a constitution of government, especially those which concern the general administration of the affairs of a country, its finances, trade, defence &c ought to be construed liberally, in advancement of the public good. This rule does not depend on the particular form of a government or on the particular demarkation of the boundaries of its powers, but on the nature and objects of government itself.[14] The means by which national exigencies are to be provided for, national inconveniencies obviated, national prosperity promoted, are of such

[12] Hamilton points out that, according to Jefferson's rationale, many of the powers currently exercised by the state governments, such as the establishment of state banks, could be challenged as illegitimate. Ultimately, if taken to its logical conclusion, Jefferson's reasoning could be used to deprive all levels of government of any sovereignty whatsoever.

[13] Hamilton points to the current construction of lighthouses, beacons, buoys, and piers to illustrate the flaws in Jefferson's reasoning. While such objects were not, strictly, absolutely necessary, they were constitutionally justified by the fact that were useful for the regulation of trade and the collection of federal customs.

[14] An overly "restrictive interpretation of the word necessary" violates the sound maxim that governments must be empowered to meet their obligations. A government that lacks the ability to respond with discretion to the various unknown exigencies, challenges, and emergencies it will inevitably face is one that cannot fulfill its purpose. In this sense, the federal government must be entrusted with the means necessary to oversee the affairs of the nation as a whole—such as its finances, trade, and defense.

infinite variety, extent and complexity, that there must, of necessity, be great latitude of discretion in the selection & application of those means. Hence consequently, the necessity & propriety of exercising the authorities intrusted to a government on principles of liberal construction. . .

[15] Hamilton concludes his defense of implied powers by reiterating that he does not advocate unlimited sovereignty but only that the federal government remain sovereign over the specific objects entrusted to its care.

But the doctrine which is contended for is not chargeable with the consequence imputed to it. It does not affirm that the National government is sovereign in all respects, but that it is sovereign to a certain extent: that is, to the extent of the objects of its specified powers.[15]

It leaves therefore a criterion of what is constitutional, and of what is not so. This criterion is the *end* to which the measure relates as a *mean*. If the end be clearly comprehended within any of the specified powers, & if the measure have an obvious relation to that end, and is not forbidden by any particular provision of the constitution—it may safely be deemed to come within the compass of the national authority. There is also this further criterion which may materially assist the decision. Does the proposed measure abridge a preexisting right of any State, or of any individual? If it does not, there is a strong presumption in favour of its constitutionality; & slighter relations to any declared object of the constitution may be permitted to turn the scale.

The general objections which are to be inferred from the reasonings of the Secretary of State and of the Attorney General to the doctrine which has been advanced, have been stated and it is hoped satisfactorily answered.

CONCLUSION

In the end, Hamilton's *Report on the Constitutionality of a Bank* served its intended effect. Washington, sufficiently convinced by Hamilton's defense, signed the bank bill into law the next day. Years later, Hamilton's arguments inspired John Marshall's famous defense of the bank in the well-known case of *McCulloch v. Maryland* (1819). Furthermore, both Madison and Jefferson, in spite of their fervent opposition to the establishment of the bank, eventually accepted the bank's existence during their own presidencies. Madison even signed a bill chartering the Second Bank of the United States when the original charter expired.

Source: George Washington Papers, Library of Congress.

Report of the Secretary of the Treasury on the Subject of Manufactures

December 5, 1791

INTRODUCTION

Early in Washington's first administration, the House of Representatives asked Hamilton to advise Congress on the state of America's manufacturing capability. Thus, in addition to his other responsibilities, Hamilton spent his first two years as Treasury secretary studying the current status of manufacturing in the states. Finally, in early December 1791, Hamilton submitted the *Report on the Subject of Manufactures* to Congress. Deviating somewhat from Hamilton's general advocacy of free markets, based on a strict enforcement of contracts and property rights, his report called for government encouragement of domestic manufacturing through protective duties and government subsidies.

The Secretary of the Treasury in obedience to the order of the House of Representatives, of the 15th day of January 1790, has applied his attention, at as early a period as his other duties would permit, to the subject of Manufactures; and particularly to the means of promoting such as will tend to render the United States, independent on foreign nations, for military and other essential supplies.[1] And he there[fore] respectfully submits the following Report.

The expediency of encouraging manufactures in the United States, which was not long since deemed very questionable, appears at this time to be pretty generally admitted. . . . There still are, nevertheless, respectable patrons of opinions, unfriendly to the encouragement of manufactures. The following are, substantially, the arguments, by which these opinions are defended.[2]

"In every country (say those who entertain them) Agriculture is the most beneficial and *productive* object of human industry. This position, generally, if not universally true, applies with peculiar emphasis to the United States, on account of their immense tracts of fertile territory, uninhabited and unimproved. . ."

[1] Hamilton opens his report by identifying that the main objective of government support for domestic manufacturing is to promote the nation's long-term security and independence by reducing its reliance on foreign nations for "military and other essential supplies."

[2] Hamilton anticipates four major objections to government support for manufacturing, which he proceeds to summarize: first, that agriculture is more productive and beneficial than manufacturing; second, that government support for manufacturing amounts to an artificial and counterproductive interference in the economy; third, that the country's manufacturing needs are already supplied by European nations; and fourth, that government support of manufacturing introduces a favoritism for particular classes.

"To endeavor by the extraordinary patronage of Government, to accelerate the growth of manufactures, is in fact, to endeavor, by force and art, to transfer the natural current of industry, from a more, to a less beneficial channel. . ."

"This policy is not only recommended to the United States, by considerations which affect all nations, it is, in a manner, dictated to them by the imperious force of a very peculiar situation . . . the prospect of a successful competition with the manufactures of Europe must be regarded as little less than desperate. . ."

"If contrary to the natural course of things, an unseasonable and premature spring can be given to certain fabrics, by heavy duties, prohibitions, bounties, or by other forced expedients; this will only be to sacrifice the interests of the community to those of particular classes. . ."

In order to [obtain] an accurate judgement how far that which has been just stated ought to be deemed liable to a similar imputation, it is necessary to advert carefully to the considerations, which plead in favour of manufactures, and which appear to recommend the special and positive encouragement of them; in certain cases, and under certain reasonable limitations.[3]

It ought readily to be conceded, that the cultivation of the earth—as the primary and most certain source of national supply—as the immediate and chief source of subsistence to man—as the principal source of those materials which constitute the nutriment of other kinds of labor—as including a state most favourable to the freedom and independence of the human mind—one, perhaps, most conducive to the multiplication of the human species—has *intrinsically a strong claim to pre-eminence over every other kind of industry.*

But, that it has a title to anything like an exclusive predilection, in any country, ought to be admitted with great caution.[4] That it is even more productive than every other branch of Industry requires more evidence, than has yet been given in support of the position. That its real interests, precious and important as without the help of exaggeration, they truly are, will be advanced, rather than injured by the due encouragement of manufactures, may, it is believed, be satisfactorily demonstrated. And it is also believed that the expediency of such

3 Hamilton says he will examine the validity of these objections in his effort to demonstrate why government support of manufacturing "in certain cases and under reasonable limitations" will benefit the nation as a whole.

4 After conceding the importance of a strong system of agriculture, Hamilton denies that agriculture should be exclusively preferred to other productive pursuits. In what follows, he highlights the interdependence of agriculture and manufacturing and the benefits of a diverse economy.

encouragement in a general view may be shewn to be recommended by the most cogent and persuasive motives of national policy. . .

It is now proper to proceed a step further, and to enumerate the principal circumstances, from which it may be inferred—That manufacturing establishments not only occasion a possitive augmentation of the Produce and Revenue of the Society, but that they contribute essentially to rendering them greater than they could possibly be, without such establishments.[5] These circumstances are—

1. The division of Labour.
2. An extension of the use of Machinery.
3. Additional employment to classes of the community not ordinarily engaged in the business.
4. The promoting of emigration from foreign Countries.
5. The furnishing greater scope for the diversity of talents and dispositions which discriminate men from each other.
6. The affording a more ample and various field for enterprize.
7. The creating in some instances a new, and securing in all, a more certain and steady demand for the surplus produce of the soil.

Each of these circumstances has a considerable influence upon the total mass of industrious effort in a community. Together, they add to it a degree of energy and effect, which are not easily conceived. Some comments upon each of them, in the order in which they have been stated, may serve to explain their importance.

I. As to the Division of Labour.[6]

It has justly been observed, that there is scarcely any thing of greater moment in the economy of a nation, than the proper division of labour. The seperation of occupations causes each to be carried to a much greater perfection, than it could possible acquire, if they were blended. This arises principally from three circumstances.

1st—The greater skill and dexterity naturally resulting from a constant and undivided application to a single object. . .

2nd. The economy of time—by avoiding the loss of it, incident to a frequent transition from one operation to another of a different nature. . .

[5] Hamilton contends that the growth of manufacturing will increase, rather than detract from, agricultural productivity. He then lists seven reasons why industrial development would contribute to growth in the economy as a whole.

[6] Hamilton first argues that manufacturing contributes to productivity by allowing a greater concentration of skill. Individuals are able to focus their talents and energies more efficiently in a single pursuit than when they are engaged in several, dissimilar operations. This efficiency is enhanced by the development and use of machinery.

3rd. An extension of the use of Machinery. . .

And from these causes united, the mere separation of the occupation of the cultivator, from that of the Artificer, has the effect of augmenting the *productive powers* of labour, and with them, the total mass of the produce or revenue of a Country. . .

II. As to an extension of the use of Machinery a point which though partly anticipated requires to be placed in one or two additional lights.[7]

The employment of Machinery forms an item of great importance in the general mass of national industry. 'Tis an artificial force brought in aid of the natural force of man; and, to all the purposes of labour, is an increase of hands; an accession of strength, *unincumbered too by the expence of maintaining the laborer* . . .

III. As to the additional employment of classes of the community, not ordinarily engaged in the particular business.[8]

This is not among the least valuable of the means, by which manufacturing institutions contribute to augment the general stock of industry and production. In places where those institutions prevail, besides the persons regularly engaged in them, they afford occasional and extra employment to industrious individuals and families, who are willing to devote the leisure resulting from the intermissions of their ordinary pursuits to collateral labours, as a resource of multiplying their acquisitions or enjoyments. The husbandman himself experiences a new source of profit and support from the encreased industry of his wife and daughters; invited and stimulated by the demands of the neighboring manufactories. . .

Besides this advantage of occasional employment to classes having different occupations, there is another of a nature allied to it of a similar tendency. This is—the employment of persons who would otherwise be idle (and in many cases a burthen on the community), either from the byass of temper, habit, infirmity of body, or some other cause, indisposing, or disqualifying them for the toils of the Country. . .

IV. As to the promoting of emigration from foreign Countries.[9] Men reluctantly quit one course of occupation and livelihood for another,

[7] Hamilton next argues that machines increase the availability and cost-effectiveness of physical labor by adding artificial productivity to the natural productivity of human labor.

[8] Hamilton reasons that manufacturing will provide greater access to productive pursuits for those currently unengaged in business—namely women, children, vagabonds, and the indigent. Not anticipating the abuse of child labor that would later occur at the height of industrialization, Hamilton is perhaps contemplating how important employment at a young age had been to his own success.

[9] American political and economic freedom, along with the employment opportunities created by manufacturing, would encourage large-scale immigration.

unless invited to it by very apparent and proximate advantages. Many, who would go from one country to another, if they had a prospect of continuing with more benefit the callings, to which they have been educated, will often not be tempted to change their situation, by the hope of doing better, in some other way. Manufacturers, who listening to the powerful invitations of a better price for their fabrics, or their labour, of greater cheapness of provisions and raw materials, of an exemption from the chief part of the taxes burthens and restraints, which they endure in the old world, of greater personal independence and consequence, under the operation of a more equal government, and of what is far more precious than mere religious toleration—a perfect equality of religious privileges; would probably flock from Europe to the United States to pursue their own trades or professions, if they were once made sensible of the advantages they would enjoy, and were inspired with an assurance of encouragement and employment, will, with difficulty, be induced to transplant themselves, with a view to becoming Cultivators of Land. . .

V. As to the furnishing greater scope for the diversity of talents and dispositions, which discriminate men from each other. . .[10]

It is a just observation, that minds of the strongest and most active powers for their proper objects fall below mediocrity and labour without effect, if confined to uncongenial pursuits. And it is thence to be inferred, that the results of human exertion may be immensely increased by diversifying its objects. When all the different kinds of industry obtain in a community, each individual can find his proper element, and can call into activity the whole vigour of his nature. And the community is benefitted by the services of its respective members, in the manner, in which each can serve it with most effect. . .

VI. As to the affording a more ample and various field for enterprise. . .[11]

To cherish and stimulate the activity of the human mind, by multiplying the objects of enterprise, is not among the least considerable of the expedients, by which the wealth of a nation may be promoted. Even things in themselves not positively advantageous, sometimes become so, by their tendency to provoke exertion. Every new scene, which is opened to the busy nature of man to rouse and exert itself, is the addition of a new energy to the general stock of effort. . .

[10] A diversified economy would multiply the arts and occupations in which individuals could usefully employ their skills, thereby producing a more opportunistic and efficient marketplace.

[11] The increased objects of enterprise and greater opportunity in a diverse economy would also expand human capacity by stimulating entrepreneurship.

VII. As to the creating, in some instances, a new, and securing in all a more certain and steady demand, for the surplus produce of the soil. . .[12]

This is among the most important of the circumstances which have been indicated. It is a principal mean, by which the establishment of manufactures contributes to an augmentation of the produce or revenue of a country, and has an immediate and direct relation to the prosperity of Agriculture. . .

Previously to a further discussion of the objections to the encouragement of manufactures which have been stated, it will be of use to see what can be said, in reference to the particular situation of the United States, against the conclusions appearing to result from what has been already offered. . .

If the system of perfect liberty to industry and commerce were the prevailing system of nations—the arguments which dissuade a country in the predicament of the United States, from the zealous pursuits of manufactures would doubtless have great force. . . . But the system which has been mentioned, is far from characterising the general policy of Nations.[13]

The consequence of it is, that the United States are to a certain extent in the situation of a country precluded from foreign Commerce. They can indeed, without difficulty obtain from abroad the manufactured supplies, of which they are in want; but they experience numerous and very injurious impediments to the emission and vent of their own commodities. Nor is this the case in reference to a single foreign nation only. The regulations of several countries, with which we have the most extensive intercourse, throw serious obstructions in the way of the principal staples of the United States.

In such a position of things, the United States cannot exchange with Europe on equal terms; and the want of reciprocity would render them the victim of a system, which should induce them to confine their views to Agriculture and refrain from Manufactures. . .

The remaining objections to a particular encouragement of manufactures in the United States now require to be examined.

13 Hamilton contends that European nations have stunted the growth of manufacturing by imposing "numerous and very injurious impediments" on the sale of American commodities. Consequently, government assistance is necessary to invigorate American manufacturing and make it more competitive.

One of these turns on the proposition, that Industry, if left to itself, will naturally find its way to the most useful and profitable employment: whence it is inferred, that manufactures without the aid of government will grow up as soon and as fast, as the natural state of things and the interest of the community may require.[14]

Against the solidity of this hypothesis, in the full latitude of the terms, very cogent reasons may be offered. These have relation to—the strong influence of habit and the spirit of imitation—the fear of want of success in untried enterprises—the intrinsic difficulties incident to first essays towards a competition with those who have previously attained to perfection in the business to be attempted—the bounties premiums and other artificial encouragements, with which foreign nations second the exertions of their own Citizens in the branches, in which they are to be rivalled.

Experience teaches, that men are often so much governed by what they are accustomed to see and practice, that the simplest and most obvious improvements, in the [most] ordinary occupations, are adopted with hesitation, reluctance and by slow gradations. The spontaneous transition to new pursuits, in a community long habituated to different ones, may be expected to be attended with proportionably greater difficulty.[15] When former occupations ceased to yield a profit adequate to the subsistence of their followers, or when there was an absolute deficiency of employment in them, owing to the superabundance of hands, changes would ensue; but these changes would be likely to be more tardy than might consist with the interest either of individuals or of the Society. In many cases they would not happen, while a bare support could be ensured by an adherence to ancient courses; though a resort to a more profitable employment might be practicable. To produce the desireable changes, as early as may be expedient, may therefore require the incitement and patronage of government.

The apprehension of failing in new attempts is perhaps a more serious impediment.[16] There are dispositions apt to be attracted by the mere novelty of an undertaking—but these are not always those best calculated to give it success. To this, it is of importance that the confidence of cautious sagacious capitalists both citizens and foreigners, should be excited. And to inspire this description of persons with confidence, it is essential, that they should be made to see in any

[14] Although Hamilton identifies himself as a supporter of free markets, he lists several reasons why private interest alone cannot be relied on to promote the initial development of domestic manufacturing.

[15] First, Hamilton argues that ingrained habits often deter individuals from seeking more profitable means of employment and, thus, are an impediment to developing new means of production. Government can spur changes in habitual modes of occupation by increasing the financial attraction and lessening the risk of engaging in new enterprises.

[16] Second, Hamilton argues that the spontaneous development of manufacturing is hindered by the risk of engaging in new enterprises. Individuals frequently remain in a less-profitable occupation to avoid the possibility of failure in a new one.

project, which is new, and for that reason alone, if, for no other, precarious, the prospect of such a degree of countenance and support from government, as may be capable of overcoming the obstacles, inseperable from first experiments.

The superiority antecedently enjoyed by nations, who have preoccupied and perfected a branch of industry, constitutes a more formidable obstacle, than either of those, which have been mentioned, to the introduction of the same branch into a country, in which it did not before exist.[17] To maintain between the recent establishments of one country and the long matured establishments of another country, a competition upon equal terms, both as to quality and price, is in most cases impracticable. The disparity in the one, or in the other, or in both, must necessarily be so considerable as to forbid a successful rivalship, without the extraordinary aid and protection of government.

But the greatest obstacle of all to the successful prosecution of a new branch of industry in a country, in which it was before unknown, consists, as far as the instances apply, in the bounties premiums and other aids which are granted, in a variety of cases, by the nations, in which the establishments to be imitated are previously introduced.[18] It is well known (and particular examples in the course of this report will be cited) that certain nations grant bounties on the exportation of particular commodities, to enable their own workmen to undersell and supplant all competitors, in the countries to which those commodities are sent. Hence the undertakers of a new manufacture have to contend not only with the natural disadvantages of a new undertaking, but with the gratuities and remunerations which other governments bestow. To be enabled to contend with success, it is evident, that the interference and aid of their own government are indispensible. . .

There remains to be noticed an objection to the encouragement of manufactures, of a nature different from those which question the probability of success. This is derived from its supposed tendency to give a monopoly of advantages to particular classes at the expence of the rest of the community, who, it is affirmed, would be able to procure the requisite supplies of manufactured articles on better terms from foreigners, than from our own Citizens, and who it is alledged, are reduced to a necessity of paying an enhanced price for whatever

[17] Third, Hamilton maintains that infant American manufacturers need assistance to reach the superior level of development in technology and practice that industries in other nations have already achieved.

[18] Finally, Hamilton contends that in order to compete successfully in the global market, American industries will need government support to counteract the bounties and tariffs liberally adopted by European nations to prop up their own industries.

they want, by every measure, which obstructs the free competition of foreign commodities.

It is not an unreasonable supposition, that measures, which serve to abridge the free competition of foreign Articles, have a tendency to occasion an enhancement of prices and it is not to be denied that such is the effect in a number of Cases; but the fact does not uniformly correspond with the theory.[19] A reduction of prices has in several instances immediately succeeded the establishment of a domestic manufacture. Whether it be that foreign Manufacturers endeavour to supplant by underselling our own, or whatever else be the cause, the effect has been such as is stated, and the reverse of what might have been expected.

But though it were true, that the immediate and certain effect of regulations controuling the competition of foreign with domestic fabrics was an increase of price, it is universally true, that the contrary is the ultimate effect with every successful manufacture. When a domestic manufacture has attained to perfection, and has engaged in the prosecution of it a competent number of Persons, it invariably becomes cheaper. Being free from the heavy charges, which attend the importation of foreign commodities, it can be afforded, and accordingly seldom or never fails to be sold Cheaper, in process of time, than was the foreign Article for which it is a substitute. The internal competition, which takes place, soon does away everything like Monopoly, and by degrees reduces the price of the Article to the *minimum* of a reasonable profit on the Capital employed. This accords with the reason of the thing and with experience. . .

It is not uncommon to meet with an opinion that though the promoting of manufactures may be the interest of a part of the Union, it is contrary to that of another part. The Northern & southern regions are sometimes represented as having adverse interests in this respect. Those are called Manufacturing, these Agricultural states; and a species of opposition is imagined to subsist between the Manufacturing and Agricultural interests. . .

Ideas of a contrariety of interests between the Northern and southern regions of the Union, are in the Main as unfounded as they are mischievous. The diversity of Circumstances on which such

[19] Hamilton responds to the charge that government support of manufacturing would benefit particular classes of the community at the expense of others by arguing that promotion of domestic manufacturing would increase internal competition, which would eventually cause the price of commodities to drop.

[20] Hamilton likewise responds to the assertion that his plan would benefit the North at the expense of the South by denying that the two regions have completely unrelated economic interests. He once again emphasizes that the advancement of manufacturing creates new markets, which will inevitably improve the aggregate prosperity of those employed in agriculture.

[21] Hamilton admonishes appeals to regionalism for undermining the harmony, well-being, and prosperity of the union as a whole.

[22] Hamilton lists various regulations and incentives that might encourage the growth of the infant manufacturing industry in America.

[23] Hamilton emphasizes that financial incentives, or government bounties, are preferable to regulations or prohibitions against competing goods, which often lead to higher prices and scarcity. He concludes that moderate duties on foreign goods could finance government subsidies for domestic production.

contrariety is usually predicated, authorises a directly contrary conclusion. Mutual wants constitute one of the strongest links of political connection, and the extent of these bears a natural proportion to the diversity in the means of mutual supply.[20]

Suggestions of an opposite complexion are ever to be deplored, as unfriendly to the steady pursuit of one great common cause, and to the perfect harmony of all the parts. . .[21]

In order to a better judgment of the Means proper to be resorted to by the United states, it will be of use to Advert to those which have been employed with success in other Countries.[22] The principal of these are.

I   Protecting duties—or duties on those foreign articles which are the rivals of the domestic ones, intended to be encouraged. . .
II   Prohibitions of rival articles or duties equivalent to prohibitions. . .
III Prohibitions of the exportation of the materials of manufactures. . .
IV   Pecuniary bounties

This has been found one of the most efficacious means of encouraging manufactures, and it is in some views, the best. . .[23]

Its advantages, are these—

1 It is a species of encouragement more positive and direct than any other, and for that very reason, has a more immediate tendency to stimulate and uphold new enterprises, increasing the chances of profit, and diminishing the risks of loss, in the first attempts.
2. It avoids the inconvenience of a temporary augmentation of price, which is incident to some other modes, or it produces it to a less degree; either by making no addition to the charges on the rival foreign article, as in the Case of protecting duties, or by making a smaller addition. . .
3 Bounties have not like high protecting duties, a tendency to produce scarcity. . .
4. Bounties are sometimes not only the best, but the only proper expedient, for uniting the encouragement of a new object of agriculture, with that of a new object of manufacture. It is the Interest of the farmer to have the production of the raw material

promoted, by counteracting the interference of the foreign material of the same kind. . .

It cannot escape notice, that a duty upon the importation of an article can no[t] otherwise aid the domestic production of it, than giving the latter greater advantages in the home market. It can have no influence upon the advantageous sale of the article produced, in foreign markets; no tendency, therefore to promote its exportation.

The true way to conciliate these two interests, is to lay a duty on foreign *manufactures* of the material, the growth of which is desired to be encouraged, and to apply the produce of that duty by way of bounty, either upon the production of the material itself or upon its manufacture at home or upon both. . .

A Question has been made concerning the Constitutional right of the Government of the United States to apply this species of encouragement, but there is certainly no good foundation for such a question. The National Legislature has express authority "To lay and Collect taxes, duties, imposts and excises, to pay the debts and provide for the *Common defence* and *general welfare*" with no other qualifications than that "all duties, imposts and excises, shall be *uniform* throughout the United states, that no capitation or other direct tax shall be laid unless in proportion to numbers ascertained by a census or enumeration taken on the principles prescribed in the Constitution," and that "no tax or duty shall be laid on articles exported from any state."[24] These three qualifications excepted, the power to *raise money* is *plenary*, and *indefinite*; and the objects to which it may be *appropriated* are no less comprehensive, than the payment of the public debts and the providing for the common defence and "*general Welfare.*" The terms "*general Welfare*" were doubtless intended to signify more than was expressed or imported in those which Preceded; otherwise numerous exigencies incident to the affairs of a Nation would have been left without a provision. The phrase is as comprehensive as any that could have been used; because it was not fit that the constitutional authority of the Union, to appropriate its revenues shou'd have been restricted within narrower limits than the "General Welfare" and because this necessarily embraces a vast variety of particulars, which are susceptible neither of specification nor of definition.

[24] Hamilton concludes his argument by maintaining that Congress's constitutional authority to issue government bounties is derived from its mandate to "provide for the *Common defense* and *general welfare*." Furthermore, he asserts that although Congress's power to tax is explicitly restricted in a number of ways, its power to appropriate money is limited only in the sense that such appropriations must relate to one or more of Congress's enumerated powers and must promote a *general* rather than a parochial objective or interest.

Congress eventually adopted modest protective tariffs, but it never even considered Hamilton's proposals for government bounties. In the meantime, Hamilton helped found the government-subsidized Society for the Establishment of Useful Manufactures to promote manufacturing in New Jersey, but corruption and poor decision-making on behalf of the organization's politically appointed leadership eventually led to the organization's bankruptcy and closure in 1795.

In his assessment of Hamilton's report, Thomas G. West (2017) contends that government bounties and other state-sponsored privileges ultimately proved unnecessary for industrial development in America, illustrated by the fact that "the first successful large-scale manufacturing enterprise in America was established without government subsidy by a group of private investors, the Boston Associates, who set up profitable cotton mills in Lowell, Massachusetts, in the 1820s" (382). Nevertheless, as Karl-Friedrich Walling (2003) observes, Hamilton's funding system helped generate the capital necessary for the Industrial Revolution (179).

Nevertheless, although never fully adopted, the modest proposals contained in Hamilton's report increased Madison's and Jefferson's animosity toward him and his policies and further advanced the formation of the nation's first political parties.

Source: Original Reports of the Secretary of the Treasury, 1791–1792. *National Archives.*

SECTION VIII

The Rise and Fall of the Federalists

Letter to Edward Carrington on Political Adversaries

May 26, 1792

INTRODUCTION

By 1792, the conflict over the nation's fiscal and economic policies, between Jefferson and Madison on the one side and Hamilton on the other, gave way to full-scale political warfare. Hamilton and his allies donned the title Federalists, while Jefferson and Madison became de facto leaders of the Democratic-Republicans.

Earlier the previous year, Jefferson and Madison established the *National Gazette*, to oppose the pro-Hamilton stance of the *Gazette of the United States*, a paper Jefferson accused of "disseminating the doctrines of monarchy, aristocracy, and the exclusion of the influence of the people" (Chernow 2004, 396). Madison and Jefferson enlisted former poet laureate Philip Freneau to serve as editor of the *National Gazette* and secured him a foreign translator position at the state department to supplement his meager salary.

In early 1792, a financial credit crisis hit New York, caused in large part by the corrupt and reckless speculation of former assistant Treasury secretary William Duer. Hamilton, with the consent of bank trustees, quickly averted the crisis by purchasing large numbers of government securities with a fund established for such purposes. Nevertheless, Jefferson and Madison began using the *National Gazette* and other forms of communication to imply that Hamilton had corruptly used federal funds to protect speculators. As attacks on Hamilton's policies deteriorated into full-scale character assassination, Hamilton responded with a series of public and private essays. In a letter to an old Revolutionary War friend, Edward Carrington, Hamilton laments the alliance between his former political ally, James Madison, and Secretary of State Thomas Jefferson and harshly critiques the views and motives of his now openly hostile political adversaries.

My Dear Sir

Believing that I possess a share of your personal friendship and confidence and yielding to that which I feel towards you—persuaded also that our political creed is the same on *two essential points*, 1st the necessity of *Union* to the respectability and happiness of this Country and 2 the necessity of an *efficient* general government to maintain

[1] Hamilton opens his letter by identifying the twin tenets of his political creed: the belief that a firm union of states is necessary for the "respectability and happiness" of the country and the belief that an energetic central government is necessary to preserve such a union. In the remainder of the letter, he contends that Madison and Jefferson, in seeking to undermine his particular policies, are also undermining the principles of political action necessary to preserve the union.

[2] Hamilton explains that when he accepted the position of secretary of Treasury he had assumed that James Madison, his former political ally and colleague, would support and assist him. He was thus surprised and dismayed when Madison conspired with Jefferson to form a hostile faction that Hamilton argues will subvert the principles of good government and the nation's future peace and prosperity. In what follows, Hamilton critiques Madison and Jefferson's personal opposition and the logic of their political views.

[3] Hamilton argues that if the political principles informing Jefferson's opposition to federal funding of the national debt were universalized they would sap the national government of legitimate authority and impair the entire basis of the union.

[4] Hamilton accuses Jefferson of attempting to undermine his reputation and policies by spreading rumors at home and abroad about his private motives and conduct.

that Union[1]—I have concluded to unbosom myself to you on the present state of political parties and views. . .

When I accepted the Office, I now hold, it was under a full persuasion, that from similarity of thinking, conspiring with personal goodwill, I should have the firm support of Mr. Madison, in the *general course* of my administration. Aware of the intrinsic difficultties of the situation and of the powers of Mr. Madison, I do not believe I should have accepted under a different supposition. . .

It was not 'till the last session that I became unequivocally convinced of the following truth—"*That Mr. Madison cooperating with Mr. Jefferson is at the head of a faction decidedly hostile to me and my administration, and actuated by views in my judgment subversive of the principles of good government and dangerous to the union, peace and happiness of the Country. . .*"[2]

This conviction in my mind is the result of a long train of circumstances; many of them minute. To attempt to detail them all would fill a volume. I shall therefore confine myself to the mention of a few.

First—As to the point of opposition to me and my administration.

Mr. Jefferson with very little reserve manifests his dislike of the funding system generally; calling in question the expediency of funding a debt at all. . . . I do not mean, that he advocates directly the undoing of what has been done, but he censures the whole on principles, which if they should become general, could not but end in the subversion of the system.[3]

In various conversations with *foreigners* as well as citizens, he has thrown censure on my *principles* of government and on my measures of administration. . . . Some of those, whom he *immediately* and *notoriously* moves, have *even* whispered suspicions of the rectitude of my motives and conduct . . .[4] When any turn of things in the community has threatened either odium or embarrassment to me, he has not been able to suppress the satisfaction which it gave him.

A part of this is of course information, and might be misrepresentation. But it comes through so many channels and so well accords with what falls under my own observation that I can entertain no doubt.

I find a strong confirmation in the following circumstances. *Freneau* the present Printer of the National Gazette . . . was brought to Philadelphia by Mr. Jefferson to be the conductor of a News Paper. It is notorious that cotemporarily with the commencement of his paper he was a Clerk in the department of state for foreign languages. Hence a clear inference that his paper has been set on foot and is conducted under the patronage & not against the views of Mr. Jefferson. What then is the complexion of this paper? Let any impartial man peruse all the numbers down to the present day; and I never was more mistaken, if he does not pronounce that it is a paper devoted to the subversion of me & the measures in which I have had an Agency; and I am little less mistaken if he do not pronounce that it is a paper of a tendency *generally unfriendly* to the Government of the U States. . .[5]

With regard to Mr. Madison—the matter stands thus . . . I cannot persuade myself that Mr. Madison and I, whose politics had formerly so much the *same point of departure*, should now diverge so widely in our opinions of the measures which are proper to be pursued. The opinion I once entertained of the candour and simplicity and fairness of Mr. Madisons character has, I acknowledge, given way to a decided opinion that *it is one of a peculiarly artificial and complicated kind.* . .[6]

When the department of the Treasury was established Mr. Madison was an unequivocal advocate of the principles which prevailed in it and of the powers and duties which were assigned by it to the head of the department. This appeared both from his private and public discourses; and I will add, that I have personal evidence that Mr. Madison is as well convinced as any man in the U States of the necessity of the arrangement which characterizes that establishment to the orderly conducting of the business of the Finances.

Mr. Madison nevertheless opposed directly a reference to me to report *ways & means* for the Western expedition, & combatted *on principle* the propriety of such references.

He well knew, that, if he had prevailed, a certain consequence was, my *resignation*—that I would not be fool enough to make pecuniary sacrifices and endure a life of extreme drudgery without opportunity either to do material good or to acquire reputation; and frequently with a responsibility in reputation for measures in which I had no

[5] Hamilton classifies the *National Gazette* as a paper hostile to the general government and devoted to the opposition of Hamilton and his measures. He implies that Jefferson—in personally supporting the paper and providing its editor Philip Freneau with a paid position at the state department—was improperly working internally to subvert the very administration he currently served.

[6] Hamilton laments the fact that his former ally Madison, whom he greatly admired as a man of good character, was now allied with Jefferson in an effort to undermine the vitality of the national government.

7 As Treasury secretary, Hamilton often introduced legislative suggestions directly to Congress. Seeking to cut off Hamilton's close working relationship with Congress, Madison introduced a resolution that would require Hamilton to go through President Washington before making any requests of Congress for supplying federal troops on the Western frontiers. Hamilton argues that Madison knew full well that Hamilton would be unwilling to make the pecuniary sacrifices required of public office if he were not empowered to acquire his own reputation for promoting the public good. Thus, Madison was essentially raising a vote of no confidence in order to push Hamilton into retirement. To Madison's chagrin, the House narrowly rejected his resolution by a four-vote margin.

8 Unlike Jefferson, who openly challenged the legitimacy of laws passed for funding the national debt, Madison argued publically that he did not favor repealing any previously agreed to financial obligations. Hamilton points out, however, that in private conversation Madison had favored the claim made by Representative John Mercer that future generations were not required to fulfill the obligations of their predecessors.

hand, and in respect to which, the part I had acted, if any, could not be known. . .[7]

My overthrow was anticipated as certain and Mr. Madison, *laying aside his wonted caution*, boldly led his troops as he imagined to a certain victory. He was disappointed. Though, *late* I became apprized of the danger. Measures of counteraction were adopted, & when the Question was called, Mr. Madison was confounded to find characters voting against him, whom he had counted upon as certain. . .

Secondly As to the tendency of the views of the two Gentlemen who have been named.

Mr. Jefferson is an avowed enemy to a funded debt. Mr. Madison disavows in public any intention to *undo* what has been done; but in a private conversation with Mr. Charles Carroll (Senator) . . . he favoured the sentiment in Mr. Mercers speech that a Legislature had no right to *fund* the debt by mortgaging permanently the public revenues because they had no right to bind posterity. The inference is that what has been unlawfully done may be undone.[8]

The discourse of partizans in the Legislature & the publications in the party news-papers direct their main battery against the *principle* of a funded debt, & represent it in the most odious light as a perfect *Pandoras box* . . .

Whatever were the original merits of the funding system, after having been so solemly adopted, & after so great a transfer of property under it, what would become of the Government should it be reversed? What of the National Reputation? Upon what system of morality can so atrocious a doctrine be maintained? In me, I confess it excites *indignation* & *horror*!

What are we to think of those maxims of Government by which the power of a Legislature is denied to bind the Nation by a *Contract* in an affair of *property* for twenty four years? For this is precisely the case of the debt. What are to become of all the legal rights of property, of all charters to corporations, nay, of all grants to a man his heirs & assigns for ever, if this doctrine be true? What is the term for which a government is in capacity to *contract?* Questions might be multiplied without end to demonstrate the perniciousness & absurdity of such a doctrine.[9]

In almost all the questions great & small which have arisen, since the first session of Congress, Mr. Jefferson & Mr. Madison have been found among those who were disposed to narrow the Federal authority.[10] The question of a National Bank is one example. The question of bounties to the Fisheries is another. Mr. Madison resisted it on the ground of constitutionality, 'till it was evident, by the intermediate questions taken, that the bill would pass & he then under the wretched subterfuge of a change of a single word "bounty" for "allowance" went over to the Majority & voted for the bill. In the Militia bill & in a variety of minor cases he has leaned to abridging the exercise of foederal authority, & leaving as much as possible to the States & he has lost no opportunity of *sounding the alarm* with great affected solemnity at encroachments meditated on the rights of the States, & of holding up the bugbear of a faction in the Government having designs unfriendly to Liberty.

This kind of conduct has appeared to me the more extraordinary on the part of Mr. Madison as I know for a certainty it was a primary article in his Creed that the real danger in our system was the subversion of the National authority by the preponderancy of the State Governments.[11] All his measures have proceeded on an opposite supposition. . .

In respect to our foreign politics the views of these Gentlemen are in my judgment equally unsound & dangerous. *They have a womanish attachment to France and a womanish resentment against Great Britain.*[12] They would draw us into the closest embrace of the former & involve us in all the consequences of her politics, & they would risk the peace of the country in their endeavours to keep us at the greatest possible distance from the latter. This disposition goes to a length particularly in Mr. Jefferson of which, till lately, I had no adequate Idea. Various circumstances prove to me that if these Gentlemen were left to pursue their own course there would be in less than six months *an open War between the U States & Great Britain.*

I trust I have a due sense of the conduct of France towards this Country in the late Revolution, & that I shall always be among the foremost in making her every suitable return; but there is a wide

[9] Hamilton asks a series of questions to highlight the radical implications of the Jeffersonian view that the present generation has no authority to bind its posterity. Such a stance would undermine not only public faith in the nation's credit but also the just foundation for private property rights, in which legally binding titles to property are valid in perpetuity.

[10] Hamilton observes that, since the convening of the first Congress, Jefferson and Madison, as a matter of practice rather than true principle, had stood with those who sought to abridge federal authority.

[11] Hamilton points out that Madison's current opposition to federal authority is a direct reversal of his previous stance in *The Federalist,* in which he had emphasized that the real threat to the viability of union and good government would be the subversion of national authority by the states.

[12] Although his letter deals most directly with disagreements over domestic policy, Hamilton foreshadows conflicts pertaining to the hostilities between Britain and France. Hamilton argues that Madison and Jefferson had developed an affection for France and hatred for Britain proceeding more from the heart than the head. If not restrained, the inevitable conclusion of such irrational love and aversion would be full-scale war with Great Britain.

difference between this & implicating ourselves in all her politics; between bearing good will to her, & hating and wranggling with all those whom she hates. . .

Having now delineated to you what I conceive to be the true complexion of the politics of these Gentlemen, I will now attempt a solution of these strange appearances.

Mr. Jefferson, it is known, did not in the first instance cordially acquiesce in the new constitution for the U States; he had many doubts & reserves. He left this Country before we had experienced the imbicillities of the former.[13]

In France he saw government only on the side of its abuses. He drank deeply of the French Philosophy, in Religion, in Science, in politics. He came from France in the moment of a fermentation which he had had a share in exciting, & in the passions and feelings of which he shared both from temperament and situation.[14]

He came here probably with a too partial idea of his own powers, and with the expectation of a greater share in the direction of our councils than he has in reality enjoyed. I am not sure that he had not peculiarly marked out for himself the department of the Finances. . .[15]

Mr. Madison had always entertained an exalted opinion of the talents, knowledge and virtues of Mr. Jefferson. The sentiment was probably reciprocal. A close correspondence subsisted between them during the time of Mr. Jefferson's absence from this country. A close intimacy arose upon his return.

Whether any peculiar opinions of Mr. Jefferson concerning the public debt wrought a change in the sentiments of Mr. Madison . . . or whether Mr. Madison seduced by the expectation of popularity and possibly by the calculation of advantage to the state of Virginia was led to change his own opinion—certain it is, that a very material *change* took place, & that the two Gentlemen were united in the new ideas. . .[16]

Subsequent events have increased the Spirit of opposition and the feelings of personal mortification on the part of these Gentlemen.

[13] Hamilton attributes Jefferson's views in part to his ambition and in part to his personal experience. In 1784, Jefferson had traveled to France to serve on a diplomatic mission before he was able to personally observe or fully experience the failures of the trepid government under the Articles of Confederation. On the other hand, while in France, he had witnessed firsthand the abuses of an overly powerful, central authority. This experience fostered in Jefferson an irrational fear of the energetic government that Hamilton sought to promote.

[14] Furthermore, Jefferson, an ideologue with a zealous attachment to liberty, was personally moved by the revolutionary spirit taking over France, and his passions were thus drawn to the philosophy and outcome of the insurrection.

[15] Hamilton contends that Jefferson's opposition was motivated by both ideology and personal ambition. He even speculates that Jefferson might have sought for himself the position of Treasury secretary.

[16] Hamilton conjectures that Madison's ideological turnabout likely resulted from his high regard for Jefferson and his expectation that his new outlook would be more popular and politically advantageous in his home state of Virginia.

A mighty stand was made on the affair of the Bank. There was much *commitment* in that case. I prevailed.

On the Mint business I was opposed from the same Quarter, & with still less success. In the affair of ways & means for the Western expedition—on the supplementary arrangements concerning the debt except as to the additional assumption, my views have been equally prevalent in opposition to theirs. This current of success on one side & defeat on the other have rendered the Opposition furious, & have produced a disposition to subvert their Competitors even at the expence of the Government. . .[17]

A word on another point. I am told that serious apprehensions are disseminated in your state as to the existence of a Monarchical party meditating the destruction of State & Republican Government. If it is possible that so absurd an idea can gain ground it is necessary that it should be combatted. I assure you on my *private faith* and *honor* as a Man that there is not in my judgment a shadow of foundation of it. . .

As to the destruction of State Governments, the *great* and *real* anxiety is to be able to preserve the National from the too potent and counteracting influence of those Governments. As to my own political Creed, I give it to you with the utmost sincerity. I am *affectionately* attached to the Republican theory. I desire *above all things* to see the *equality* of political rights exclusive of all *hereditary* distinction firmly established by a practical demonstration of its being consistent with the order and happiness of society . . . but in candor I ought also to add that I am far from being without doubts. I consider its success as yet a problem.[18]

It is yet to be determined by experience whether it be consistent with that *stability* and *order* in Government which are essential to public strength & private security and happiness. On the whole, the only enemy which Republicanism has to fear in this Country is in the Spirit of faction and anarchy. If this will not permit the ends of Government to be attained under it—if it engenders disorders in the community, all regular & orderly minds will wish for a change—and the demagogues who have produced the disorder will make it for their own aggrandizement. This is the old Story.

[17] Hamilton maintains that the success of his early measures, which Madison and Jefferson had staked their political reputation on openly opposing, had only increased their desire to subvert anything associated with him.

[18] Madison and Jefferson had become so inflamed by their animosity toward Hamilton that they had convinced themselves and others of the absurd proposition that Hamilton was part of a concerted effort to overthrow both the state governments and republicanism. In response, Hamilton reiterates his commitment to republicanism based on equality of political rights but emphasizes that the successful establishment of such a government is not guaranteed. Furthermore, he contends that the danger to such a system lies not in the overthrow of the long-established institutions of local government but in the collapse of the national government, weak in its infancy.

[19] Hamilton declares that if his true intention were to overthrow the state governments and impose a monarchy, he would have adopted methods of a populist demagogue, fermenting the people by appealing directly to their immediate passions and desires. While Hamilton stops short of explicitly accusing Madison and Jefferson of such demagoguery, he does identify Jefferson as "a man of profound ambition & violent passions."

If I were disposed to promote Monarchy & overthrow State Governments, I would mount the hobby horse of popularity—I would cry out usurpation—danger to liberty &c. &c—I would endeavour to prostrate the National Government—raise a ferment—and then "ride in the Whirlwind and direct the Storm."[19] That there are men acting with Jefferson & Madison who have this in view I verily believe. I could lay my finger on some of them. That Madison does *not* mean it I also verily believe, and I rather believe the same of Jefferson; but I read him upon the whole thus—"A man of profound ambition & violent passions."

You must be by this time tired of my epistle. Perhaps I have treated certain characters with too much severity. I have however not meant to do them injustice—and from the bottom of my soul believe I have drawn them truly and that it is of the utmost consequence to the public weal they should be viewed in their true colors. I yield to this impression. I will only add that I make no clandestine attacks on the gentlemen concerned. They are both apprized indirectly from myself of the opinion I entertain of their views. With the truest regard and esteem.

CONCLUSION

Dismayed by the political feuds that were fomenting within his own cabinet, President Washington pleaded with Jefferson and Hamilton to cease their public assaults. Reconciliation, however, was never achieved, and the animosity between the two cabinet secretaries continued to grow. Nevertheless, both camps, recognizing that Washington was the main force preventing disunion, and possibly even civil war, urged him to stay on as chief executive for a second term.

In spite of Washington's unanimous reelection in the Electoral College, the political warfare that had erupted over domestic policies during Washington's first term only increased in his second, as public opinion further divided over America's appropriate response to the political convulsions in Europe caused in large part by the onset of the French Revolution.

Source: John C. Hamilton. *History of the Republic of the United States of America, as Traced in the Writings of Alexander Hamilton and of His Contemporaries*, vol. IV. Philadelphia: J.B. Lippincott & Co., 1864, 520–540.

Pacificus No. I on Neutrality

June 29, 1793

On September 20, 1792, French revolutionaries overthrew the French monarchy and pronounced France a republic. Following the execution of King Louis XVI in January 1793, France declared war on an alliance of European monarchies, including Great Britain. Now a republic in need of finances, France appealed to the treaty of alliance forged with the United States during the American Revolution and requested that its fellow American republic quickly repay its war debts.

Although members of Washington's cabinet agreed that America should avoid military involvement in the European conflict, they were bitterly divided over the appropriate response to France. Jefferson—who, like many Americans, was thrilled by the prospect of a European republic—advocated full payment of debts and openly sympathized with the French revolutionaries. He opposed an explicit statement of neutrality, argued that previous treaties with France should remain in full force, and favored accepting a French foreign minister to the United States without restrictions.

Hamilton, on the other hand, was one of the few political leaders to publically doubt France's future prospect as a free nation and was therefore more hesitant to recognize the legitimacy of the French republic. In contrast with the American Revolution, in which the demand for liberty was moderated by a respect for order, religious and moral obligation, and property rights, Hamilton believed that the French Revolution was rooted in fanaticism, lawlessness, and cruelty. On these grounds, he sought to distance the United States from the chaos in France. He, therefore, held that the treaty of alliance with France should be provisionally suspended, since it had been negotiated with the now-overthrown French monarchy. He further advocated only a qualified acceptance of a French foreign minister and warned that publically siding with France would invite an adversarial relationship with Great Britain, which would threaten beneficial trade with England.

Washington, like Jefferson and Madison, maintained that the treaty of alliance was still valid, arguing that it was an agreement with the nation of France, not with the monarchy per se. Nevertheless, he concurred with Hamilton that showing favoritism toward the French would expose the young American republic to significant political and economic risk. Thus, Washington sought to honor the obligations of the defensive alliance with France, while still avoiding U.S. involvement in its growing offensive war. As the friction in his cabinet grew, Washington sought to advert a constitutional crisis by announcing that the United States would maintain a "friendly and impartial" policy between the warring nations. This pronouncement, which was titled the Neutrality Proclamation of 1793, enraged Madison and Jefferson, who contended that the policy was biased toward Great Britain and an unconstitutional executive encroachment on the Senate's power to ratify treaties and the power of Congress to declare war.

Hamilton responded to such charges in a series of public essays, written under the pseudonym Pacificus, which defended Washington's proclamation on pragmatic and constitutional grounds. In the first of his Pacificus essays, Hamilton defends the constitutionality of the Neutrality Proclamation through a broad interpretation of the president's executive and diplomatic powers.

---

[1] Hamilton speculates that the highly bitter and critical opposition to the Neutrality Proclamation is motivated not only by disapproval of the particular policy but also by a desire to undermine President Washington and the general government. Hence, those who seek to preserve the peace and the U.S. Constitution must strive to undercut the influence of such opposition.

As attempts are making very dangerous to the peace, and it is to be feared not very friendly to the constitution of the UStates—it becomes the duty of those who wish well to both to endeavour to prevent their success.

The objections which have been raised against the Proclamation of Neutrality lately issued by the President have been urged in a spirit of acrimony and invective, which demonstrates, that more was in view than merely a free discussion of an important public measure; that the discussion covers a design of weakening the confidence of the People in the author of the measure; in order to remove or lessen a powerful obstacle to the success of an opposition to the Government. . .[1]

This Reflection adds to the motives connected with the measure itself to recommend endeavours by proper explanations to place it in a just light. Such explanations at least cannot but be satisfactory to those who may not have leisure or opportunity for pursuing themselves an investigation of the subject, and who may wish to perceive that the policy of the Government is not inconsistent with its obligations or its honor.

The objections in question fall under four heads—

1 That the Proclamation was without authority
2 That it was contrary to our treaties with France

3 That it was contrary to the gratitude, which is due from this to that country; for the succours rendered us in our own Revolution.
4 That it was out of time & unnecessary.

In order to judge of the solidity of the first of these objections, it is necessary to examine what is the nature and design of a proclamation of neutrality.[2]

The true nature & design of such an act is—to *make known* to the powers at War and to the Citizens of the Country, whose Government does the Act that such country is in the condition of a Nation at Peace with the belligerent parties, and under no obligations of Treaty, to become an *associate in the war* with either of them; that this being its situation its intention is to observe a conduct conformable with it and to perform towards each the duties of neutrality; and as a consequence of this state of things, to give warning to all within its jurisdiction to abstain from acts that shall contravene those duties, under the penalties which the laws of the land (of which the law of Nations is a part) annexes to acts of contravention.

This, and no more, is conceived to be the true import of a Proclamation of Neutrality.

It does not imply, that the Nation which makes the declaration will forbear to perform to any of the warring Powers any stipulations in Treaties which can be performed without rendering it an *associate* or *party* in the War. . .[3]

But no special aids, succours or favors having relation to war, not positively and precisely stipulated by some Treaty of the above description, can be afforded to either party, without a breach of neutrality.

In stating that the Proclamation of Neutrality does not imply the non performance of any stipulations of Treaties which are not of a nature to make the Nation an associate or party in the war, it is conceded that an execution of the clause of Guarantee contained in the 11th article of our Treaty of Alliance with France would be contrary to the sense and spirit of the Proclamation;[4] because it would engage us with our whole force as an *associate* or *auxiliary* in the War; it would be much more than the case of a definite limited succour, previously ascertained.

[2] After summarizing the legal, moral, and pragmatic objections to the Neutrality Proclamation, Hamilton responds directly to the charge that the president lacks the legal authority to issue such a proclamation. First, he examines the "nature and design" of the proclamation and explains that it merely announces to the parties at war and to U.S. citizens that the U.S. government is at peace with both of the combatants and will not become "an associate in the war with either."

[3] Hamilton stresses that the United States will continue to meet the obligations of current treaties so long as they do not require the United States to become a belligerent party or to issue special aid or favors to one of the warring powers.

[4] Hamilton concedes that the Article 11 clause of guarantee in the Treaty of Alliance with France, which requires the United States to aid France as a partner in war, undermines the spirit of the neutrality.

It follows that the Proclamation is virtually a manifestation of the sense of the Government that the UStates are, *under the circumstances of the case, not bound* to execute the clause of Guarantee.[5]

If this be a just view of the true force and import of the Proclamation, it will remain to see whether the President in issuing it acted within his proper sphere, or stepped beyond the bounds of his constitutional authority and duty.

It will not be disputed that the management of the affairs of this country with foreign nations is confided to the Government of the UStates.

It can as little be disputed, that a Proclamation of Neutrality, when a Nation is at liberty to keep out of a War in which other Nations are engaged and means so to do, is a *usual* and a *proper* measure. . .

An object this of the greatest importance to a Country whose true interest lies in the preservation of peace.

6 After affirming that the power over diplomacy and foreign policy belongs to the federal government, Hamilton turns to the question of which branch is best suited to issue declarations of neutrality. The legislative branch, he points out, cannot bear responsibility for interpreting and maintaining the obligations of peace with other nations, since it neither makes nor interprets treaties. Moreover, although the judiciary possesses the authority to interpret the requirements of treaties in specific cases and controversies, it has no influence over the establishment and execution of political relationships between governments. Consequently, the authority to define and enforce conditions of peace with other nations belongs to the executive.

The inquiry then is—what department of the Government of the UStates is the proper one to make a declaration of Neutrality in the cases in which the engagements of the Nation permit and its interests require such a declaration.[6]

A correct and well informed mind will discern at once that it can belong neither to the Legislative nor Judicial Department and of course must belong to the Executive.

The Legislative Department is not the *organ* of intercourse between the UStates and foreign Nations. It is charged neither with *making* nor *interpreting* Treaties. It is therefore not naturally that Organ of the Government which is to pronounce the existing condition of the Nation, with regard to foreign Powers, or to admonish the Citizens of their obligations and duties as founded upon that condition of things. Still less is it charged with enforcing the execution and observance of these obligations and those duties.

It is equally obvious that the act in question is foreign to the Judiciary Department of the Government. The province of that Department is to decide litigations in particular cases. It is indeed charged with the interpretation of treaties; but it exercises this function only in the litigated cases; that is where contending parties bring before it a specific controversy. It has no concern with pronouncing upon the external political relations of Treaties between Government and Government. This position is too plain to need being insisted upon.

It must then of necessity belong to the Executive Department to exercise the function in Question—when a proper case for the exercise of it occurs. . .

This view of the subject is so natural and obvious—so analogous to general theory and practice—that no doubt can be entertained of its justness, unless such doubt can be deduced from particular provisions of the Constitution of the UStates.

Let us see then if cause for such doubt is to be found in that constitution.

The second Article of the Constitution of the UStates, section 1st, establishes this general Proposition, That "The EXECUTIVE POWER shall be vested in a President of the United States of America."[7]

The same article in a succeeding Section proceeds to delineate particular cases of Executive Power. It declares among other things that the President shall be Commander in Chief of the army and navy of the UStates and of the Militia of the several states when called into the actual service of the UStates, that he shall have power by and with the advice and consent of the senate to make treaties; that it shall be his duty to receive ambassadors and other public Ministers and to take care that the laws be faithfully executed.

It would not consist with the rules of sound construction to consider this enumeration of particular authorities as derogating from the more comprehensive grant contained in the general clause, further than as it may be coupled with express restrictions or qualifications; as in regard to the cooperation of the Senate in the appointment of Officers and the making of treaties; which are qualifications of the general executive powers of appointing officers and making treaties: Because the difficulty of a complete and perfect specification of all the cases of Executive authority would naturally dictate the use of

[7] After establishing that the power to negotiate and maintain the conditions of peace with other nations is a natural function of executive authority, Hamilton inquires whether this reasoning is also justified by the explicit provisions of the U.S. Constitution. Hamilton begins by citing Article II's opening line, which vests executive power in the president. He then summarizes several of the specifically delineated powers, including the power to "be commander in chief," the "power by and with the consent of the senate to make treaties," the "duty to receive ambassadors and other public ministers," and the responsibility "to take care that the laws be faithfully executed."

[8] Hamilton contends that, since it would be impossible for the Constitution to list all instances of executive power, the "vesting clause" of Article II grants the president open-ended authority to respond to national contingencies, domestic and foreign. Whereas Article I explicitly limits Congress to those legislative powers "herein granted," Article II lists the "executive power" vested in the president as a singular unit. Consequently, the subsequent listing of particular executive powers in Article II was intended to illustrate specific instances of executive power, not to limit its scope. Thus, the general grant of executive power was limited only by the explicitly mentioned "restrictions and qualifications"—such as the power of Congress to declare war and the power of the Senate to ratify treaties.

[9] Hamilton points out that Congress had already acted on a broad view of the president's executive authority when it determined that the power to remove subordinate executive branch officials, although not explicitly listed in the Constitution, is a natural function of the Constitution's general grant of executive power.

general terms—and would render it improbable that a specification of certain particulars was designd as a substitute for those terms, when antecedently used.[8] The different mode of expression employed in the constitution in regard to the two powers the Legislative and the Executive serves to confirm this inference. In the article which grants the legislative powers of the Governt. the expressions are— "*All Legislative powers herein granted shall be vested in a Congress of the UStates*"; in that which grants the Executive Power the expressions are, as already quoted "The EXECUTIVE POWER shall be vested in a President of the UStates of America."

The enumeration ought rather therefore to be considered as intended by way of greater caution, to specify and regulate the principal articles implied in the definition of Executive Power; leaving the rest to flow from the general grant of that power, interpreted in conformity to other parts of the constitution and to the principles of free government.

The general doctrine then of our constitution is, that the EXECUTIVE POWER of the Nation is vested in the President; subject only to the *exceptions* and *qualifications* which are expressed in the instrument.

Two of these have been already noticed—the participation of the Senate in the appointment of Officers and the making of Treaties. A third remains to be mentioned the right of the Legislature "to declare war and grant letters of marque and reprisal."

With these exceptions the EXECUTIVE POWER of the Union is completely lodged in the President. This mode of construing the Constitution has indeed been recognized by Congress in formal acts, upon full consideration and debate. The power of removal from office is an inportant instance.[9]

And since upon general principles for reasons already given, the issuing of a proclamation of neutrality is merely an Executive Act; since also the general Executive Power of the Union is vested in the President, the conclusion is, that the step, which has been taken by him, is liable to no just exception on the score of authority.

It may be observed that this Inference would be just if the power of declaring war had not been vested in the Legislature, but that this power naturally includes the right of judging whether the Nation is under obligations to make war or not.[10]

The answer to this is, that however true it may be, that the right of the Legislature to declare war includes the right of judging whether the Nation be under obligations to make War or not—it will not follow that the Executive is in any case excluded from a similar right of Judgment, in the execution of its own functions.

If the Legislature have a right to make war on the one hand—it is on the other the duty of the Executive to preserve Peace till war is declared; and in fulfilling that duty, it must necessarily possess a right of judging what is the nature of the obligations which the treaties of the Country impose on the Government; and when in pursuance of this right it has concluded that there is nothing in them inconsistent with a *state* of neutrality, it becomes both its province and its duty to enforce the laws incident to that state of the Nation. The Executive is charged with the execution of all laws, the laws of Nations as well as the Municipal law, which recognises and adopts those laws. It is consequently bound, by faithfully executing the laws of neutrality, when that is the state of the Nation, to avoid giving a cause of war to foreign Powers. . .[11]

Those who object to the proclamation will readily admit that it is the right and duty of the Executive to judge of, or to interpret, those articles of our treaties which give to France particular privileges, in order to the enforcement of those privileges: But the necessary consequence of this is, that the Executive must judge what are the proper bounds of those privileges—what rights are given to other nations by our treaties with them—what rights the law of Nature and Nations gives and our treaties permit, in respect to those Nations with whom we have no treaties;[12] in fine what are the reciprocal rights and obligations of the United States & of all & each of the powers at War. . .

The President is the constitutional EXECUTOR of the laws. Our Treaties and the laws of Nations form a part of the law of the land. He who is to execute the laws must first judge for himself of their meaning. In order to the observance of that conduct, which the laws of nations combined with our treaties prescribed to this country, in reference to the present War in Europe, it was necessary for the President to judge for himself whether there was any thing in our

[10] Hamilton next responds to the objection that the Constitution explicitly gave Congress the power to declare war and that Congress, not the executive, rightly possesses the authority to determine the obligations of war and peace and whether the obligations of treaties should continue to be upheld.

[11] After conceding that the congressional power to declare war includes the authority to determine whether the nation is obligated to enter into a state of war on behalf of another, Hamilton argues that this authority does not supersede the right of the president to make similar judgments in regard to executive functions. Until Congress formally declares war, the law of the land is peace. The president is thus responsible for determining how to interpret and execute international laws and treaties in a way that best preserves that peace.

[12] Hamilton points out that opponents of the Neutrality Proclamation acknowledge that the president has a "right and duty" to interpret the requirements of treaties that establish a privileged relationship with other countries in order to enforce those requirements. The consequence of this, however, is that the president must determine not only the proper bounds of privileges given to a particular country but also the obligations the United States might have toward other sovereign nations under treaties made with them or under "the law of Nature and Nations."

treaties incompatible with an adherence to neutrality. Having judged that there was not, he had a right, and if in his opinion the interests of the Nation required it, it was his duty, as Executor of the laws, to proclaim the neutrality of the Nation, to exhort all persons to observe it, and to warn them of the penalties which would attend its non observance.

The Proclamation has been represented as enacting some new law. This is a view of it entirely erroneous. It only proclaims a *fact* with regard to the *existing state* of the Nation, informs the citizens of what the laws previously established require of them in that state, & warns them that these laws will be put in execution against the Infractors of them.

CONCLUSION

Hamilton's immediate purpose for defending Washington's Neutrality Proclamation was to promote America's unity, strength, and independence by preventing the young nation from becoming entangled in a European war. Nevertheless, his argument for broad executive authority in the realm of foreign affairs deeply disturbed and startled Madison and Jefferson, who believed that it signified a dangerous step in the direction of monarchial government.

At the behest of Jefferson, Madison reluctantly took up his pen and responded with his own series of essays. Writing under the pseudonym Helvidius, Madison argued that Congress, not the president, rightfully possessed the authority to determine the direction of foreign policy. Although Madison's argument more likely represented the sense of those who authored the Constitution, he failed to adequately explain how Congress, as a multiple-headed body, could efficiently or successfully conduct national diplomacy (Cooke 1982). Thus, while Hamilton's defense of energetic executive authority was one of the most controversial acts of his political career, it eventually established an important precedent for presidential leadership in foreign affairs.

Jefferson, frustrated by Hamilton's influence over Washington, resigned his post as secretary of state at the end of the year, determined to lead Democratic-Republican opposition from outside the administration.

Source: *Gazette of the United States*, Philadelphia, June 29, 1793.

Tully No. II on the Whiskey Rebellion

August 26, 1794

INTRODUCTION

In the summer of 1794, just prior to his retirement from Washington's cabinet, Hamilton helped suppress an armed rebellion against constitutionally imposed excise taxes. Both he and Washington feared the insurrection, although provincial at the time, would ultimately threaten the legitimacy and longevity of the federal government under the U.S. Constitution.

Early on in his tenure as Treasury secretary, Hamilton had suggested an excise tax on alcohol and other luxuries to ease the revenue burden required from duties on imports. In response, Congress approved a modest excise tax on domestic distilled spirits in 1791. While pockets of resistance toward the excise tax popped up around the country, violence toward federal tax collectors in Western Pennsylvania became common. Seeking conciliation, Hamilton convinced Congress to make several modifications to the tax law in the subsequent years, including lowering domestic rates and raising taxes on imported spirits. But nothing short of complete repeal would appease the most ardent opponents.

In July 1794, Western Pennsylvania erupted in violent protest. Fueled by local politicians, who characterized the excise tax as a tool of tyranny designed to oppress the people for the benefit of the rich, thousands of rebels besieged the property of the local federal excise inspector, attacked the stills of those who complied with the tax, intercepted the federal mail en route from west Pennsylvania to Philadelphia, and threatened to burn Pittsburgh to the ground.

Washington sought to act quickly against the rebellion, but he received mixed advice from his cabinet. Whereas Hamilton, Secretary of War Henry Knox, and Attorney General William Bradford urged military intervention, Jefferson's replacement as secretary of state, Edmund Randolph, worried that a show of force would alienate the people. He instead suggested sending commissioners to negotiate with the insurgents. Washington chose to exercise diplomacy, with the option of military force if necessary. In mid-August, he warned the rebel forces to cease and desist by September 1 or face a militia, and he correspondingly sent a three-man commission to determine the likelihood of a peaceful solution.

As the commissioners prepared to meet with citizens in Pittsburgh, Hamilton published a series of essays, arguing that the insurrection in Western Pennsylvania was, in essence, a crisis of constitutional government. Hamilton wrote these essays under the pen name "Tully," a nickname for Cicero, one of the most well-known and eloquent defenders of the Roman republic.

For the American Daily Advertiser.
To the PEOPLE *of the* UNITED STATES.
LETTER II.

It has been observed that the means most likely to be employed to turn the insurrection in the western country to the detriment of the government, would be artfully calculated among other things "to divert your attention from the true question to be decided."

Let us see then what is this question. It is plainly this—shall the majority govern or be governed? shall the nation rule, or be ruled? shall the general will prevail, or the will of a faction? shall there be government, or no government?[1]

It is impossible to deny that this is the true, and the whole question. No art, no sophistry can involve it in the least obscurity.

The Constitution *you* have ordained for yourselves and your posterity contains this express clause, "The Congress *shall have power* to lay and collect taxes, duties, imposts, and *Excises*, to pay the debts, and provide for the common defence and general welfare of the United States." You have then, by a solemn and deliberate act, the most important and sacred that a nation can perform, pronounced and decreed, that your Representatives in Congress shall have power to lay Excises.[2] You have done nothing since to reverse or impair that decree.

Your Representatives in Congress, pursuant to the Commission derived from you, and with a full knowledge of the public exigencies have laid an excise.[3] At three suceeding Sessions they have revised that act, and have as often, with a degree of unanimity not common, and after the best opportunities of knowing your sense, renewed their sanction to it, you have acquiesced in it, it has gone into general operation: and *you* have actually paid more than a million dollars on account of it.

But the four western counties of Pennsylvania, undertake to rejudge and reverse your decrees, you have said, "The Congress *shall have power* to lay *Excises*." They say, "The Congress *shall not have* this power." Or what is equivalent—they shall not exercise it:—for a *power* that may not be exercised is a nullity.[4] Your Representatives have said, and four times repeated it, "an excise on distilled spirits *shall* be collected." They say it *shall not* be collected. We will

[1] Hamilton bluntly argues that the viability of constitutional democracy is at stake in the battle over compliance with excise taxes. At the heart of the rebellion is the unequivocal question of whether the majority should govern through constitutionally enacted laws or whether domestic factions should be permitted to impose their own arbitrary will on the nation through the use of force—in which case government itself becomes futile.

[2] Hamilton explains that the Constitution, adopted by the people as the perpetual law of the land, contains an express clause granting Congress the power to "lay and collect taxes, duties, imposts, and *Excises*." Thus, in ratifying the Constitution the people unambiguously endowed their representatives in Congress with the authority to impose excise taxes. The people have since taken no action to revoke or amend that authority.

[3] Hamilton expounds on his argument for the constitutional legitimacy of the excise tax by pointing out that representatives, electorally accountable to the people, adopted the excise tax and then revised and reinstituted it three times in a process fully open to popular sanction.

[4] By refusing to allow enforcement of constitutionally enacted laws, a factious minority in four counties is, in effect, asserting that sovereignty lies not with the majority acting under a limited constitution but with the arbitrary whims of an armed minority, willing to league itself with foreign powers against their fellow citizens. Stephen F. Knott and Tony Williams (2015) point out that this question of whether "an armed minority [has] the right to defy laws enacted through constitutionally approved procedures through the use of violence" is the same question that was again "tested some eighty years later during the American Civil War" (200).

punish, expel, and banish the officers who shall attempt the collection. We will do the same by every other person who shall dare to comply with your decree expressed in the Constitutional character; and with that of your Representative expressed in the Laws. The sovereignty shall not reside with you, but with us. If you presume to dispute the point by force—we are ready to measure swords with you; and if unequal ourselves to the contest we will call in the aid of a foreign nation. We will league ourselves with a foreign power.

If there is a man among us who shall affirm that the question is not what it has been stated to be—who shall endeavour to perplex it, by ill timed declamations against excise laws—who shall strive to paralise the efforts of the community by invectives, or insinuations against the government—who shall inculcate directly, or indirectly, that force ought not to be employed to compel the Insurgents to a submission to the laws, if the pending experiment to bring them to reason (an experiment which will immortalize the moderation of the government) shall fail; such a man is not a good Citizen; such a man however he may prate and babble republicanism, is not a republican; he attempts to set up the *will* of a part against the *will* of the whole, the *will* of a *faction*, against the *will* of *nation*, the pleasure of a *few* against *your* pleasure; the violence of a lawless combination against the sacred authority of laws pronounced under your indisputable commission.[5]

Mark such a man, if such there be. The occasion may enable you to discriminate the *true* from *pretended Republicans*; *your* friends from the friends of *faction*. 'Tis in vain that the latter shall attempt to conceal their pernicious principles under a crowd of odious invectives against the laws. *Your* answer is this: "*We* have already in the Constitutional act decided the point against you, and against those for whom you apologize. *We* have pronounced that *excises* may be laid and consequently that they are not as you say inconsistent with Liberty. Let our will be first obeyed and then we shall be ready to consider the reason which can be afforded to prove our judgement has been erronious. . . . In a full respect for the laws we discern the reality of our power and the means of providing for our welfare as occasion may require; in the contempt of the laws we see the annihilation of our power; the possibility, and the danger of its being usurped by others & of the despotism of individuals succeeding to the regular authority of the nation."[6]

That a fate like this may never await *you*, let it be deeply imprinted in your minds and handed down to your latest posterity, that there

[5] Hamilton highlights the hypocrisy of political leaders who portray the lawless whiskey rebels and their sympathizers as the true representatives of democracy. A political system in which an armed minority faction is permitted to forcefully overrule the constitutionally enacted will of the majority is not democracy but tyranny.

[6] The maintenance of popular government, Hamilton argues, requires consistent enforcement of laws legitimately enacted by the representatives of the people. The proper mode of contesting constitutionally enacted laws is to reform and repeal them through the legal process. Permitting minority factions to forcefully resist valid laws leads to anarchy, which ultimately ends in tyranny.

is no road to *despotism* more sure or more to be dreaded than that which begins at *anarchy*.

TULLY.

CONCLUSION

As Hamilton's Tully letters appeared in print, the three commissioners issued a series of bleak reports from Western Pennsylvania. Their attempts at a peaceful solution had only emboldened the most violent insurgents. Determined to enforce compliance with the law and diffuse the rebellion, Washington ordered a militia of over 12,000 men from Pennsylvania and three other states to march into Western Pennsylvania under the leadership of Virginia governor and general Henry Lee. To emphasize the seriousness and prestige of the mission, Washington personally attended the assembly of the militia in Carlisle, Pennsylvania, and then gave Hamilton authority to escort General Lee and his troops into the hub of the rebellion and to direct the mission.

The massive militia had its intended effect. Faced with federal forces, the rebellion dissipated and most of the rebels fled into nearby Ohio. Washington eventually pardoned all those who had been taken into custody and charged with instigating the insurrection. While Jefferson and Madison were highly critical of the mission, arguing that Washington had become a tool of "a dictatorially inclined Hamilton," the public at large was highly impressed with the federal exhibition of both strength and clemency, and the Federalists were overwhelmingly returned to power in congressional elections that year. Chernow (2004) highlights the overall significance of the event, explaining that in their effort to restore the rule of law, "Washington and Hamilton had brought new prestige to the government and shown how a democratic society could handle popular disorder without resorting to despotic methods" (477).

With the nation's finances in good order and its laws on solid ground, Hamilton resigned as secretary of the Treasury and returned to his family and law practice in early 1795. In a nod of recognition to Hamilton's valuable contributions, Washington replaced him with his former undersecretary, Oliver Wolcott.

In spite of Hamilton's retirement from the president's cabinet, Washington continued to rely on his advice and support. Most notably, Hamilton helped to resolve diplomatically several outstanding disputes with Great Britain by leading the successful campaign to ratify the extremely controversial Jay Treaty. In one last tribute to his former mentor and friend, Hamilton drafted Washington's Farewell Address, which stressed the blessings of the union that the two had fought so hard to build and preserve.

Source: *American Daily Advertiser*, Philadelphia, August 26, 1794.

Letter Concerning the Public Conduct and Character of John Adams

October 24, 1800

In contrast to Hamilton's intimate and amicable relationship with Washington, his relationship with the nation's second president, fellow Federalist John Adams, was largely hostile. Adams disdained Hamilton, whom he berated for his illegitimate, foreign birth, weakness for women, and burning ambition. Adams additionally resented Hamilton's close relationship with Washington and believed that Hamilton had purposely sought to keep him from the top of the presidential ticket. Nevertheless, Adams was eventually compelled to invite Hamilton to assume a prominent role in his administration, during what was termed the Quasi-War with France.

Early on in the Adams administration, tensions with France increased as French ships expanded the practice of pirating American ships carrying goods for Great Britain. In hopes of avoiding a full-scale war, Adams sent emissaries John Marshall, Charles Cotesworth Pinckney, and Elbridge Gerry on a diplomatic mission to France. To the mortification of the United States, French officials humiliated and rejected these well-respected and distinguished delegates. In response to France's blatant disregard for U.S. attempts at diplomacy and increasing popular support for war, Adams approved an unofficial military buildup. He further requested that Washington return from retirement to once again oversee the armed forces. Washington accepted this commission only on the precondition that Hamilton serve as his second in command. Adams was thus, begrudgingly, forced to appoint Hamilton inspector general of the army with the rank of major general.

Late the following year, Adams shocked the nation by dispatching a special envoy to France, against the advice and knowledge of his cabinet. In late 1799, the envoy reached a peace agreement with Napoleon Bonaparte—who had come to power in a successful coup d'état. The agreement, which was overwhelmingly lopsided in favor of the French, inflamed and divided the Federalist Party. It also doomed the army, which Congress ordered disbanded in early 1800—a charge that Hamilton, to his credit, promptly worked to accomplish, even though it spelled the end to his much-longed-for military career.

Following Washington's death in December 1799, Adams unleashed a slew of personal and public attacks against Hamilton, at one point referring to him as "a bastard brat of a Scottish peddler." In early 1800, Adams further enraged the increasingly unhinged Hamilton when he spitefully fired a couple members of his cabinet and branded Hamilton as the head of a "British faction." Incensed, Hamilton wrote Adams demanding an explanation for the "British faction" charge, which Hamilton viewed as tantamount to an allegation of treason. When Adams refused to reply, Hamilton responded with a letter of his own. On the eve of the presidential election of 1800, he wrote a fifty-two-page diatribe to Federalist leaders condemning Adams's character flaws and failures in executive leadership. A short selection of this lengthy letter is included here.

Sir,

Some of the warm personal friends of Mr. ADAMS are taking unwearied pains to disparage the motives of those Federalists, who advocate the equal support of Gen. PINCKNEY, at the approaching election of President and Vice-President. . .

It is necessary, for the public cause, to repel these slanders; by stating the real views of the persons who are calumniated, and the reasons of their conduct. . .

1 Hamilton opens by acknowledging Adams's patriotism and integrity but then immediately alleges that Adams is deficient in character and not well suited for the presidency.

Not denying to Mr. ADAMS patriotism and integrity, and even talents of a certain kind, I should be deficient in candor, were I to conceal the conviction, that he does not possess the talents adapted to the *Administration* of Government, and that there are great and intrinsic defects in his character, which unfit him for the office of Chief Magistrate.[1]

To give a correct idea of the circumstances which have gradually produced this conviction, it may be useful to retrospect to an early period.

2 Hamilton concedes that he once held Adams in high esteem for his contributions to the early stages of the American Revolution. He then proceeds to recount his growing disillusionment.

I was one of that numerous class who had conceived a high veneration for Mr. ADAMS, on account of the part he acted in the first stages of our revolution.[2] My imagination had exalted him to a high eminence, as a man of patriotic, bold, profound, and comprehensive mind. . .

In this disposition I was, when just before the close of the war, I became a member of Congress. . .

I then adopted an opinion, which all my subsequent experience has confirmed, that he is a man of an imagination sublimated and eccentric; propitious neither to the regular display of sound judgment, nor to steady perseverance in a systematic plan of conduct; and I began to perceive what has been since too manifest, that to this defect are added the unfortunate foibles of a vanity without bounds, and a jealousy capable of discoloring every object. . .[3]

The remaining causes of dissatisfaction with him respect his conduct in the office of President; which, in my opinion, has been a heterogeneous compound of right and wrong, of wisdom and error. . .

It is in regard to our foreign relations, that the public measures of Mr. ADAMS first attract criticism. . .[4]

Mr. ADAMS precipitately nominated Mr. MURRAY as Envoy to the French Republic, without previous consultation with any of his Ministers. The nomination itself was to each of them, even to the Secretary of State, his Constitutional Counsellor, in similar affairs, the first notice of the project.

Thus was the measure wrong, both as to mode and substance.

A President is not bound to conform to the advice of his Ministers. He is even under no positive injunction to ask or require it. But the Constitution presumes that he will consult them; and the genius of our government and the public good recommend the practice. . .

The ablest men may profit by advice. Inferior men cannot dispense with it; and if they do not get it through legitimate channels, it will find its way to them, through such as are clandestine and impure.

Very different from the practice of Mr. ADAMS was that of the modest and sage WASHINGTON. He consulted much, pondered much, resolved slowly, resolved surely.[5]

And as surely, Mr. ADAMS might have benefited by the advice of his ministers. . .

The circumstance, which next presents itself to examination, is the dismission of the two Secretaries, PICKERING and M'HENRY. This circumstance, it is known, occasioned much surprise, and a strong sensation to the disadvantage of Mr. ADAMS.[6]

[3] Hamilton argues that he first witnessed Adams's defects in character—including his extreme vanity, poor judgment, and jealousy—on full display while serving as a delegate to the Continental Congress in the early 1780s.

[4] Hamilton begins to overview Adams's failures as president by highlighting his dissatisfying foreign policy. Hamilton specifically critiques Adams's unilateral decision to dispatch a peace mission to France.

[5] After criticizing Adams for failing to consult with or to seek the advice of members of his own cabinet, Hamilton contrasts Adams's arrogance and rashness with the humility and prudence of Washington.

[6] Hamilton reproaches Adams for firing Secretary of War James McHenry and Secretary of State Timothy Pickering on baseless charges. He explains that Adams was infuriated by unexpected Federalist Party losses in New York, which gave Republicans control of the legislature and thereby diminished his chance of winning New York's Electoral College votes. Adams irrationally charged Hamilton with tinkering with the election in a sinister plot to overthrow him. Then, in an illogical and abusive tirade, he fired those in his cabinet that he suspected of allying with Hamilton.

It happened at a peculiar juncture, immediately after the unfavorable turn of the election in New-York, and had much the air of an explosion of combustible materials which had been long prepared, but which had been kept down by prudential calculations respecting the effect of an explosion upon the friends of those Ministers in the State of New-York...

One fact, however, is understood to be admitted, namely, that neither of the dismissed Ministers had given any new or recent cause for their dismission.

A primary cause of the state of things which led to this event, is to be traced to the ungovernable temper of Mr. ADAMS. It is a fact that he is often liable to paroxisms of anger, which deprive him of self command, and produce very outrageous behaviour to those who approach him. Most, if not all his Ministers, and several distinguished Members of the two Houses of Congress, have been humiliated by the effects of these gusts of passion...

On other topics, my sensations are far less neutral. If, as I have been assured from respectable authorities, Mr. ADAMS has repeatedly indulged himself in virulent and indecent abuse of me; if he has denominated me a man destitute of every moral principle; if he has stigmatised me as the leader of a British Faction;[7] then certainly I have right to think that I have been most cruelly and wickedly traduced; then have I right to appeal to all those who have been spectators of my public actions; to all who are acquainted with my private character, in its various relations, whether such treatment of me, by Mr. ADAMS, is of a nature to weaken or to strengthen his claim to the approbation of wise and good men...

It is time to conclude—The statement, which has been made, shews that Mr. ADAMS has committed some positive and serious errors of Administration; that in addition to these, he has certain fixed points of character which tend naturally to the detriment of any cause of which he is the chief, of any Administration of which he is the head; that by his ill humors and jealousies he has already divided and distracted the supporters of the Government; that he has furnished deadly weapons to its enemies by unfounded accusations, and has weakened the force of its friends by decrying

[7] In his enumeration of Adams's failures as a president, Hamilton pettily airs his personal grievances, recounting how Adams publically berated him and accused him of leading a "British faction."

some of the most influential of them to the utmost of his power; and let it be added, as the necessary effect of such conduct, that he has made great progress in undermining the ground which was gained for the government by his predecessor, and that there is real cause to apprehend, it might totter, if not fall, under his future auspices. . .

Yet with this opinion of Mr. ADAMS, I have finally resolved not to advise the withholding from him a single vote.[8] The body of Federalists, for want of sufficient knowledge of facts, are not convinced of the expediency of relinquishing him. It is even apparent, that a large proportion still retain the attachment which was once a common sentiment. Those of them, therefore, who are dissatisfied, as far as my information goes, are, generally speaking, willing to forbear opposition, and to acquiesce in the equal support of Mr. ADAMS with Mr. PINCKNEY, whom they prefer. . . . Especially, since by doing this, they will increase the probability of excluding a third candidate, of whose unfitness all sincere federalists are convinced. If they do not pursue this course, they will certainly incur an immense responsibility to their friends and to the Government.

To promote this co-operation, to defend my own character, to vindicate those friends, who with myself have been unkindly aspersed, are the inducements for writing this letter. Accordingly, it will be my endeavor to regulate the communication of it in such a manner as will not be likely to deprive Mr. ADAMS of a single vote. Indeed, it is much my wish that its circulation could forever be confined within narrow limits. . . . To refrain from a decided opposition to Mr. ADAMS's re-election has been reluctantly sanctioned by my judgment; which has been not a little perplexed between the unqualified conviction of his unfitness for the station contemplated, and a sense of the great importance of cultivating harmony among the supporters of the Government; on whose firm union hereafter will probably depend the preservation of order, tranquillity, liberty, property; the security of every social and domestic blessing.

[8] After questioning Adams's fitness for office, Hamilton defies the logic of his previous charges by declaring that he does not wish to deprive Adams of a single vote. Instead, he encourages Federalist electors to vote equally for Adams and Pinckney, in order to accomplish the primary goal of keeping Jefferson from the presidency. He concludes the letter with the disingenuous claim that he seeks to cultivate harmony in the party. This was likely part of Hamilton's overall scheme to convince Federalists to favor Pinckney, so that Adams would be elected vice president instead of president.

CONCLUSION

Although Hamilton's letter enumerating Adams's "defects of character" was meant as a private circular to leading Federalists, a copy of the letter eventually fell into the hands of Aaron Burr. Delighted by the prospect of exposing division within the Federalist Party, Burr ensured the letter's publication in newspapers all around the country.

Shortly later, Adams and Pinckney narrowly lost the election to the Republican Jefferson-Burr slate. While it is unclear whether Hamilton's letter affected the electoral outcome, the letter was clearly a disaster for Hamilton's own political career. Many of his former Federalist allies now reproached him for acting impulsively on the basis of his wounded ambition and pride. Unfortunately for Hamilton, the letter also spelled the demise of the party he had helped create, and the Federalists never again won a presidential election.

Source: *Letter from Alexander Hamilton, Concerning the Public Conduct and Character of John Adams, Esq. President of the United States.* New York: Printed for John Lang, by George F. Hopkins, 1800.

Letter to James A. Bayard Favoring Jefferson over Burr

January 16, 1801

INTRODUCTION

As a result of the division and diminished popularity of the Federalist Party, the Republicans achieved a narrow victory in the presidential election of 1800. This victory, however, presented a crisis: Aaron Bur and Thomas Jefferson had each received seventy-three electoral votes. Although Thomas Jefferson was the candidate clearly intended for the presidency, Burr did not concede, and the election for president was thrown into the lame-duck Federalist-controlled House of Representatives.

With the election deadlocked, many Federalists decided to cast their lot with Burr, whom they hoped would be more malleable than the dogmatic Jefferson. Hamilton, however, feared Burr more than he loathed Jefferson. Hamilton held that Burr's lack of principle would make him less restrained than Jefferson in achieving his malicious goals. He was, therefore, more of a threat to the constitutional order. From mid-December to mid-January, Hamilton worked incessantly to convince Federalists in Congress to throw away their votes rather than cast them for Burr.

On January 16, 1801, Hamilton made a final appeal to Congressman James Bayard. His letter to Bayard bore particular significance. Bayard, as Delaware's only representative, had the sole power to cast his state delegation's vote and could, therefore, break the deadlock in Congress.

New-York Jany. 16th. 1801.

I was glad to find my dear sir, by your letter, that you had not yet determined to go with the current of the Fœderal Party in the support of Mr *Burr* & that you were resolved to hold yourself disengaged till the moment of final decision. Your resolution to separate yourself, in this instance, from the Fœderal Party if your conviction shall be strong of the unfitness of Mr Burr, is certainly laudable. So much does it coincide with my ideas, that if the Party Shall by supporting Mr Burr as President adopt him for their official Chief—I shall be obliged to consider myself as an *isolated*

[1] Hamilton acknowledges that, in supporting his arch rival Jefferson over Burr, he would have to retract many of the prejudices and criticisms against Jefferson that he had himself helped promulgate. He summarizes many of his previous critiques and then proceeds to admit that Jefferson possesses some good qualities as well. Among his enumeration of Jefferson's virtues, Hamilton argues that Jefferson, aware that he might someday occupy the presidency, had always been more amenable to executive power than many people thought. Hamilton further contends that Jefferson's actions would likely be more temperate than his rhetoric. Although Jefferson opposed the adoption of the Constitution, he was prudent enough to recognize that his good reputation would best be served by sustaining the system of government it established.

[2] In sum, Hamilton argues that Jefferson, in spite of his flaws, would likely be sensible in the exercise of power. Hamilton further trusted that Jefferson's moderation would be complemented by the fact that he is not susceptible to corruption.

[3] Hamilton proceeds to make the case that Burr, in contrast to Jefferson, would be unrestrained and dangerous. Hamilton reasons that since Burr's ambition is not constrained by principle, there would be no boundaries to the measures he might impose or the destruction he might cause in an effort to obtain and maintain power. In other words, whereas Hamilton sought to gratify his own ambition with the successful establishment and preservation of a republic, he worried that Burr's Napoleonic ambition might eventually lead him to seek that same government's overthrow.

man. It will be impossible for me to reconcile with my notions of *honor* or policy, the continuing to be of a Party which according to my apprehension will have degraded itself & the country. I am sure nevertheless that the motives of many will be good, and I shall never cease to esteem the individuals, tho' I shall deplore a step which I fear experience will show to be a very fatal one. Among the letters which I receive assigning the reasons *pro* & *con* for prefering Burr to J. I observe no small exaggeration to the prejudice of the latter & some things taken for granted as to the former which are at least questionable. Perhaps myself the first, at some expence of popularity, to unfold the true character of Jefferson, it is too late for me to become his apologist. Nor can I have any disposition to do it. I admit that his politics are tinctured with fanaticism, that he is too much in earnest in his democracy, that he has been a mischevous enemy to the principle measures of our past administration, that he is crafty & persevering in his objects, that he is not scrupulous about the means of success, nor very mindful of truth, and that he is a contemptible hypocrite.[1] But it is not true as is alleged that he is an enemy to the power of the Executive. . . . I have more than once made the reflection that viewing himself as the reversioner, he was solicitous to come into possession of a Good Estate. Nor is it true that Jefferson is zealot enough to do anything in pursuance of his principles which will contravene his popularity, or his interest. He is as likely as any man I know to temporize—to calculate what will be likely to promote his own reputation and advantage; and the probable result of such a temper is the preservation of systems, though originally opposed, which being once established, could not be overturned without danger to the person who did it. To my mind a true estimate of Mr J.'s character warrants the expectation of a temporizing rather than a violent system. . . . Add to this that there is no fair reason to suppose him capable of being corrupted, which is a security that he will not go beyond certain limits. . .[2]

As to Burr these things are admitted and indeed cannot be denied, that he is a man of *extreme* & *irregular* ambition—that he is *selfish* to a degree which excludes all social affections & that he is decidedly *profligate*. . . .[3] The truth is that *Burr* is a man of a very subtile imagination, and a mind of this make is rarely free from ingenious whimsies. Yet I admit that he has no fixed theory & that his peculiar notions will easily give way to his interest. But is it a recommendation to have *no theory*? Can that man be a systematic or able statesman who has none? I believe not. *No general principles* will hardly work much better than erroneous ones. . . . It is demonstrated by recent facts that Burr is *solicitous* to *keep* upon *Antifœderal ground*, to avoid compromitting himself by any engagements with the Fœderalists. With or without such engagements he will easily persuade his former friends that he does stand on that ground, & after their first resentment they will be glad to rally under him. In the mean time he will take care not to disoblige them & he will always court those among them who are best fitted for tools. He will never choose to lean on good men because he knows that they will never support his bad projects: but instead of this he will endeavour to disorganize both parties & to form out of them a third composed of men fitted by their characters to be conspirators, & instruments of such projects. That this will be his future conduct may be inferred from his past plan, & from the admitted quality of irregular ambition. Let it be remembered that Mr Burr has never appeared solicitous for fame, & that great Ambition unchecked by principle, or the love of Glory, is an unruly Tyrant which never can keep long in a course which good men will approve . . .

But there is one point of view which seems to me decisive. If the Antifœderalists who prevailed in the election are left to take their own man, they remain responsible, and the Fœderalists remain *free united* and without *stain*, in a situation to resist with effect pernicious measures. If the Fœderalists substitute Burr, they adopt him and become answerable for him. . . . Can there be any serious question between the policy of leaving the Antifœderalists to be answerable for the elevation of an exceptionable man, & that of adopting ourselves & becoming answerable for a man who on all hands is acknowledged to be a complete *Cataline* in his practice & principles?. . .[4]

Your's very truly,
A H

[4] Hamilton warns Bayard that if the Federalists explicitly advocate for Burr they will be answerable for any pernicious measure he might advance. It would be unwise, Hamilton asserts, to align with a man who, in "practice and principles," resembles Catiline, the degraded Roman senator best known for his role in the conspiracy to overthrow the Roman republic.

CONCLUSION

When Congress reconvened in mid-February to resolve the deadlocked election, James Bayard finally agreed to cast a blank ballot, thereby allowing Jefferson to be elected president. In the end, Hamilton helped hand the election to one of his most formidable political foes, never again to hold public office himself. In spite of the vicious partisan squabbles that had taken place in the years leading up to the election, however, Jefferson's inauguration marked one of the first times in history that power was peacefully transferred between opposing parties through an electoral process. Furthermore, although Hamilton feared that a Republican victory would endanger the institutions he had helped construct, many scholars have noted that "Jefferson the president turned out to be more Hamiltonian than Hamilton could have imagined at the time, and the institutions and practices that Washington and Hamilton put in place were more resilient than expected" (Knott and Williams 2015, 228).

Source: Hamilton Papers, Library of Congress.

SECTION IX

The Nation's First Sex Scandal

The Reynolds Pamphlet

July 1797

INTRODUCTION

In mid-summer 1791, Hamilton's wife and children returned to New York while he remained in Philadelphia to continue preparing his Report on Manufacturers. One sweltering day in July, twenty-three-year-old Maria Reynolds called at the Hamilton residence. She told Hamilton that her abusive husband had left her penniless and appealed to Hamilton for a loan, so she might return to her family in New York. Although Hamilton thought her story was "odd," he was easily swayed by beautiful women in distress. After securing a bank bill, he returned to Maria's lodging that evening, where he thus began his liaison with her. The affair between the two continued uninterrupted until her husband James Reynolds returned to Philadelphia that December, apparently seeking to reconcile with his wife. After supposedly discovering the affair, however, he actually encouraged it to continue and resorted to bribing Hamilton for hush money. Eventually, Hamilton, recognizing that husband and wife were in concert, ended the affair and the corresponding payments to James Reynolds.

In December 1792, James Reynolds and his business partner Jacob Clingman were arrested and charged with perjury and attempting to defraud the federal government. After being released on bail, Clingman sought to avoid further imprisonment by appealing to his former employer, Speaker of the House Frederick Muhlenberg. Clingman informed Muhlenberg that he had evidence of corruption at the highest level of the Treasury department. Clingman subsequently presented Muhlenberg with proof that Hamilton had made payments to Reynolds, which he claimed were for illicit speculation. Muhlenberg shared this information with Senator James Monroe and Congressman Abraham Venable. The three decided to confront Hamilton with the charges made against him before sharing the revelations with Washington. In a meeting with the congressional delegation, Hamilton confessed his entire affair with Maria Reynolds and presented evidence successfully vindicating himself of the charge that he had illicitly used Treasury funds and information.

Years later in 1797, Republican journalist and gossipmonger James Callender published a series of pamphlets titled *The History of the United States for 1796*, in which he charged that Hamilton not only engaged in an extramarital affair with Maria but also participated in corrupt speculations with her husband James. Hamilton, fearing that the resurrected charges of public corruption would fatally undermine the financial system he had worked so hard to erect, decided to vindicate his service as Treasury secretary by publically confessing the details of his affair in what became known as *The Reynolds Pamphlet*.

THE spirit of jacobinism, if not entirely a new spirit, has at least been cloathed with a more gigantic body and armed with more powerful weapons than it ever before possessed. . .[1]

Not content with traducing their best efforts for the public good, with misrepresenting their purest motives, with inferring criminality from actions innocent or laudable, the most direct falsehoods are invented and propagated, with undaunted effrontery and unrelenting perseverance. Lies often detected and refuted are still revived and repeated, in the hope that the refutation may have been forgotten or that the frequency and boldness of accusation may supply the place of truth and proof.[2] The most profligate men are encouraged, probably bribed, certainly with patronage if not with money, to become informers and accusers. And when tales, which their characters alone ought to discredit, are refuted by evidence and facts which oblige the patrons of them to abandon their support, they still continue in corroding whispers to wear away the reputations which they could not directly subvert. . .

Of all the vile attempts which have been made to injure my character that which has been lately revived in No. V and VI, of the history of the United States for 1796 is the most vile. . .[3] This it will be impossible for any *intelligent*, I will not say *candid*, man to doubt, when he shall have accompanied me through the examination. . .

The charge against me is a connection with one James Reynolds for purposes of improper pecuniary speculation. My real crime is an amorous connection with his wife, for a considerable time with his privity and connivance, if not originally brought on by a combination between the husband and wife with the design to extort money from me.[4]

This confession is not made without a blush. I cannot be the apologist of any vice because the ardour of passion may have made it mine. I can never cease to condemn myself for the pang, which it may inflict in a bosom eminently intitled to all my gratitude, fidelity and love. But that bosom will approve, that even at so great an expence, I should effectually wipe away a more serious stain from a name, which it cherishes with no less elevation than tenderness.[5] The public too will I trust excuse the confession. The necessity of it to my defence against a more heinous charge could alone have extorted from me so painful an indecorum.

[1] Hamilton equates his adversaries' methods with the spirit of the French Jacobins who sought to destroy and execute their political opponents.

[2] Hamilton contends that, although he had repeatedly disproved allegations that he had engaged in corrupt dealings as secretary of the Treasury, his enemies were now reviving fabricated charges in hopes that if they were continually repeated with confidence, the people would start to believe them.

[3] Of all the attempts to injure his reputation, Hamilton maintains that the allegations of public corruption laid out in installments V and VI of James Callender's *The History of the United States for 1796* were the most heinous.

[4] Hamilton identifies the principal purpose of his exposé—to demonstrate that his "real crime" was not "improper pecuniary speculations" with James Reynolds as charged but rather an illicit amorous relationship with James's wife, Maria.

[5] Hamilton recognizes the humiliation and pain that his detailed confession will inevitably cause his wife and family, yet he contends that they will understand his need to salvage his public reputation. Thus, Hamilton reveals his belief that public corruption is a more serious charge against a public servant than adultery.

Before I proceed to an exhibition of the positive proof which repels the charge, I shall analize the documents from which it is deduced, and I am mistaken if with discerning and candid minds more would be necessary. But I desire to obviate the suspicions of the most suspicious.

The first reflection which occurs on a perusal of the documents is that it is morally impossible I should have been foolish as well as depraved enough to employ so vile an instrument as *Reynolds* for such *insignificant ends*, as are indicated by different parts of the story itself. . . . All the documents shew, and it is otherwise matter of notoriety, that Reynolds was an obscure, unimportant and profligate man. . . . It is very extraordinary, if the head of the money department of a country, being unprincipled enough to sacrifice his trust and his integrity, could not have contrived objects of profit sufficiently large to have engaged the co-operation of men of far greater importance than Reynolds, and with whom there could have been due safety, and should have been driven to the necessity of unkennelling such a reptile to be the instrument of his cupidity.[6]

But, moreover, the scale of the concern with Reynolds, such as it is presented, is contemptibly narrow for a rapacious speculating secretary of the treasury. *Clingman, Reynolds* and his wife were manifestly in very close confidence with each other. It seems there was a free communication of secrets. Yet in clubbing their different items of information as to the supplies of money which Reynolds received from me, what do they amount to? *Clingman* states, that Mrs. Reynolds told him, that at a certain time her husband had received from me upwards of eleven hundred dollars. A note is produced which shews that at one time fifty dollars were sent to him, and another note is produced, by which and the information of Reynolds himself through Clingman, it appears that at another time 300 dollars were asked and refused. Another sum of 200 dollars is spoken of by *Clingman* as having been furnished to Reynolds at some other time. What a scale of speculation is this for the head of a public treasury, for one who in the very publication that brings forward the charge is represented as having procured to be funded at forty millions a debt which ought to have been discharged at ten or fifteen millions for the criminal purpose of enriching himself and his friends? He must have been a clumsy knave, if he did not secure enough of this excess of twenty five or thirty millions, to have taken away all inducement to risk his character in such bad hands and in

[6] Hamilton demonstrates the implausibility of Callender's charges by referring to documents outlining Reynolds's sultry character and the small sums of money he had paid to Reynolds. It would be senseless, Hamilton argues, for the head of the federal Treasury, with millions at his disposal, to have risked his position and reputation by dealing with an obscure, incompetent figure like James Reynolds and for such paltry sums.

so huckstering a way—or to have enabled him, if he did employ such an agent, to do it with more means and to better purpose. . .

The accusation against me was never heard of 'till Clingman and Reynolds were under prosecution by the treasury for an infamous crime.[7] It will be seen by the document No. 1 (a) that during the endeavours of *Clingman* to obtain relief, through the interposition of Mr. Mughlenberg, he made to the latter the communication of my pretended criminality. It will be further seen by document No. 2 [(a)] that Reynolds had while in prison conveyed to the ears of Messrs. Monroe and Venable that he could give intelligence of my being concerned in speculation, and that he also supposed that he was kept in prison by a design on my part to oppress him and drive him away. And by his letter to *Clingman* of the 13 of December, after he was released from prison, it also appears that he was actuated by a spirit of revenge against me; for he declares that he will have *satisfaction* from me *at all events*; adding, as addressed to *Clingman*, "And *you only I trust.*" . . . These circumstances, according to every estimate of the credit due to accusers, ought to destroy their testimony. To what credit are persons intitled, who in telling a story are governed by the double motive of escaping from disgrace and punishment and of gratifying revenge? As to Mrs. Reynolds, if she was not an accomplice, as it is too probable she was, her situation would naturally subject her to the will of her husband. But enough besides will appear in the sequel to shew that her testimony merits no attention. . .

I proceed in the next place to offer a frank and plain solution of the enigma, by giving a history of the origin and progress of my connection with Mrs. Reynolds, of its discovery, real and pretended by the husband, and of the disagreeable embarrassments to which it exposed me.[8] This history will be supported by the letters of Mr. and Mrs. Reynolds, which leave no room for doubt of the principal facts, and at the same time explain with precision the objects of the little notes from me which have been published, shewing clearly that such of them as have related to money had no reference to any concern in speculation. As the situation which will be disclosed, will fully explain every ambiguous appearance, and meet satisfactorily the written documents, nothing more can be requisite to my justification. . .

Some time in the summer of the year 1791 a woman called at my house in the city of Philadelphia and asked to speak with me in

[7] Hamilton points out that Reynolds and Clingman did not present their allegations against him until they themselves were being prosecuted and imprisoned for a federal crime. He further explains that they made their accusations with the direct purpose of negotiating their own release. Thus, the circumstances discredit the veracity of their testimony.

[8] After discounting the evidence presented by Reynolds and Clingman, Hamilton pledges to give a thorough account of his relationship with Maria Reynolds and the origins of the false charges to which this relationship exposed him.

private.[9] I attended her into a room apart from the family. With a seeming air of affliction she informed that she was a daughter of a Mr. Lewis, sister to a Mr. G. Livingston of the State of New-York, and wife to a Mr. Reynolds whose father was in the Commissary Department during the war with Great Britain, that her husband, who for a long time had treated her very cruelly, had lately left her, to live with another woman, and in so destitute a condition, that though desirous of returning to her friends she had not the means—that knowing I was a citizen of New-York, she had taken the liberty to apply to my humanity for assistance.

I replied, that her situation was a very interesting one—that I was disposed to afford her assistance to convey her to her friends, but this at the moment not being convenient to me (which was the fact) I must request the place of her residence, to which I should bring or send a small supply of money. She told me the street and the number of the house where she lodged. In the evening I put a bank-bill in my pocket and went to the house. I inquired for Mrs. Reynolds and was shewn up stairs, at the head of which she met me and conducted me into a bed room. I took the bill out of my pocket and gave it to her. Some conversation ensued from which it was quickly apparent that other than pecuniary consolation would be acceptable.

After this, I had frequent meetings with her, most of them at my own house; Mrs. Hamilton with her children being absent on a visit to her father. In the course of a short time, she mentioned to me that her husband had solicited a reconciliation, and affected to consult me about it. I advised to it, and was soon after informed by her that it had taken place. She told me besides that her husband had been engaged in speculation, and she believed could give information respecting the conduct of some persons in the department which would be useful. I sent for Reynolds who came to me accordingly.[10]

In the course of our interview, he confessed that he had obtained a list of claims from a person in my department which he had made use of in his speculations. I invited him, by the expectation of my friendship and good offices, to disclose the person. After some affectation of scruple, he pretended to yield, and ascribed the infidelity to Mr. Duer from whom he said he had obtained the list in New-York, while he (Duer) was in the department.

[9] Hamilton begins his personal confession, by recounting the origins of his affair with Maria Reynolds. He explains that Maria Reynolds had approached him and, after establishing her social credentials, had recounted her ill-fate and requested a loan so she might return to her family. According to Hamilton, when he delivered the requested funds to Maria's chambers, she deliberately seduced him and the affair thus commenced.

[10] Hamilton reports that, after a short time, Maria informed him that her husband, James, had returned and was seeking to reconcile, which Hamilton says he encouraged. Maria also told Hamilton that James had information that would expose illicit speculation by an employee of the Treasury department. After arranging a meeting, James Reynolds informed Hamilton that William Duer, former assistant Treasury secretary, had illegally given him a list of government securities that could be purchased from veterans below value. This information was of little worth to Hamilton, considering Duer no longer worked for the Treasury. Nevertheless, Hamilton explains that his passions motivated him to maintain an amicable relationship with James Reynolds, and he, therefore, thanked him and told him that he would be in his future service.

As Mr. Duer had resigned his office some time before the seat of government was removed to Philadelphia; this discovery, if it had been true, was not very important—yet it was the interest of my passions to appear to set value upon it, and to continue the expectation of friendship and good offices. Mr. Reynolds told me he was going to Virginia, and on his return would point out something in which I could serve him. I do not know but he said something about employment in a public office.

On his return he asked employment as a clerk in the treasury department. The knowledge I had acquired of him was decisive against such a request.[11] I parried it by telling him, what was true, that there was no vacancy in my immediate office, and that the appointment of clerks in the other branches of the department was left to the chiefs of the respective branches. . . . Some material reflections will occur here to a discerning mind. Could I have preferred my private gratification to the public interest, should I not have found the employment he desired for a man, whom it was so convenient to me, on my own statement, to lay under obligations. Had I had any such connection with him, as he has since pretended, is it likely that he would have wanted other employment? Or is it likely that wanting it, I should have hazarded his resentment by a persevering refusal? This little circumstance shews at once the delicacy of my conduct, in its public relations, and the impossibility of my having had the connection pretended with Reynolds.

The intercourse with Mrs. Reynolds, in the mean time, continued; and, though various reflections, (in which a further knowledge of Reynolds' character and the suspicion of some concert between the husband and wife bore a part) induced me to wish a cessation of it; yet her conduct, made it extremely difficult to disentangle myself.[12] All the appearances of violent attachment, and of agonizing distress at the idea of a relinquishment, were played off with a most imposing art. This, though it did not make me entirely the dupe of the plot, yet kept me in a state of irresolution. My sensibility, perhaps my vanity, admitted the possibility of a real fondness; and led me to adopt the plan of a gradual discontinuance rather than of a sudden interruption, as least calculated to give pain, if a real partiality existed.[13]

Mrs. Reynolds, on the other hand, employed every effort to keep up my attention and visits. Her pen was freely employed, and her letters

[11] Reynolds subsequently requested a job working as a clerk for the Treasury department, which Hamilton promptly refused based on his perception of Reynolds's devious character. Hamilton's refusal to offer Reynolds employment indicates his high regard for the integrity of the Treasury department, especially considering how eager he must have been to pacify James Reynolds.

[12] Although Hamilton suspected "some concert" between the wife and husband to entrap him, he argues that Maria, appealing to his sympathy with fits of agonizing distress, made it difficult for him to end the affair.

[13] In a moment of self-reflection, Hamilton admits that perhaps his vanity prevented him from admitting to himself that he had been bamboozled by such sultry characters.

were filled with those tender and pathetic effusions which would have been natural to a woman truly fond and neglected.

One day, I received a letter from her, which is in the appendix (No. I. b) intimating a discovery by her husband. It was matter of doubt with me whether there had been really a discovery by accident, or whether the time for the catastrophe of the plot was arrived.

The same day, being the 15th of December 1791, I received from Mr. Reynolds the letter (No. II. b) by which he informs me of the detection of his wife in the act of writing a letter to me, and that he had obtained from her a discovery of her connection with me, suggesting that it was the consequence of an undue advantage taken of her distress.[14]

In answer to this I sent him a note, or message desiring him to call upon me at my office, which I think he did the same day.

He in substance repeated the topics contained in his letter, and concluded as he had done there, that he was resolved to have satisfaction.

I replied that he knew best what evidence he had of the alleged connection between me and his wife, that I neither admitted nor denied it—that if he knew of any injury I had done him, intitling him to satisfaction, it lay with him to name it. . .[15]

On the 19th, I received the promised letter (No. IV. b) the essence of which is that he was willing to take a thousand dollars as the plaister of his wounded honor.

I determined to give it to him, and did so in two payments, as per receipts (No. V and VI) dated the 22d of December and 3d of January. It is a little remarkable, that an avaricious speculating secretary of the treasury should have been so straitened for money as to be obliged to satisfy an engagement of this sort by two different payments![16]

On the 17th of January, I received the letter No. V. by which Reynolds invites me to *renew my visits to his wife*. He had before requested that I would see her no more. The motive to this step appears in the conclusion of the letter, "*I rely* upon your befriending me, *if there*

[14] Shortly after he refused Reynolds a job as a Treasury clerk, Hamilton reports that he received two letters which he preserved and presented as evidence—one from Maria, indicating that her husband had discovered their affair, and the other from James, who maintained that he had learned of Hamilton's affair with his wife due to her extreme state of distress at Hamilton's neglect.

[15] While neither admitting nor denying the affair, Hamilton agreed to a meeting with James and invited him to request amends for any injury he might have caused. James predictably responded with a letter requesting a bribe of $1,000.

[16] Hamilton, unable to pay the whole amount all at once, arranged to pay in two separate installments. He argues that his shortage of funds is in itself evidence that he had not been involved in avaricious speculation.

should any thing offer that should be to my advantage, as you *express a wish to befriend me.*" Is the pre-existence of a speculating connection reconcileable with this mode of expression?

If I recollect rightly, I did not immediately accept the invitation, nor 'till after I had received several very importunate letters from Mrs. Reynolds—See her letters No. VIII, (b) IX, X.

On the 24th of March following, I received a letter from *Reynolds,* No. XI, and on the same day one from his wife, No. XII. These letters will further illustrate the obliging co-operation of the husband with his wife to aliment and keep alive my connection with her.

The letters from Reynolds, No. XIII to XVI, are an additional comment upon the same plan. It was a persevering scheme to spare no pains to levy contributions upon my passions on the one hand, and upon my apprehensions of discovery on the other. . .[17]

It has been seen that an explanation on the subject was had cotemporarily that is in December 1792, with three members of Congress—F. A. Muhlenberg, J. Monroe, and A. Venable. It is proper that the circumstances of this transaction should be accurately understood. . .[18]

But on the morning of the 15th of December 1792, the above mentioned gentlemen presented themselves at my office. Mr. Muhlenberg was then speaker. He introduced the subject by observing to me, that they *had discovered a very improper connection* between me and a Mr. Reynolds: extremely hurt by this mode of introduction, I arrested the progress of the discourse by giving way to very strong expressions of indignation. The gentlemen explained, telling me in substance that I had misapprehended them—that they did not intend to take the fact for established—that their meaning was to apprise me that unsought by them, information had been given them of an improper pecuniary connection between Mr. Reynolds and myself; that they had thought it their duty to pursue it and had become possessed of some documents of a suspicious complexion—that they had contemplated the laying the matter before the President, but before they did this, they thought it right to apprise me of the affair and to afford an opportunity of explanation; declaring at the same time that their agency in the matter was influenced solely by a sense of public duty and by no motive of personal ill will. If my

[17] After relating subsequent letters from James and Maria, who had separately encouraged the continuation of the affair, Hamilton concludes that the two continued to take advantage of him by appealing to his desire for Maria on the one hand and his fear of being discovered on the other.

[18] Hamilton next recounts the circumstances of his encounter with House Speaker Frederick Muhlenberg, Senator James Monroe, and Congressman Abraham Venable in December 1792. During this meeting he had satisfactorily exonerated himself of the charge that he had used Treasury department funds and information to engage in corrupt speculations with James Reynolds.

memory be correct, the notes from me in a disguised hand were now shewn to me which without a moment's hesitation I acknowledged to be mine.

I replied, that the affair was now put upon a different footing—that I always stood ready to meet fair inquiry with frank communication—that it happened, in the present instance, to be in my power by written documents to remove all doubt as to the real nature of the business, and fully to convince, that nothing of the kind imputed to me did in fact exist. The same evening at my house was by mutual consent appointed for an explanation.

I immediately after saw Mr. Wolcott, and for the first time informed him of the affair and of the interview just had; and delivering into his hands for perusal the documents of which I was possessed, I engaged him to be present at the intended explanation in the evening.

In the evening the proposed meeting took place, and Mr. Wolcott according to my request attended. The information, which had been received to that time, from *Clingman, Reynolds* and his wife was communicated to me and the notes were I think again exhibited.

I stated in explanation, the circumstances of my affair with Mrs. Reynolds and the consequences of it and in confirmation produced the documents (No. I. b, to XXII). . . . The result was a full and unequivocal acknowlegement on the part of the three gentlemen of perfect satisfaction with the explanation and expressions of regret at the trouble and embarrassment which had been occasioned to me. Mr. Muhlenberg and Mr. Venable, in particular manifested a degree of sensibility on the occasion. Mr. Monroe was more cold but intirely explicit. . .[19]

Some days after the explanation I wrote to the three gentlemen the letter No. XXVI already published. That letter evinces the light in which I considered myself as standing in their view.

I received from Mr. Muhlenberg and Mr. Monroe in answer the letters No. XXVII and XXVIII.

Thus the affair remained 'till the pamphlets No. V and VI of the history of the U. States for 1796 appeared. . . . I acknowledge that I was

[19] Hamilton explains that after he had given a thorough confession of his relationship with the Reynolds, the three interrogators were completely satisfied that he had not committed fraud and that the affair was a matter of personal rather than public concern. Although Monroe exhibited a frostier demeanor than Muhlenberg and Venable, all three explicitly confirmed their conviction that Hamilton was innocent of the charges against him and apologized for any embarrassment they might have caused. Hamilton cites additional letters received from Muhlenberg and Monroe reaffirming their previously expressed convictions.

20 The affair remained hidden from the public until years later when James Callender
published his pamphlet, *The History of the
United States for 1796*. Hamilton expresses
astonishment at the quote from Muhlenberg, Monroe, and Venable, published
in installments V and VI of the pamphlet,
implying that they had merely left Hamilton
with the impression that they were satisfied
with the evidence he presented, when in
fact they were not convinced.

21 Upon reading Callender's astonishing
account, Hamilton immediately sought
confirmation from his former interrogators
that he had previously convinced them of
his integrity in administering the Treasury
and its funds. Muhlenberg and Venable
complied, but Monroe did not.

22 After recounting a series of unsatis-
factory correspondence with Monroe,
Hamilton explains that he had decided to
publicize the evidence of his affair, in order
to redeem his integrity as a public official in
the court of public opinion.

astonished when I came to read in the pamphlet No. VI the conclusion of the document No. V, containing the equivocal phrase "*We left
him under an impression our suspicions were removed,*" which seemed
to imply that this had been a mere piece of management, and that
the impression given me had not been reciprocal.[20] The appearance
of duplicity incensed me; but resolving to proceed with caution and
moderation, I thought the first proper step was to inquire of the
gentlemen whether the paper was genuine. . .

I afterwards received from Messrs. Muhlenberg and Venable the
letters No. XXIX, XXX, and XXXI. Receiving no answer from
Mr. Monroe, and hearing of his arrival at New-York I called upon
him.[21] The issue of the interview was that an answer was to be given
by him, in conjunction with Mr. Muhlenberg and Mr. Venable on
his return to Philadelphia, he thinking that as the agency had been
joint it was most proper the answer should be joint, and informing
me that Mr. Venable had told him he would wait his return.

I came to Philadelphia accordingly to bring the affair to a close; but
on my arrival I found Mr. Venable had left the city for Virginia.

Mr. Monroe reached Philadelphia according to his appointment.
And the morning following wrote me the note No. XXXII. While
this note was on its way to my lodgings I was on my way to his. I had
a conversation with him from which we separated with a repetition
of the assurance in the note. In the course of the interviews with
Mr. Monroe, the *equivoque* in document No. V, (a) and the paper of
January 2d, 1793, under his signature were noticed.

I received the day following the letter No. XXXIII, to which
I returned the answer No. XXXIV,—accompanied with the letter No.
XXXV which was succeeded by the letters No. XXXVI—XXXVII—
XXXVIII—XXXIX—XL. In due time the sequel of the correspon-
dence will appear.

Though extremely disagreeable to me, for very obvious reasons, I at
length determined in order that no cloud whatever might be left on
the affair, to publish the documents which had been communicated
to Messrs. Monroe, Muhlenberg and Venable, all which will be seen
in the appendix from No. I, (b) to No. XXII, inclusively. . .[22]

Thus has my desire to destroy this slander, completely, led me to a more copious and particular examination of it, than I am sure was necessary. The bare perusal of the letters from Reynolds and his wife is sufficient to convince my greatest enemy that there is nothing worse in the affair than an irregular and indelicate amour. For this, I bow to the just censure which it merits. I have paid pretty severely for the folly and can never recollect it without disgust and self condemnation. It might seem affectation to say more. . .

ALEXANDER HAMILTON.
Philadelphia, July, 1797.

CONCLUSION

To the embarrassment of his friends and delight of his enemies, Hamilton's detailed public confession of his affair with Maria Reynolds failed to serve its intended effect. The pamphlet shocked the sensibilities of public opinion and provided Hamilton's adversaries with the ammunition needed to destroy his political reputation. Furthermore, his public confession did not alleviate suspicions that Hamilton had engaged in corrupt dealings as Treasury secretary. On becoming president, Jefferson directed his incoming Treasury secretary Albert Gallatin to conduct a thorough investigation of department files, believing they would contain proof of Hamilton's corruption. To Jefferson's great disappointment, however, Gallatin found no evidence of duplicity, and the investigation eventually served to vindicate Hamilton of the charges against him. Nevertheless, Hamilton's self-revelation of the long-ended Reynolds affair destroyed much of his remaining political credibility and, consequently, terminated any aspirations he might have retained for higher office.

In the wake of the Reynolds' scandal, two individuals continued to stand by Hamilton's side—his wife Eliza and former president George Washington. In a telling letter sent to Hamilton, along with the gift of a wine cooler, Washington—without mentioning the affair—expressed his desire that Hamilton "would be persuaded, that with every sentiment of the highest regard, I remain your sincere friend, and affectionate H[um]ble Servant."

Source: *Observations on Certain Documents Contained in No. V & VI of "The History of the United States for the Year 1796," In Which the Charge of Speculation against Alexander Hamilton, Late Secretary of the Treasury, Is Fully Refuted. Written by Himself.* Philadelphia: Printed for John Fenno, by John Bioren, 1797.

SECTION X

Death

Letter to Aaron Burr Refusing to Disavow

June 20, 1804

Following the presidential election of 1800, in which Hamilton had successfully lobbied for Jefferson, Vice President Aaron Burr found himself increasingly alienated from his own party. His loss of influence became even more apparent when Jefferson, preparing to run for a second term, decided to replace Burr as his vice-presidential running mate with New York governor George Clinton. Thus, looking for a way to revive his fledgling political career, Burr turned to the gubernatorial race in his home state of New York.

The situation in New York seemed favorable for Burr's political comeback. By early 1804, many Northern Federalists—angered by the Louisiana Purchase, which they feared would solidify the political influence of Republicans and the Southern slave-holding class—began to advocate that the New England states and New York should secede from the union and form a country of their own. When Hamilton adamantly rejected the scheme, disgruntled Federalists decided to cast their lot with the more pliable Aaron Burr. Although Burr never overtly committed himself to the breakaway plan, he catered to such extremists in an attempt to form a coalition of disaffected Federalists and Republicans. Hamilton, horrified at the prospect that a Burr victory might ultimately lead to the dismemberment of the union, campaigned wholeheartedly in favor of Burr's opponent, Republican Morgan Lewis. In spite of the fact that Hamilton's contributions to Lewis's overwhelming victory were likely minimal, Burr was convinced that Hamilton had ruined his political prospects and became consumed with a desire for revenge.

In the aftermath of the governor's race, Burr found the opportunity to retaliate when he discovered a letter by Dr. Charles D. Cooper that had been published in the *Albany Register* during the gubernatorial campaign. In the letter, Dr. Cooper recalled an exchange during a dinner, in which Hamilton had referred to Burr as "a dangerous man . . . who ought not be trusted with the reins of government." Without providing specific details, Cooper further asserted that Hamilton had offered "a still more despicable opinion . . . of Mr. Burr." Burr believed that this statement, though vague, was provocative enough to warrant a duel. He, therefore, sent an emissary, William P. Van Ness, with a message to Hamilton demanding "a prompt and *unqualified* acknowledgement or denial of any expression which would warrant the assertions of Dr. Cooper."

Hamilton briefly considered the matter and then composed a letter refusing Burr's petition.

New York June 20. 1804
Sir

I have maturely reflected on the subject of your letter of the 18th instant; and the more I have reflected the more I have become convinced, that I could not, without manifest impropriety, make the avowal or disavowal which you seem to think necessary.[1]

The clause pointed out by Mr. Van Ness is in these terms "I could detail to you a *still more despicable opinion*, which General Hamilton has expressed of Mr. Burr." To endeavour to discover the meaning of this declaration, I was obliged to seek in the antecedent part of the letter, for the opinion to which it referred, as having been already disclosed. I found it in these words "General Hamilton and Judge Kent have declared, *in substance*, that they looked upon Mr. Burr to be *a dangerous man*, and one *who ought not to be trusted with the reins of Government*." The language of Doctor Cooper plainly implies, that he considered this opinion of you, which he attributes to me, as a *despicable* one; but he affirms that I have expressed some other *still more despicable*; without however mentioning to whom, when, or where. 'Tis evident, that the phrase "still more dispicable" admits of infinite shades, from very light to very dark. How am I to judge of the degree intended? Or how shall I annex any precise idea to language so indefinite? . . . How could you be sure, that even this opinion had exceeded the bounds which you would yourself deem admissible between political opponents?

But I forbear further comment on the embarrassment to which the requisition you have made naturally leads. The occasion forbids a more ample illustration, though nothing would be more easy than to pursue it.

Repeating, that I cannot reconcile it with propriety to make the acknowlegement, or denial, you desire—I will add, that I deem it inadmissible, on principle, to consent to be interrogated as to the justness of the *inferences*, which may be drawn by *others*, from whatever I may have said of a political opponent in the course of a fifteen years competition.[2] If there were no other objection to it, this is sufficient, that it would tend to expose my sincerity and delicacy to injurious imputations from every person, who may at any time have conceived the import of my expressions differently from what I may then have intended, or may afterwards recollect.

[1] After reflecting on Burr's demands, Hamilton concludes that the allegations were too vague and undefined to warrant an explanation or apology.

[2] Hamilton refuses to confirm or deny Dr. Cooper's ambiguous statement, since, he argues, it might refer to a wide range of insults that he had lobbied against Burr over the course of their fifteen-year political rivalry.

I stand ready to avow or disavow promptly and explicitly any precise or definite opinion, which I may be charged with having declared of any Gentleman. More than this cannot fitly be expected from me; and especially it cannot reasonably be expected, that I shall enter into an explanation upon a basis so vague as that which you have adopted. I trust, on more reflection, you will see the matter in the same light with me. If not, I can only regret the circumstance, and must abide the consequences.[3]

The publication of Doctor Cooper was never seen by me 'till after the receipt of your letter.

I have the honor to be   Sir   Your obed. servt
A Hamilton

[3] Hamilton announces that, unless Burr provided more precise details, he would refrain from confirming or disavowing the charges. He also acknowledges that Burr would likely reject this response and that he would have to abide by the consequences—implying his awareness that his refusal to comply with Burr's demands would ultimately lead to a duel.

CONCLUSION

After corresponding back and forth for over a week with no resolution, Burr issued an ultimatum that Hamilton disavow any statement he might have made implying that Burr's character was "despicable." Hamilton, recognizing the dishonor that such a disavowal would entail, refused to retract any offending statements. In response, Burr extended an invitation for a duel, and Hamilton accepted, asking only that he be given a short delay to put his affairs in order. The two, thus, agreed that they would meet for a duel on the morning of July 11, 1804.

Source: *The Burr-Hamilton Duel, with Correspondence Preceding Same.* Compiled by Irving C. Gaylord, 1889, 6–9.

Statement on the Impending Duel with Aaron Burr

June 28–July 10, 1804

INTRODUCTION

Following the death of his son Philip in a duel, Hamilton repeatedly made clear that he abhorred the custom of dueling. In fact, just months prior to Burr's challenge, Hamilton had publically declared in a court of law that the practice violates "the principle of natural justice, that no man shall be the avenger of his own wrongs" (Brookhiser 1999, 196). Nevertheless, when faced with his own challenge, Hamilton refused to negotiate a solution to avert a duel with Aaron Burr.

In the days leading up to the impending duel, Hamilton penned a statement, to be enclosed with his will, justifying his decision to proceed with the "interview."

On my expected interview with Col Burr, I think it proper to make some remarks explanatory of my conduct, motives and views.

I am certainly desirous of avoiding this interview, for the most cogent reasons.[1]

[1] Hamilton expresses his internal conflict in deciding whether or not to proceed with the duel. He explains that the "interview" would violate his religious and moral principles, threaten the well-being of his beloved family, and expose his creditors to risk. He further asserts that, in spite of opposing Burr politically, he holds no personal ill will toward him and would stand to gain little from the conflict.

1 My religious and moral principles are strongly opposed to the practice of Duelling, and it would even give me pain to be obliged to shed the blood of a fellow creature in a private combat forbidden by the laws.
2 My wife and Children are extremely dear to me, and my life is of the utmost importance to them, in various views.
3 I feel a sense of obligation towards my creditors; who in case of accident to me, by the forced sale of my property, may be in some degree sufferers. I did not think my self at liberty, as a man of probity, lightly to expose them to this hazard.
4 I am conscious of no *ill-will* to Col Burr, distinct from political opposition, which, as I trust, has proceeded from pure and upright motives.

Lastly, I shall hazard much, and can possibly gain nothing by the issue of the interview.

But it was, as I conceive, impossible for me to avoid it. There were *intrinsick* difficulties in the thing, and *artificial* embarrassments, from the manner of proceeding on the part of Col Burr.

Intrinsick—because it is not to be denied, that my animadversions on the political principles character and views of Col Burr have been extremely severe, and on different occasions, I, in common with many others, have made very unfavourable criticisms on particular instances of the private conduct of this Gentleman.[2]

In proportion as these impressions were entertained with sincerity and uttered with motives and for purposes, which might appear to me commendable, would be the difficulty (until they could be removed by evidence of their being erroneous), of explanation or apology. The disavowal required of me by Col Burr, in a general and indefinite form, was out of my power, if it had really been proper for me to submit to be so questionned; but I was sincerely of opinion, that this could not be, and in this opinion, I was confirmed by that of a very moderate and judicious friend whom I consulted. Besides that Col Burr appeared to me to assume, in the first instance, a tone unnecessarily peremptory and menacing, and in the second, positively offensive. Yet I wished, as far as might be practicable, to leave a door open to accommodation. . .[3]

It is not my design, by what I have said to affix any odium on the conduct of Col Burr, in this case. He doubtless has heared of animadversions of mine which bore very hard upon him; and it is probable that as usual they were accompanied with some falshoods. He may have supposed himself under a necessity of acting as he has done. I hope the grounds of his proceeding have been such as ought to satisfy his own conscience. . .

[B]ecause it is possible that I may have injured Col Burr, however convinced myself that my opinions and declarations have been well founded, as from my general principles and temper in relation to similar affairs—I have resolved, if our interview is conducted in the usual manner, and it pleases God to give me the opportunity, to *reserve* and *throw away* my first fire, and I *have thoughts* even of *reserving* my second fire—and thus giving a double opportunity to Col Burr to pause and to reflect.[4]

[2] In spite of his reticence, however, Hamilton argues that several factors make it impossible for him to avoid Burr's challenge. First of all, Hamilton candidly admits that, due to his intense political opposition to Burr, he had at times maligned even his personal conduct. Hamilton maintains, however, that it would be improper for him to disavow or apologize for such critiques, since they were made for valid reasons based on pure motives.

[3] Hamilton additionally argues that Burr's manner and tone in approaching the supposed offense were needlessly insulting and malicious. Nevertheless, Hamilton still hoped for an amicable solution.

[4] In an effort to reconcile his decision to proceed with the duel with his religious and moral opposition to the practice of dueling, Hamilton announces that he will throw away his first and second shot. He expresses hope that the conflict might ultimately be resolved without bloodshed.

It is not however my intention to enter into any explanations on the ground. Apology, from principle I hope, rather than Pride, is out of the question.

To those, who with me abhorring the practice of Duelling may think that I ought on no account to have added to the number of bad examples—I answer that my *relative* situation, as well in public as private aspects, enforcing all the considerations which constitute what men of the world denominate honor, impressed on me (as I thought) a peculiar necessity not to decline the call. The ability to be in future useful, whether in resisting mischief or effecting good, in those crises of our public affairs, which seem likely to happen, would probably be inseparable from a conformity with public prejudice in this particular.[5]

AH

[5] Responding to those who, like himself, abhor the practice of dueling, Hamilton utters a telling explanation of why he felt compelled to proceed with this particular challenge. Hamilton ultimately recognizes that if he were to refuse to face Burr's fire, he would lose all credibility in the eyes of public opinion. Hamilton emphasizes that his continued political usefulness in promoting good and averting mischief in the crises facing the nation (i.e., the threat of a Northern breakaway confederacy) requires that he maintain a reputation for honor and courage.

CONCLUSION

In his last days, Hamilton ultimately recognized that maintaining his own political credibility and usefulness would require him to face Burr's fire, yet he also foresaw that Burr had nothing to gain from murdering him based on such a vague offense. While Burr did shoot to kill, Hamilton still emerged victorious in terms of his ultimate goal. By reserving his own shot, Hamilton maintained his honor while publically revealing Burr's unprincipled, nefarious character. He, therefore, succeeded in politically defanging the man he viewed as the greatest threat to his beloved union. Commentating on the political significance of the Hamilton–Burr duel, historian Joanne Freeman (2001) notes, "Ultimately, it was Hamilton's apologia that ensured Burr's downfall. Hamilton closed his life with an intimate, heartfelt statement that professed his willingness to die for the public good; he depicted himself as an exemplary man of honor, compelled to fight, unwilling to kill, gaining nothing, sacrificing all. There was no more effective way to prove oneself a martyr and one's foe, by necessity, a fiend" (197).

Source: *New-York Evening Post*, July 16, 1804.

Letters to Elizabeth Hamilton Delivered after the Duel

July 4 and 10, 1804

INTRODUCTION

In the days leading up to his impending duel with Aaron Burr, Hamilton calmly went about his daily life. He attended to his law practice, participated in social gatherings, and drew up a will. Hamilton also wrote two letters to his wife, which were to be delivered following the duel.

This letter, my very dear Eliza, will not be delivered to you, unless I shall first have terminated my earthly career; to begin, as I humbly hope from redeeming grace and divine mercy, a happy immortality.

If it had been possible for me to have avoided the interview, my love for you and my precious children would have been alone a decisive motive. But it was not possible, without sacrifices which would have rendered me unworthy of your esteem. I need not tell you of the pangs I feel, from the idea of quitting you and exposing you to the anguish which I know you would feel. Nor could I dwell on the topic lest it should unman me.

The consolations of Religion, my beloved, can alone support you; and these you have a right to enjoy. Fly to the bosom of your God and be comforted.[1] With my last idea; I shall cherish the sweet hope of meeting you in a better world.

[1] Should he be killed, Hamilton encourages Eliza to find solace in her faith.

Adieu best of wives and best of Women. Embrace all my darling Children for me.

Ever yours

A H
July 4. 1804

Mrs. Hamilton
My beloved Eliza

[2] Hamilton emphasizes his indebtedness to his maternal cousin Ann Lytton Mitchell and instructs Eliza to see to her care. Although little is known of Ann Mitchell, the fact that Hamilton—at the end of his life—identifies a specific obligation to her above all others, suggests that she must have played a crucial role in helping him overcome the tribulations of his youth.

[3] Hamilton was convinced that preserving his reputation and thereby his ability to serve the public good would require him to proceed with the duel, yet "the Scruples of a Christian" made him wish to avoid the guilt of killing another. Thus, he informs Eliza of his intention to withhold his fire, even though such action would inevitably increase the hazard to his own life.

Mrs. Mitchel is the person in the world to whom as a friend I am under the greatest Obligations. I have not hitherto done my duty to her. But resolved to repair my omission as much as possible,[2] I have encouraged her to come to this Country and intend, if it shall be in my power to render the Evening of her days comfortable. But if it shall please God to put this out of my power and to inable you hereafter to be of service to her, I entreat you to do it and to treat her with the tenderness of a Sister.

This is my second letter.

The Scruples of a Christian have determined me to expose my own life to any extent rather than subject my self to the guilt of taking the life of another.[3] This must increase my hazards & redoubles my pangs for you. But you had rather I should die innocent than live guilty. Heaven can preserve me and I humbly hope will but in the contrary event, I charge you to remember that you are a Christian. God's Will be done. The will of a merciful God must be good.

Once more Adieu My Darling darling Wife
A H

CONCLUSION

On the morning of July 11, Hamilton and Burr met in Weehawken, New Jersey. The two exchanged fire almost simultaneously. Burr's bullet ripped through Hamilton's liver and embedded in his spine, while Hamilton's merely split an overhead branch. The following day, surrounded by grieving friends and family members, Hamilton received the Eucharist and died. He was only forty-nine years old.

Betsy, who outlived Hamilton by fifty years, spent the remainder of her life editing his papers, working to ensure he received the recognition he deserved for the instrumental role he had played in establishing and preserving the American republic.

Source: Hamilton Papers, Library of Congress.

Timeline of Events

1757

Alexander Hamilton is born on the island of Nevis in the West Indies on January 11. Although some authorities report his birth in 1755, Hamilton himself maintained that he was born in 1757.

1765

James Hamilton travels with Rachel Fawcett Lavien and their two sons, Alexander and James, to St. Croix to collect a debt on behalf of his employer.

1766

After completing his business in St. Croix, James Hamilton returns to St. Kitts alone, leaving behind his family never to return.

Young Alexander begins helping his mother clerk her provision store and shortly later is hired at Beekman and Cruger's mercantile house.

1768

Rachel Fawcett Lavien dies of fever, effectively orphaning James and Alexander.

1769

Alexander Hamilton's uncle and cousin both die leaving him and his brother without a caretaker.

1771

Hamilton begins managing Nicholas Cruger's mercantile house in St. Croix, while Cruger is away in New York City.

1772

A devastating hurricane strikes St. Croix in late August. Hamilton writes a letter to his absent father describing the hurricane's ravaging effects.

This letter is published in *The Royal Danish American Gazette*.

Hamilton leaves the West Indies and arrives in New York. He then enrolls in preparatory school in Elizabethtown, New Jersey.

1773

After being denied the opportunity to engage in an accelerated learning plan at Princeton, Hamilton enrolls in King's College New York.

The Boston Tea Party protest occurs in mid-December.

1774

Parliament shuts down the port of Boston and passes other Coercive Acts.

The First Continental Congress meets in Philadelphia. It condemns the Coercive Acts and adopts an embargo on commercial relations with Great Britain.

Hamilton publishes his first major political tract, *A Full Vindication of the Measures of Congress*.

Hamilton begins drilling with a local militia company, the Corsicans.

1775

Hamilton publishes his second major pamphlet, *The Farmer Refuted*, in response to Samuel Seabury's "A View of the Controversy."

The Revolutionary War officially begins with the Battles of Lexington and Concord in April.

The Continental Congress appoints George Washington as commander in chief of the Continental Army.

Hamilton publically condemns Sons of Liberty leader Isaac Sears and his men for raiding the press of well-known Tory James Rivington.

1776

Hamilton is commissioned as captain of the New York Provincial Artillery Company.

The British invade New York, and the Declaration of Independence is signed in Philadelphia.

Hamilton and his company cross the Delaware with George Washington in the surprise attack on the Hessians in Trenton, New Jersey.

1777

Washington invites Hamilton to join his staff.

Hamilton is commissioned as an aide-de-camp to Washington and promoted to the rank of lieutenant colonel in early March.

The Continental Congress approves a draft of the Articles of Confederation and submits it to the states for adoption.

1780

Hamilton repeatedly requests reassignment to field command and is rebuffed.

Hamilton marries Elizabeth Schuyler, the daughter of General Philip Schuyler.

1781

Hamilton resigns from Washington's staff in April and is eventually assigned field command that summer.

The Articles of Confederation are officially ratified.

Hamilton leads a battalion and acquits himself bravely in the successful Battle of Yorktown.

Hamilton commences legal studies.

1782

Hamilton's oldest son Philip is born in January.

Hamilton receives his first political appointment as receiver of Continental taxes for New York.

Hamilton begins practicing law and is selected by the New York legislature to serve as a delegate to the Continental Congress.

Preliminary terms of the Paris Peace Treaty to end the war with Great Britain are negotiated.

Hamilton starts calling for a convention of the states to amend the Articles of Confederation.

1783

Hamilton leaves Congress and returns to full-time law practice, establishing a law office in New York City.

The final treaty of peace is signed in Paris in September.

The British officially relinquish control of Manhattan on November 25. The day was commemorated in New York as Evacuation Day.

The New York legislature—adding to an earlier series of Anti-Loyalist laws, such as the Confiscation Act and the Citation Act—passes the Trespass Act, which authorized those whose property had been held by Tories during British occupation to sue for back rent and damages.

1784

The Confederation Congress ratifies the peace treaty.

Hamilton publishes his Phocion letters defending the rights of Tories and rebuking the New York legislature for violating the terms of the peace treaty.

Hamilton questions the validity of New York's Trespass Act and argues for judicial review in the case of *Rutgers v. Waddington*.

Hamilton's daughter Angelica is born.

1785

Hamilton becomes a founding member of the New York Society for Promoting the Manumissions of Slaves.

1786

Hamilton is elected to the New York legislature.

Hamilton's third child, Alexander Jr., is born.

Hamilton is selected as a delegate to the Annapolis Convention, where he calls for a Constitutional Convention.

1787

Hamilton serves as a delegate to the Constitutional Convention in Philadelphia.

The Constitutional Convention concludes in September after adopting the Constitution and submitting it to the states for ratification.

Hamilton begins writing the *Federalist*, essays in defense of the proposed Constitution, along with coauthors John Jay and James Madison.

1788

Hamilton is once again elected as a New York delegate to the Continental Congress.

Hamilton's fourth child, James, is born.

Hamilton leads the fight for constitutional ratification in New York as a delegate to the state's ratifying convention.

New York ratifies the Constitution.

1789

The Constitution goes into effect, and George Washington is elected the nation's first president.

Washington appoints Hamilton secretary of Treasury. Hamilton immediately begins working to stabilize national finances.

1790

Hamilton submits his first and second "Report on the Public Credit" to Congress and leads the campaign for Congress to pass debt assumption measures.

1791

Hamilton defends the constitutionality of a national bank.

Washington signs the bill creating the first bank of the United States on February 24.

The *National Gazette* is founded as a Republican rival to the Federalist-sponsored *Gazette of the United States*.

Hamilton begins his affair with Maria Reynolds.

Hamilton submits his "Report on Manufacturers" to Congress.

1792

Speaker of the House Frederick Muhlenberg, Senator James Monroe, and Representative Abraham Venable visit Hamilton to inquire into his dealings with Maria Reynolds's husband James.

Hamilton's fifth child, John, is born.

The French monarchy is overthrown, and the French republic is established.

1793

Revolutionaries execute King Louis XVI and the French republic declares war on Great Britain and an alliance of European powers.

Washington is inaugurated for a second term.

Washington announces that the United States will remain neutral in the war between Great Britain and France.

Hamilton defends Washington's Neutrality Proclamation on pragmatic and constitutional grounds.

Jefferson resigns as secretary of state on December 31.

1794

Hamilton and Washington lead a militia of troops from several states into Western Pennsylvania and successfully quell the Whiskey Rebellion.

1795

Hamilton resigns as secretary of Treasury on January 31 and returns to his law practice in New York.

Hamilton leads the campaign in support of the Jay Treaty with Great Britain, and the U.S. Senate narrowly ratifies the treaty in June.

1796

Hamilton drafts Washington's Farewell Address, which Washington delivers on September 19.

John Adams is elected second president of the United States and Thomas Jefferson is elected vice president.

1797

President Adams sends Elbridge Gerry, Charles C. Pinckney, and John Marshall on a diplomatic mission to France.

Hamilton's sixth child, William, is born.

Hamilton publishes the *Reynolds Pamphlet* disclosing the details of his extramarital affair with Maria Reynolds.

1798

Adams reports the details of the failed diplomatic mission to France, known as the XYZ Affair, to the House of Representatives.

Congress passes and Adams signs the Alien and Sedition Acts.

George Washington leaves retirement to command the newly expanded army in July.

Hamilton is appointed inspector general of the army.

1799

President Adams, against the advice of his cabinet, sends commissioners to France.

Hamilton's father James dies on the British West Indies island of St. Vincent.

Napoleon overthrows the French Directory and establishes the consulate under his leadership.

Hamilton's seventh child, Elizabeth, is born.

Washington dies on December 19.

1800

Congress votes to disband the army, and Hamilton resigns as inspector general.

The Treaty of Mortefontaine is negotiated ending the Quasi-War with France.

Hamilton pens an attack on the character and conduct of President John Adams.

The presidential election of 1800 is deadlocked as Thomas Jefferson and Aaron Burr tie with seventy-three electoral votes each.

Hamilton sides with Jefferson against Burr.

1801

The House of Representatives elects Thomas Jefferson president.

Hamilton establishes the *New York Evening Post*.

Hamilton's oldest son Philip is mortally wounded in a duel.

1802

Hamilton's eighth child, Phillip II, is born.

1804

Hamilton defends freedom of the press in the case of *People v. Croswell*.

Hamilton leads the campaign against Aaron Burr in the New York gubernatorial election.

Hamilton is mortally wounded in a duel with Aaron Burr and dies the following day on July 12.

Further Reading

Ambrose, Douglas, and Martin, Robert W.T. 2006. *The Many Faces of Alexander Hamilton: The Life & Legacy of America's Most Elusive Founding Father*. New York: New York University Press.

Bailey, Ralph Edward. 1933. *An American Colossus: The Singular Career of Alexander Hamilton*. Boston: Lothrop, Lee & Shepard Company.

Bowers, Claude. 1941. *Jefferson and Hamilton: The Struggle for Democracy in America*. Boston: Houghton Mifflin Company.

Brookhiser, Richard. 1999. *Alexander Hamilton: American*. New York: Simon & Schuster.

Chernow, Ron. 2004. *Alexander Hamilton*. New York: Penguin Books.

Cooke, Jacob Ernest. 1982. *Alexander Hamilton*. New York: Charles Scribner's Sons.

Edling, Max M. 2007. "'So Immense a Power in the Affairs of War': Alexander Hamilton and the Restoration of Public Credit." *William and Mary Quarterly* 64 (2): 287–327.

Ellis, Joseph J. 2016. *The Quartet: Orchestrating the Second American Revolution, 1783–1789*. New York: Vintage Books.

Federici, Michael P. 2012. *The Political Philosophy of Alexander Hamilton*. Baltimore: The Johns Hopkins University Press.

Flaumenhaft, Harvey. 1992. *The Effective Republic: Administration and Constitution in the Thought of Alexander Hamilton*. Durham, NC: Duke University Press.

Flexner, James Thomas. 1998. *Young Hamilton: A Biography*, 2nd edition. New York: Fordham University Press.

Freeman, Joanne. 2001. *Affairs of Honor: National Politics in the New Republic*. New Haven, CT: Yale University Press.

Fritz, Jean. 2012. *Alexander Hamilton: The Outsider*. New York: The Penguin Group.

Goebel, Julius, Jr. 1964. *The Law Practice of Alexander Hamilton: Documents and Commentary*, 5 vols. New York: Columbia University Press.

Gordon, John Steele. 1997. *Hamilton's Blessing: The Extraordinary Life and Times of Our National Debt*. New York: Walker & Company.

Hamilton, Alexander. 1961. *The Papers of Alexander Hamilton*. Edited by Harold C. Syrett and Jacob E. Cooke. New York: Columbia University Press.

Hamilton, Alexander. 1985. *Selected Writings and Speeches of Alexander Hamilton*. Edited by Morton J. Frisch. Washington, DC: AEI Press.

Hamilton, Alexander. 2001. *Hamilton: Writings*. Edited by Joanne Freeman. New York: Library of America.

Hamilton, Alexander. 2008. *The Revolutionary Writings of Alexander Hamilton*. Edited by Richard B. Vernier. Indianapolis: Liberty Fund, Inc.

Hamilton, Alexander. 2017. *The Essential Hamilton: Letters and Other Writings*. Edited by Joanne Freeman. New York: Library of America.

Hamilton, Alexander. 2017. *The Political Writings of Alexander Hamilton*. Edited by Carson Holloway. New York: Cambridge University Press.

Harper, John Lamberton. 2004. *American Machiavelli: Alexander Hamilton and the Origins of U.S. Foreign Policy*. Cambridge, MA: Cambridge University Press.

Hendrickson, Robert A. 1981. *The Rise and Fall of Alexander Hamilton*. New York: Van Nostrand Reinhold Company.

Hoffer, Peter Charles. 2016. *Rutgers v. Waddington: Alexander Hamilton, the End of the War for Independence, and the Origins of Judicial Review*. Lawrence: University of Kansas Press.

Holloway, Carson. 2015. *Hamilton versus Jefferson in the Washington Administration: Completing the Founding or Betraying the Founding*. New York: Cambridge University Press.

Kessler, Charles. 1987. *Saving the Revolution: The Federalist Papers and the American Founding*. New York: The Free Press.

Knott, Stephen. 2002. *Alexander Hamilton and the Persistence of Myth*, Revised edition. Lawrence: University of Kansas Press.

Knott, Stephen, and Williams, Tony. 2015. *Washington and Hamilton: The Alliance That Forged America*. Naperville, IL: Sourcebooks.

Locke, John. 1690. Essay Concerning the True Original, Extent, and End of Government. London: Amen-Corner.

Lodge, Henry Cabot. 2016. *American Statesman: Alexander Hamilton*. Victoria, Australia: Leopold Classic Library, Reprint.

Lycan, Gilbert. 1970. *Alexander Hamilton and American Foreign Policy*. Norman: University of Oklahoma Press.

McDonald, Forrest. 1979. *Alexander Hamilton: A Biography*. New York: W.W. Norton and Company.

McNamara, Peter. 1998. *Political Economy and Statesmanship: Smith, Hamilton, and the Foundation of the Commercial Republic*. DeKalb: Northern Illinois Press.

Miranda, Lin-Manuel, and McCarter, Jeremy. 2016. *Hamilton: The Revolution*. New York: Grand Central Publishing.

Newton, Michael E. 2015. *Alexander Hamilton: The Formative Years*. Phoenix: Eleftheria Publishing.

Owens, Mackubin T. 1986. "Alexander Hamilton on Natural Rights and Prudence." *Interpretation* 14 (2): 331–351.

Randall, Willard Sterne. 2003. *Alexander Hamilton: A Life*. New York: Harper Collins.

Read, James H. 2000. *Power versus Liberty: Madison, Hamilton, Wilson, Jefferson*. Charlottesville: University Press of Virginia.

Rogow, Arnold A. 1998. *A Fatal Friendship: Alexander Hamilton and Aaron Burr*. New York: Hill & Wang, Inc.

Rosano, Michael J. 2003. "Liberty, Nobility, Philanthropy, and Power in Alexander Hamilton's Conception of Human Nature." *American Journal of Political Science* 47 (1): 61–74.

Rossiter, Clinton. 1964. *Alexander Hamilton and the Constitution*. New York: Harcourt, Brace & World, Inc.

Schachner, Nathan. 1947. "Alexander Hamilton Viewed by His Friends: The Narratives of Robert Troup and Hercules Mulligan." *William and Mary Quarterly* 4 (2): 203–225.

St. George, Judith. 2016. *The Duel: The Parallel Lives of Alexander Hamilton and Aaron Burr*. New York: SPEAK.

Stoner, James. 2003. "The New Constitutionalism of Publius." *History of American Political Thought*. Edited by Bryan-Paul Frost and Jeffrey Sikkenga. Lanham, MD: Lexington Books, 230–247.

Stourzh, Gerald. 1970. *Alexander Hamilton and the Idea of Republican Government*. Stanford, CA: Stanford University Press.

Walling, Karl. 1999. *Republican Empire: Alexander Hamilton on War and Free Government*. Lawrence: University of Kansas Press.

Walling, Karl-Friedrich. 2003. "Alexander Hamilton on the Strategy of American Free Government." In *History of American Political Thought*. Edited by Bryan-Paul Frost and Jeffrey Sikkenga. Lanham, MD: Lexington Books, 167–191.

West, Thomas G. 2017. *The Political Theory of the American Founding: Natural Rights, Public Policy, and the Moral Conditions of Freedom*. New York: Cambridge University Press.

Index